GERARD MANLEY HOPKINS AND THE POETRY OF RELIGIOUS EXPERIENCE

This nuanced yet accessible study is the first to examine the range of religious experience imagined in Hopkins's writing. By exploring the shifting way in which Hopkins imagines religious belief in individual history, Martin Dubois contests established views of his poetry as a unified project. Combining detailed close readings with extensive historical research, Dubois argues that the spiritual awareness manifest in Hopkins's poetry is varied and fluctuating, and that this is less a failure of his intellectual system than a sign of the experiential character of much of his poetry's thought. Individual chapters focus on biblical language and prayer, as well as on the spiritual ideal seen in the figures of the soldier and the martyr, and on Hopkins's ideas of death, judgement, heaven, and hell. Offering fresh interpretations of the major poems, this volume reveals a more diverse and exploratory poet than has been recognised.

MARTIN DUBOIS is Lecturer in Victorian Literature at Newcastle University.

CAMBRIDGE STUDIES IN NINETEENTH-CENTURY
LITERATURE AND CULTURE

General Editor
Gillian Beer, *University of Cambridge*

Editorial Board
Isobel Armstrong, *Birkbeck, University of London*
Kate Flint, *University of Southern California*
Catherine Gallagher, *University of California, Berkeley*
D.A. Miller, *University of California, Berkeley*
J. Hillis Miller, *University of California, Irvine*
Daniel Pick, *Birkbeck, University of London*
Mary Poovey, *New York University*
Sally Shuttleworth, *University of Oxford*
Herbert Tucker, *University of Virginia*

Nineteenth-century British literature and culture have been rich fields for interdisciplinary studies. Since the turn of the twentieth century, scholars and critics have tracked the intersections and tensions between Victorian literature and the visual arts, politics, social organization, economic life, technical innovations, scientific thought – in short, culture in its broadest sense. In recent years, theoretical challenges and historiographical shifts have unsettled the assumptions of previous scholarly synthesis and called into question the terms of older debates. Whereas the tendency in much past literary critical interpretation was to use the metaphor of culture as 'background', feminist, Foucauldian, and other analyses have employed more dynamic models that raise questions of power and of circulation. Such developments have reanimated the field. This series aims to accommodate and promote the most interesting work being undertaken on the frontiers of the field of nineteenth-century literary studies: work which intersects fruitfully with other fields of study such as history, or literary theory, or the history of science. Comparative as well as interdisciplinary approaches are welcomed.

A complete list of titles published will be found at the end of the book.

GERARD MANLEY HOPKINS AND THE POETRY OF RELIGIOUS EXPERIENCE

MARTIN DUBOIS

Newcastle University

CAMBRIDGE
UNIVERSITY PRESS

CAMBRIDGE
UNIVERSITY PRESS

University Printing House, Cambridge CB2 8BS, United Kingdom

One Liberty Plaza, 20th Floor, New York, NY 10006, USA

477 Williamstown Road, Port Melbourne, VIC 3207, Australia

314-321, 3rd Floor, Plot 3, Splendor Forum, Jasola District Centre, New Delhi - 110025, India

79 Anson Road, #06-04/06, Singapore 079906

Cambridge University Press is part of the University of Cambridge.

It furthers the University's mission by disseminating knowledge in the pursuit of education, learning and research at the highest international levels of excellence.

www.cambridge.org
Information on this title: www.cambridge.org/9781107180451
DOI: 10.1017/9781316848036

© Martin Dubois 2017

First published 2017

A catalogue record for this publication is available from the British Library

Library of Congress Cataloging in Publication data
NAMES: Dubois, Martin, 1984– author.
TITLE: Gerard Manley Hopkins and the poetry of religious experience / Martin Dubois, University of Newcastle upon Tyne.
DESCRIPTION: New York : Cambridge University Press, 2017. | Series: Cambridge studies in nineteenth-century literature and culture ; 108
IDENTIFIERS: LCCN 2017027648 | ISBN 9781107180451 (hardback)
SUBJECTS: LCSH: Hopkins, Gerard Manley, 1844–1889 – Criticism and interpretation. | Hopkins, Gerard Manley, 1844–1889 – Religion. | Experience (Religion) in literature. | Bible – In literature. | Prayer in literature. | Spirituality in literature. | Christianity and literature – England – History – 19th century. | Christian poetry, English – 19th century – History and criticism.
CLASSIFICATION: LCC PR4803.H44 Z6243 2017 | DDC 821/.8–dc23
LC record available at https://lccn.loc.gov/2017027648

ISBN 978-1-107-18045-1 Hardback
ISBN 978-1-316-63223-9 Paperback

In memory of Elfrieda Dubois

Contents

Acknowledgements

This book has been long in the writing, and many people have helped me on the way to its completion. I particularly wish to thank Catherine Phillips, whose wise and patient mentoring of my work has done much to improve it. Two other teachers have also been important influences: Francis O'Gorman, who supervised my first attempt to write on Hopkins and has offered good advice and encouragement ever since, and Matthew Bevis, who challenged and inspired me to think in new ways about poetry. I am very grateful to those who, at various stages, read and commented on different parts of this book: Kirstie Blair, Philip Endean, S.J., Eric Griffiths, Michael Hurley, Angela Leighton, Robbie McLaughlan, Joseph Pizza, Peter Riley, Michael Rossington, Summer Star, David Stewart, Kelsey Thornton, and the anonymous readers for Cambridge University Press. I am also indebted to Lesley Higgins for answering specific queries. I thank Matthew Campbell and James Williams for permission to cite unpublished conference papers, and Michael Hurley for allowing me to read and quote from forthcoming work in advance of publication. I appreciate the advice given by Colin Kerr, who generously provided the cover image.

Much of the research for this book would not have been possible without the assistance of archivists and librarians, and I would like to acknowledge in particular the support given by Stephanie Plowman and her staff at the Foley Center Library, Gonzaga University, Spokane, Washington; Joseph Munitiz, S.J., at Campion Hall, Oxford; Damien Burke at the Irish Jesuit Archives, Dublin; Tom McCoog, S.J., and Anna Edwards at the Archive of the Jesuits in Britain, London; and Vicky Rowley, at Heythrop College Library, University of London.

An early version of Chapter 1 of this book appeared as an article published in *Victorian Poetry* in 2012. Chapters 3 and 5 adapt several paragraphs taken from my article 'Hopkins and the Burden of Security', which appeared in *Essays in Criticism* in 2013. I thank the editors and publishers for permission to reproduce material from these articles.

I owe much to my family. My dad has been a constant source of encouragement. Joseph, Sebastian, and Felicity provided ample fun and distraction whenever I was in danger of becoming too absorbed in my work. My deepest thanks go to Anna, for her love and support.

Note on Editions and Abbreviations

I have chosen to cite Hopkins's poems from Norman MacKenzie's 1990 edition *The Poetical Works of Gerard Manley Hopkins* because it includes the largest number of Hopkins's metrical marks of any edition as well as uncancelled variants in several of his poems. It is hereafter cited as *PW*. I have departed from the practice of this edition in two ways: first, in respect of caesurae, which are here marked by a double vertical bar (||) rather than a single vertical bar so that they can be differentiated from line breaks in in-text quotations; and second, in using line breaks to represent the structural divisions of the sonnet Hopkins indicated by braces in the left margin while he was in the process of drafting some later poems. I often comment upon Hopkins's metrical marks, but readers wanting further guidance should consult MacKenzie's detailed explanation in *PW*, lii–lix, or the notes given in Catherine Phillips's edition, *Gerard Manley Hopkins: The Major Works*, rev. edn (Oxford: Oxford University Press, 2002), p. 307.

The new *Collected Works of Gerard Manley Hopkins*, being published in eight volumes by Oxford University Press under the general editorship of Lesley Higgins and Michael F. Suarez, S.J., will become the standard edition. So far five volumes have appeared: volumes I and II, *Correspondence*, ed. by R. K. R. Thornton and Catherine Phillips (2013); volume III, *Diaries, Journals, and Notebooks*, ed. by Lesley Higgins (2015); volume IV, *Oxford Essays and Notes*, ed. by Lesley Higgins (2006); and volume VII, *The Dublin Notebook*, ed. by Lesley Higgins and Michael F. Suarez, S.J. (2014). These are hereafter cited as *CW*. I have used the *CW* editions wherever possible but otherwise rely on older editions (listed here). The *CW* editions preserve cancelled words and other deletions in his prose writings; the transcription of the Dublin notebook also holds to Hopkins's spacing. For clarity of text, these are only included when relevant to my argument.

CW	*The Collected Works of Gerard Manley Hopkins*, ed. by Lesley Higgins and Michael Suarez, S.J. (Oxford: Oxford University Press, 2006–)
EPM	*The Early Poetic Manuscripts of Gerard Manley Hopkins in Facsimile*, ed. by Norman H. MacKenzie (New York and London: Garland, 1989)
Gonzaga	Gerard Manley Hopkins Collection, Gonzaga University, Spokane, Washington
J&P	*The Journals and Papers of Gerard Manley Hopkins*, ed. by Humphry House and Graham Storey (London: Oxford University Press, 1959)
LPM	*The Later Poetic Manuscripts of Gerard Manley Hopkins in Facsimile*, ed. by Norman H. MacKenzie (New York and London: Garland, 1991)
MW	*Gerard Manley Hopkins: The Major Works*, ed. by Catherine Phillips (Oxford: Oxford University Press, 2002)
PW	*The Poetical Works of Gerard Manley Hopkins*, ed. by Norman H. MacKenzie (Oxford: Clarendon Press, 1990)
S	*The Sermons and Devotional Writings of Gerard Manley Hopkins*, ed. by Christopher Devlin (London: Oxford University Press, 1959)

Introduction

Gerard Manley Hopkins's last poem, the sonnet 'To R. B.', was completed on 22 April 1889. Written to make up a minor quarrel with its addressee Robert Bridges, the poem was enclosed a week later with a letter to Bridges that made brief reference to what would turn out to be Hopkins's final illness. He died of typhoid in June of that year, aged forty-four. 'To R. B.' was not intended to be valedictory, but as Bridges himself would later acknowledge, it is 'full of a strange fitness for the end':[1]

> The fine delight that fathers thought; the strong
> Spur, live and lancing like the blowpipe flame,
> Breathes once and, quenchèd faster than it came,
> Leaves yet the mind a mother of immortal song.
>
> Nine months she then, nay years, nine years she long
> Within her wears, bears, cares and combs the same:
> The widow of an insight lost she lives, with aim
> Now known and hand at work now never wrong.
>
> Sweet fire the sire of muse, my soul needs this;
> I want the one rapture of an inspiration.
> O then if in my lagging lines you miss
>
> The roll, the rise, the carol, the creation,
> My winter world, that scarcely breathes that bliss
> Now, yields you, with some sighs, our explanation.

'To R. B.' is a quieter work than is usual for Hopkins. One would not guess from it that he could be called by Elizabeth Bishop 'the most intricate of poets technically and the most taxing emotionally'.[2] In describing what his poetry lacks, however, Hopkins also manages to intimate a high aesthetic ideal, an ideal close to that envisaged in a letter of 1886: the notion that works of art 'have an absolute excellence in them and are steps in a scale of infinite and inexhaustible excellence'.[3] The *Ars Poetica* of the octave, with its allusion to Horace's idea of the long gestation of the poem, treats of the aesthetic on its own terms. 'Soul', on the other hand, at the beginning of the sestet, along with 'carol' and 'creation' in line 12, hints that the immortality of 'immortal song' may not be only aesthetic. Of course, what we encounter here are acoustic qualities (an earlier version of line 12 had read 'The wild wing, waft, cry, carol, and creation').[4] The comedown of the final line, moreover, with its flat return of 'explanation' upon 'creation', seems too humdrum to sustain a connection between the life of poetry and the life of God. Yet 'creation' still stands out, connoting less poetry's flow of words (as do 'roll', 'rise', and 'carol') than the entire act of artistic production. Conceiving of inspiration as a type of fertility, Hopkins in 'To R. B.' makes an analogy between sexual procreation and the begetting of poems. With 'creation', parallels for poetic invention extend yet more widely, so that human agency seems to reciprocate divine agency in the word's religious echoes. Despite making play of its slightness, then, the poem also edges on the idea that art's reaching for transcendence implies the sacred. Hopkins's rueful disclaiming of eloquence carries a latent aesthetical boldness.

This is an apt combination for a writer of immense daring and ambition who yet tended to be equivocal about the spiritual worth of his compositions. Bishop was right to see that for Hopkins 'to be a poet was not the be-all, end-all of existence'.[5] Seldom could he imagine his own compositions in the manner of 'To R. B.' as acts of human creation that parallel the divine creation. Instead, Hopkins worried that poetry failed to answer the special demand for ordinary service he saw God had made upon his life. Not the least of the remarkable things about his sonnet 'The Windhover', which Hopkins in 1879 considered 'the best thing I ever wrote', is that he was able several years after the poem was first composed to dedicate it in the title 'to Christ our Lord'.[6] The confidence this dedication expresses in poetry's capacity to be an authentic gift to God was usually much less entire. One reason why Hopkins was rarely seen in print until after his death, aside from a few minor verses and translations, is that his daring formal innovations baffled those who might have published his poetry; another is that Hopkins himself worried that publication would not sit well with his vocation as a Jesuit priest. For a long time even the composition of poetry seemed to him at best a distraction, and at worst improper. Before commencing his Jesuit training, and with a new poetic rhythm still haunting his ear, Hopkins burnt copies of his poems in what he theatrically called a 'Slaughter of the innocents'.[7] He then imposed almost complete written silence on himself for seven years before relenting, in a blaze, with 'The Wreck of the Deutschland' in 1875–76. 'The Wreck' inaugurates

Hopkins's poetic maturity. What it did not remove was Hopkins's caution about whether the energy he expended on poetry was well spent: 'After writing ['The Wreck'] I held myself free to compose,' he explained in a letter of 1878, 'but cannot find it in my conscience to spend time upon it; so I have done little and shall do less.'[8]

None of this has prevented Hopkins's critics from seeing his poetry as the outgrowth of a unified project of philosophical understanding. Hopkins was strongly given to intellectual speculation and is famed for the theories he developed about language and about the nature of reality. These theories guide many discussions of his work. The emphasis in such discussions is on the grand system of ideas seen to define the early phase of Hopkins's poetic maturity, occurring ahead of his ordination as a priest. Often out of view are the more incomplete and unstable perceptions of his later writing – perceptions such as that found in 'To R. B.', in which regret for a lack of creative impulse is traced with a sense of poetry's spiritual worth. Such poems fit less neatly than earlier work with the conceptual scheme with which Hopkins is usually identified, and their concern with individual spiritual history has made them appear of more limited significance than the poems of bold proclamation for which he is best known. Our sense has been that when Hopkins is not comprehensive and consolidative he is strictly inward and intimate.

This book seeks to recover the diversity in Hopkins's writing by focussing on the way in which he imagines the individual lived experience of religious belief. Such experience provides a subject for Hopkins's poetry as well as a perspective from which it is offered: there are poems inspired by incidents in priestly life, in which Hopkins searches his responses to persons to whom he had ministered, and there are those that imagine the situation of individual belief, dramatising conditions of spiritual joy and confidence as well as of dryness and difficulty. His poems of religious experience have been more reputed for their feeling than for their thought. When seen against the poised and far-reaching vision typical of the dazzling early phase of Hopkins's poetic maturity, it is all too easy to think of them as a retreat into the private drama of inward self. Thus the earliest full-length study of the poet divided his work into two classes, distinguishing between poems which 'deal in an intellectual way with something which is more or less in the nature of a maxim or aphorism' and those 'which are records of experience, which deal with moods rather than maxims'.[9] The same division has become embedded in the binary preoccupations of Hopkins criticism, drawn to concentrate either on systematic metaphysical proposition in his poetry or on how it expresses private and individual spiritual history.

Hopkins's poems of religious experience require us to move beyond this division. This book does not seek to establish another scheme by which to understand Hopkins but rather highlights what can be gained from a more flexible approach to his writing. The building of Hopkins's ideas into a tight system by his critics has certainly helped refute the old impression of the poet as wholly unable to reconcile a delight in sensuous beauty with strict religious commitment; yet it has also created an imbalance in what we appreciate of him. One obvious danger is that the effort to harmonise Hopkins's poetry with his prose writings according to a consistent intellectual programme means we neglect what is distinctive to each of the forms in which he wrote. Another is that little allowance can be made for contradiction and anomaly when all of his work is expected to adhere to a set conceptual standard. I aim to show that his poetry's thought does not run in a single pattern, but instead it takes different forms, sometimes striving for logical consistency and unifying principles, and on other occasions appearing more provisional and exploratory. Hopkins emerges here as a poet just as much occupied with the contingency of spiritual process as with the assertion of a uniform vision. This too lay within his roll, rise, carol, and creation.

Parts and Wholes of Hopkins

The first edition of Hopkins's poetry did not appear until nearly three decades after his death. Yet although largely unpublished in his lifetime, he was something other than a private poet and, at least initially, did make efforts to publish his mature work. Overcoming his scruples to begin work on 'The Wreck' needed the encouragement of his Jesuit superiors and the likely hope that the poem might eventually appear in a Jesuit journal.[10] Anxieties remained – 'You must never say that the poem is mine', Hopkins warned his mother at a point when he expected that 'The Wreck' might be published – but the prospect of honouring his religious profession by poetry appears to have been essential to Hopkins taking up his pen again after a long period when it had been largely at rest.[11] This prospect faded once another shipwreck poem, 'The Loss of the Eurydice' (1878), suffered the same fate as 'The Wreck' in finally being rejected by the same Jesuit journal. Even so, the disappointment of Hopkins's hopes for his poetry after this rejection was far from total. In 1881 Hopkins eagerly pursued the possibility of being published in an anthology of sonnets, 'even though it meant going against his stated edict not to seek, or at least force, notoriety'.[12] Again, he was turned down as a result of the novelty of his poetic methods. In retreat notes written two years later, Hopkins earnestly asked our Lord to watch over my compositions, not to preserve them from being lost or coming to nothing, for that I am very willing that they should be, but that they might not do me harm through the enmity or imprudence of any man or my own; that he should have them as his own and employ or not employ them as he should see fit.[13]

The hope that his poems might in some way render service to God may be distressingly frail here, but it remains clearly discernible – as it does also in the desire Hopkins once expressed 'that my pieces could at some time become known but in some spontaneous way, so to speak, and without my forcing', a statement which is characteristic both in the reluctance to seek fame and in the hope that recognition might arrive by means unprompted.[14]

At the same time, it is evident that the rejection of his poems for publication hardened Hopkins's feeling that such pieces were a distraction from more substantial employment. In effect, a tension seen earlier in Hopkins's creative life re-established itself in new form. Norman H. MacKenzie nicely identifies the 'curious paradox' of Hopkins's undergraduate verses as being that 'the only really telling pieces are religious, and yet his religious conscience was restraining him from composition'.[15] The poetry written later, from 'The Wreck' onwards, no longer occasioned the angst of these early verses, when poems had been interspersed with tortured confessional notes in his journal. In one sense Hopkins grew more relaxed about the time he gave to literary composition. But even if found to be less problematic, the notion he had of poetry as 'unprofessional' – the term he used in a letter of 1884 – revived strongly once 'The Loss of the Eurydice' had been rejected, even as religious belief remained Hopkins's most frequent and telling subject.[16]

These doubts about the merit of composing poetry were personal to Hopkins and did not apply to the literary labours of those with whom he corresponded. Attempting in a letter of 1878 to console a fellow poet whose work had not achieved wide fame, Hopkins felt able to declare that 'The only just judge, the only just literary critic, is Christ, who prizes, is proud of, and admires, more than any man, more than the receiver himself can, the gifts of his own making.'[17] Writing several years later on a similar theme to Robert Bridges, of Bridges's own poetry, and concluding on this occasion that works of art must be known to do good, Hopkins was equally able to find in them a spiritual virtue: a 'true rule' in the question of art and fame, Hopkins told Bridges, was 'what Christ our Lord said of virtue, Let your light shine before men that they may see your good works (say, of art) and glorify yr. Father in heaven'.[18] These pronouncements diverge: in one case, Christ's interest renders fame secondary; in the other, being known is what best honours God. Neither represents Hopkins's view of his own art. Its virtue in the eyes of God seemed to him less certain, so that the encouragement he occasionally received to seek literary recognition was once met with the rejoinder that 'there is more peace and it is the holier lot to be unknown than to be known'.[19]

The demands of Hopkins's professional life also limited his opportunity to write poetry. Hopkins's work as a Jesuit was often arduous. During his years in a vast Jesuit parish in Liverpool, he was part of a group of nine priests serving a local Roman Catholic population of nearly ten thousand; these priests sometimes collectively heard in excess of eighty thousand confessions in a single year.[20] Later, having been appointed to an academic position in Ireland, Hopkins's energies were equally stretched, especially by what he called the 'great, very great drudgery' of examination work.[21] It was difficult in these circumstances for Hopkins to find time and energy enough to compose poetry, let alone make efforts to have it published. This was to him not entirely a matter of regret. 'When a man has given himself to God's service', Hopkins once told his friend Richard Watson Dixon, 'when he has denied himself and followed Christ, he has fitted himself to receive and does receive from God a special guidance, a more particular providence':

> This guidance is conveyed partly by the action of other men, as his appointed superiors, and partly by direct lights and inspirations. If I wait for such guidance, through whatever channel conveyed, about anything, about my poetry, for instance, I do more wisely in every way than if I try to serve my own seeming interests in the matter. Now if you value what I write, if I do myself, much more does our Lord. And if he chooses to avail himself of what I leave at his disposal he can do so with a felicity and with a success which I could never command. And if he does not, then two things follow; one that the reward I shall nevertheless receive from him will be all the greater; the other that then I shall know how much a thing contrary to his will and even to my own best interests I should have done if I had taken things into my own hands and forced on publication. This is my principle and this in the main has been my practice: leading the sort of life I do here [at Roehampton, where Hopkins spent his tertianship, a year of relief from pastoral work] it seems easy, but when one mixes with the world and meets on every side its secret solicitations, to live by faith is harder, is very hard; nevertheless by God's help I shall always do so.

Hopkins's reluctance to seek fame may have served partly as a protection against the likelihood of further rejection of his work by editors. Once appointed to an academic post, Hopkins still occasionally managed to produce poems, but he was unable to complete the scholarly publications expected of him: evidently misgivings about his poetry becoming known did little to reduce the appeal of its composition. Obscurity also provided a form of validation when seen as a consequence of the novelty of his creative methods; it is no coincidence that several of Hopkins's particular heroes were figures whose originality he saw to have gone unappreciated in their own time ('I hope you will long continue to work out yr beautiful and original style', Hopkins told his favourite architect, William Butterfield, in a letter of 1877: 'I do not think this generation will ever much admire it').[22] Even so, Hopkins's desire to wait upon God's will for his writing deserves to be taken seriously on its own terms. It is not that Hopkins believed his composition of poetry was of itself sinful or corrupting; rather, it is that he required much persuasion that literary endeavours had a true relation to his religious calling. 'Our Society values, as you say, and has contributed to literature, to culture', Hopkins's letter to Dixon continues, with regard to the Jesuits, 'but only as a means to an end. Its history and its experience shew that literature proper, as poetry, has seldom been found to be to that end a very serviceable means.'[23]

Hopkins had on more than one occasion to answer the charge that he had forgone a potentially brilliant artistic career for the religious life. His reported response to such claims was disarmingly simple and typically playful: '"You wouldn't give only the dull ones to Almighty God."'[24] In one way it seems remarkable that Hopkins's Jesuit obituary makes no mention of his literary writing, commenting only that 'his acquaintance with poetry was extensive, and his judgements differed upon various poets considerably from what most people entertain'.[25] The obituary has sometimes been thought evidence of how little his literary talent was appreciated by those among whom he lived and worked; it appears to join with the sorry tale of the rejection of 'The Wreck' from publication in a Jesuit journal in the unwitting neglect of Hopkins's genius by the religious order in which he served. In another sense, though, the omission is in keeping with Hopkins's own sense that the chief purpose of his life lay elsewhere. Although often applied to Hopkins, the epithet 'priest-poet' (or its alternative: 'poet-priest') is not one that he himself would have much understood. This priest and poet rarely saw his two vocations as constituting part of the same venture.

The relation of poetry to religious duty was for a long time a main concern of Hopkins criticism. As early as 1926, eight years after the appearance of the first edition of Hopkins's poems, I. A. Richards's trailblazing essay on Hopkins in the *Dial* suggested 'that the poet in him was often oppressed and stifled by the priest' – a claim that other early studies were determined to refute.[26] The debate continued to exercise commentary on Hopkins well into the second half of the twentieth century, when the idea of 'Hopkins's commitment to religion before literature' still had prominence.[27] It has now largely disappeared from recent studies, to be replaced by the notion that poetry was for Hopkins an act of spiritual dedication and formed part of his attempt to reconcile a philosophical and theological faith in God with sensitivity to natural beauty. Hopkins's inclination for theorising in his prose writings (of which the twin concepts of 'inscape' and 'instress' are the most famous product) has in particular led a number of critics to evoke a direct and exact relation between the epistemology pursued in certain of his undergraduate essays and early journals and aspects of belief that enter into poems written across a far longer period. For some of these critics, most notably Isobel Armstrong, the potential for poetic language to trouble fixed meanings and theological prescriptions reveals the fault lines in what they declare to be Hopkins's intellectual and aesthetic scheme.[28] For others, equally taken with what they understand to be the systematic nature and orientation of his poetry's thought, it is a much more achieved project.[29] Either way, the general perception now is that, as Helen Vendler has recently proposed, 'The subjects that interested Hopkins were chiefly intellectual ones; even his most sensuous responses to the natural world were immediately referred to the intellect, which, in the poetry, meant referral to philosophical or theological thought.'[30]

This view of Hopkins is weighted towards the early phase of his poetic maturity and misses his concern with how matters of belief are received in time and combine with individual history. A different sense of Hopkins emerges from consideration of how his poetry grapples with faith as it is lived out in personal experience. The individual experience Hopkins imagines is of course never pure; it is not pre-conceptual or free from abstraction. Indeed, this book attends closely to the broad theological and spiritual resonances of Hopkins's interest in individual histories of belief. Yet it is also the case that Hopkins's poems on this topic have a less formal engagement with intellectual understanding than is suggested by Vendler's remark. The youthful poems Hopkins wrote before the advent of his poetic maturity are at once self-denying and world-denying; they tend to perceive of experience as the arena of spiritual combat, a testing ground for the life to come. This sense never disappears in Hopkins, but it is increasingly in tension with sacramental confidence that spiritual realities are to be encountered (and not only prepared for) in everyday lived circumstance. That the tension remains unresolved means that his poetry finally offers no single view of the significance of ordinary religious experience in spiritual understanding, at points appearing to embrace it, and at other times seeming to suspect its lack of grasp upon permanent and immutable truths. As such, religious experience cannot provide a key to Hopkins's thought in the manner favoured by totalising interpretations of his poetry as the elaboration of a philosophical and theological scheme. The study of religious experience in Hopkins has instead different merits, enabling detailed attention to be given to poems that usually lie outside the scope of synthesising approaches to his work, and, just as importantly, allowing for what is unresolved or elusive in Hopkins's meaning to signal more than the failure of a project of intellectual distillation.

By 'religious experience', it should be said immediately, I do not mean the private and anthropocentric experience with which the term 'spirituality' is now often associated, but rather that which for Hopkins always and finally had to be directed to self-transcendence in God. The enormous influence William James's *The Varieties of Religious Experience* (1902) has had in various fields of study means that religious experience is commonly seen in opposition to institutional religion as well as to doctrines of faith. James sets religious experience against 'theology and ceremony and ecclesiastical organization': 'In the more personal branch of religion it is on the contrary the inner dispositions of man himself which form the centre of interest, his conscience, his deserts, his helplessness, his incompleteness.'[31] The notion of religious experience appropriate to Hopkins could not be more different. In the Spiritual Exercises of the Jesuit founder, St Ignatius Loyola (1491–1556), he practised a method of prayer in which, according to a modern understanding, 'the stress is on the exercitant's distinctive experience, shaped as it is by a particular history'.[32] Yet the significance Ignatius attaches to personal experience in the Spiritual Exercises is always more than private. This experience is not meaningful for him unless sustained and guided by the doctrine and practice of the Catholic Church. The emphasis of the Spiritual Exercises on inner dispositions is intended to deepen a person's commitment to the divine: 'by means of a retreat of this kind', Ignatius observes, a person's 'intellect being less drawn in different directions than before, and his whole thought being collected and reduced to one thing, – namely to obeying God his Creator … he uses his natural powers in a freer and more unencumbered way in seeking what he so much desires'.[33]

For Hopkins there can be no dichotomy of formal truth and individual awareness. As Geoffrey Hill declares: 'To view him as an ecstatic, solipsistic rhapsodist, without reference to the solid grounding in Catholic dogmatics and the tactics of nineteenth-century Catholic proselytising, is to fail to be in earnest ... with the distinctive quality of his genius.'[34] Hopkins's poetry always has a theological and ecclesiastical discipline. This discipline takes various forms across his poetry. Some of his poems can be said to present 'stages in doctrinal discourse' (as Hill argues of 'The Windhover'), whilst others give less methodical shape to their religious thoughts.[35] Such variety means it is worth countenancing in Hopkins's writing the 'rough division' the theologian Philip Endean makes 'between approaches to the one theological mystery of God's self-gift among us focusing primarily on regulative sources and principles on the one hand ... and, on the other, those which begin from ongoing experience'.[36] Endean is referring to theology and spirituality as disciplines of study, but the distinction can also help indicate the range of insight to emerge from Hopkins's poetry. It can recall us from the wish always to organise it into a system of knowledge.

In his study of Hopkins, Philip A. Ballinger is careful to acknowledge that 'nowhere in his writings did Hopkins attempt a synthesis of his theological aesthetic'. As a result, 'the scholar is therefore required to construct a synthetic whole from bits and pieces framed in the various contexts of Hopkins' poems, sermons, letters, and personal musings', a whole from which 'there emerges the beginning of a comprehensive theological aesthetic'.[37] From this perspective, the trend of Hopkins's thought is 'anatomical', to use Carlo Ginzburg's term, and reflects on particulars by means of general, encompassing principles that are capable of being organised into a complete system.[38] It is a view of Hopkins which is profoundly in tune with 'The Wreck' as well as with certain of Hopkins's nature sonnets, especially the untitled poem which begins 'As kingfishers catch fire, dragonflies draw flame' (1877). Of the poems inspired by priestly experience, 'The Handsome Heart' (1879) is most obviously traced with a far-reaching personal metaphysic in admiring how the heart 'To its function fine it, wild and self-instressed, | Falls light as ten years long taught what and why' (ll. 7–8). This praise for the way the heart follows its natural impulse is bound up with delight in unique selfhood, selfhood which is found to be so strongly individuated that it has to be described in correspondingly particularised terms. Here too it is appropriate to speak of 'a comprehensive theological aesthetic'.

Other works, especially those written after the early phase of his poetic maturity, are less well served by the expectation that Hopkins's writing aims always to be synoptic. The claim of this book is that the effort of much of Hopkins's poetry is actually less comprehensive than has been proposed, and that the theological and spiritual awareness manifested in his writing is often more inductive and conjectural, tending to the knowledge Ginzburg describes as 'born of experience, of the concrete and individual'.[39] Such is vividly the condition of the 'terrible' or 'dark' sonnets (c. 1885–86) in their contention with spiritual dryness, and it is also recognisably that of poems on acts of priestly ministry, such as 'Felix Randal' (1880). Elsewhere, the thought of Hopkins's poetry is less obviously experiential but still, I suggest, deserves to be seen in light of the 'concrete and individual' as well as the achieved, self-complete vision more often ascribed to it.

This will be the first study of Hopkins to offer a broad account of religious experience in his poetry. Previous scholarship in this area has tended to focus either on its personal and autobiographical significance or else on the influence of Ignatius's Spiritual Exercises on the poet.[40] The influence of the Spiritual Exercises is discussed in Chapter 2, but otherwise the book attends to the more general appearance of religious experience in Hopkins's poetry. I am conscious that the term 'religious experience' can be problematic for its implication that this category is special and separate from other kinds of experience; for Hopkins, who believed God to be in all things, every part of life was informed by his faith convictions. I have retained the term because the alternatives did not seem sufficiently to indicate the book's emphasis on how Hopkins's poetry conceives of encounters with the divine in the context of specific practices of faith and in relation to particular Catholic traditions and doctrines. This emphasis provides a means of demonstrating that the inward turn taken by Hopkins's poetry after the early phase of his creative maturity does not deprive it of spiritual and theological significance. By showing that a fruitful approach to Hopkins's poetry can be made from outside the various systems proposed as keys to his thought, I also aim to open up his work to readers otherwise daunted by its weight and complexity.

The main source of the idea that Hopkins aspired always to systematic insight in his poetry is not far to seek. As the next section suggests, to oppose the view that a unified and consistent project animates all of Hopkins's poetry requires that we revisit the categories of 'inscape' and 'instress' he developed in his prose writings, categories traditionally said to be the nucleus of his poetry's vision, and the most frequent instrument of its consolidation by his critics.

Inscape and Instress

The meaning of Hopkins's terms 'inscape' and 'instress' is difficult to exhaust, a fact which also makes them hard to approach. The first term, 'inscape', signifies the unique inner essence of a thing or scene, that which constitutes the governing law or pattern of individual forms. Initially a noun, 'inscape' was soon also used as a verb by Hopkins ('to inscape'), allowing it on occasion to refer not just to the quality observed but also to the act of perception: for instance, having first recorded that he 'caught … inscape' in observing a horse at an event in 1874, Hopkins went on to note that 'I looked at the groin or flank and saw how the set of the hair symmetrically flowed outwards from it to all parts of the body, so that following that one may inscape the whole beast very simply.'[41]

'Instress' holds a double meaning, indicating at once the force of being which upholds the inscape and the effect of observing the inscape on the beholder. Like 'inscape', 'instress' first appears in Hopkins's 1868 notes on Greek philosophy, where it is defined as the energy or 'stress' of individual being, with this energy described as 'the flush and foredrawn', a dense but resonant elaboration of the term which suggests that instress is a force that is at once full and fluid, like a liquid, and yet at the same time bounded by defined limits.[42] As here, it is not always obvious that the two senses of the term go together, but go together they do, for instress, as Dennis Sobolev remarks, involves a willed act of perception to apprehend the energy of being: 'The description of the energetic impact of the world upon the mind, without which no discussion of instress is possible, requires the description of both the functioning of the mind and the energetic depths of the world.'[43] This mutual dependence is apparent in a rare appearance of the term in Hopkins's poetry, early in 'The Wreck', when it is said of Christ that 'thóugh he is únder the wórld's spléndour and wónder, | His mýstery múst be instréssed, stressed' (ll. 38–39). Here the force of divine mystery is such that its apprehension requires a special effort of the will, a notion to which Hopkins's diacritical marks seem to align: 'His mystery múst be instréssed, stressed' is emphatic in a way which itself answers to the exertion needed to feel deeply the energy of God's being.[44] As this example also suggests, part of the complexity of 'instress' as a term is that 'stress' is itself a highly evocative word in Hopkins – as indeed is the word 'scape', which also has a special use for Hopkins, indicating 'a reflection or impression of the individual quality of a thing or action' (*OED*), so that, observing a particular kind of cloud, for instance, he could remark in a journal entry of 1871 that 'its brindled and hatched scaping though difficult to catch is remarkable when seen'.[45]

Adding to the richness and density of 'inscape' and 'instress' as terms is their close relation to Hopkins's theories about the nature of language. Hopkins had a profound concern with the etymological and onomato-poetic roots of language, and his notes on Pre-Socratic philosophy made in 1868 reveal an associated conviction that words are not arbitrary signs but provide the essence of natural phenomena: 'The truth in thought is Being, stress, and each word is one way of acknowledging Being and each sentence by its copula <u>is</u> (or its equivalent) the utterance and assertion of it.'[46] This interest in the philosophical significance of language – and, especially, in the *sound* of language – was abiding. As James I. Wimsatt has demonstrated, Hopkins's prose writings arrive at a 'coherent and impressive poetics of speech sound', and this poetics bears close relation to his philosophical interests, as can be seen most clearly in the incomplete essay 'Poetry and Verse', from around 1873–74, which observes that 'Poetry is in fact speech only employed to carry the inscape of speech for the inscape's sake – and therefore the inscape must be dwelt on.'[47] It is also apparent in the typically soaring intellectual plan Hopkins later conceived of a book 'on the Dorian measure or on Rhythm in general', which was to have tackled 'almost everything elementary ... much of it physics and metaphysics'; 'It is full of new words', Hopkins told Bridges, 'without which there can be no new science.'[48] This was what Hopkins at the time believed his university position demanded, 'scientific works', as he named them in one letter, not 'luxuries like poetry', but it is surely no coincidence that Hopkins's invented terms for describing his own metrical experiments in poetry – terms such as 'hanger', 'outride', 'sprung rhythm', and 'counterpointing' – are highly figurative in just the manner of his philosophical coinages, 'inscape' and 'instress'.[49] Evidently these are parallel idioms, whose newness answers to Hopkins's profound sense of the originality of his ideas and perceptions – ideas and perceptions so original, indeed, that even his own invented vocabulary sometimes did not seem to him to be able to encompass them, as when Hopkins noticed 'coat below coat' of snow on a winter walk of 1870, 'sketched in intersecting edges bearing "idiom", all down the slope': 'I have no other word yet for that which takes the eye or mind in a bold hand or effective sketching or in marked features or again in graphic writing, which not being beauty nor true inscape yet gives interest and makes ugliness better than meaninglessness.'[50]

The roots of the personal metaphysic represented by inscape and instress lie in Hopkins's undergraduate philosophical studies, of which the 1868 notes on the Pre-Socratics are a kind of synthesis. Thereafter, most discussion of inscape and instress occurred in private reflection, meaning that Hopkins was rarely required to expound their meaning to others. Such reflection did not generally involve the elucidation of inscape and instress as concepts but rather their application to diverse subjects. In consequence, Hilary Fraser remarks, 'The critic is hence obliged to construct the theory from hints to be found in Hopkins' various writings on beauty, religion, philosophy and art', resulting in a 'necessary but artificial separation of the ideas from their context'.[51]

When this effort at constructing the theory is made, the significance of inscape and instress appears large indeed: Fraser, for instance, contends that in identifying inscape as a concept of individuation with Christ's own self-being, Hopkins finds an objective basis for his subjective perceptions of the created world, 'and in doing so solves long-standing problems of perception in Romantic aesthetics'.[52] Yet the notion that these terms provide a comprehensive explanation for all of Hopkins's writing can also be pressed too hard, giving rise to the impression that his poetry represents the culmination or even the 'outworking' of the philosophical scheme to which inscape and instress are attached, and thus that his most important poems are those which best exemplify their meaning.[53] A more balanced interpretation is given by Matthew Campbell, who observes the following:

> Hopkins' career developed into poetry and not systemised philosophy ... His poetry works to write out the rhythm which is already in the objects of a divinely created universe and which are now in turn the objects of his perceptions and thought. Of course, that poetry does work with the positions that Hopkins attempted to reach in his theological writing, no matter how unfinished that can be. Yet we can see in this writing the structures of thought and the basis of a spirituality to which the poetry gives body.[54]

The theories of self and being initiated in Hopkins's prose writings are crucial to his poetry, but the poetry does not simply continue the thinking that has already been done in other forms. This in turn suggests the need for a more flexible use of Hopkins's famous coinages to explain his poems, a use that would accept rather than attempt to surmount the raw and composite nature of the philosophical speculations from which these coinages arise, and so allow us better to countenance the range of different meanings and applications of inscape and instress that are to be found across Hopkins's oeuvre. Rather than representing a problem of definition requiring to be solved to render his work into a complete edifice, the variety in Hopkins's use of the terms helps illuminate some of the major tensions and contrasts of his writing.

A tricky balance needs to be maintained here between the tasks Hopkins determined his poetry should perform and the accidents of composition against which he battled ('The good poet ... disproves chance' is how Peter McDonald characterises Hopkins's view of rhyme, a description which might also have a more general application to his creative ideal).[55] Faced with Hopkins's carefully weighed poetics, and seeking to account for the effects of formal experimentation in his poems, a project recent criticism has revived, there can be a temptation to make of the intention a total reality, and thus to ascribe his formal practice with absolute directedness. This is particularly true in the case of sprung rhythm, 'a theory in development', as Meredith Martin notes, for which 'it has also proved impossible not to attempt to complete the theory – to come up with a way of understanding "sprung rhythm" and teaching it so that its aims and results are unmistakable'.[56] It equally applies to Hopkins's language, which has been proposed to depend so entirely on faith in God as *Logos* that his poetry can be judged by its success or failure in achieving unity between words and their referents.[57]

There are clearly connections between Hopkins's prosodic and linguistic experiments and his belief, as declared in 'The Wreck', that 'present and past, | Heaven and earth are word of, worded by' Christ (ll. 229–30). This belief frames his perception that connections between words and the world are essential rather than arbitrary, so that, as the 1868 notes on Greek philosophy put it, 'the word is the expression, uttering of the idea in the mind', a view of language which in turn prompts a determination to avoid abstraction and instead achieve a strenuous immediacy in poetic expression.[58] Yet to submit all of Hopkins's poetry to a single and unchanging standard risks a monolithic application of theories that were only partially worked out. It also assumes that Hopkins expected their realisation would be absolutely consistent. The poet himself knew otherwise: 'My meaning surely ought to appear of itself', he told Bridges in 1887, wishing it were so, 'but in a language like English, and in an age of it like the present, written words are really matter open'.[59]

Adding to the openness of Hopkins's words is that many drafts of his poems were left in an untidy state at the time of his death. There was no immediate need to ready his work for publication, and several poems have unresolved variants. In addition, the exchange of poems in manuscript and in transcription between Hopkins and his friends led him to make corrections that sometimes clarify his intention but can also confuse matters. It is difficult to tell, for instance, what exactly was meant by the correction Hopkins made to Bridges's transcription of 'The Windhover' when he deleted an ampersand Bridges had used in one line and wrote out 'AND' in capitals in the narrow space between this line and the one above it. As Randall McLeod observes, the rendering of the word in small capitals by Hopkins's editors 'is now a compelling landmark in our graphic experience of the poem' (it appears in the line 'AND the fire that breaks from thee then'), but one about which there is a good deal of uncertainty.[60] The poet had in his own earlier drafts of 'The Windhover' placed a *sforzando* symbol above the initial capital of

'And', which Bridges's use of an ampersand in his transcription appears to overlook, perhaps prompting an emphatic correction from Hopkins: 'Is Hopkins' unprecedented use of capitals (whatever their size) purely in his own voice', asks McLeod, 'or are they not provoked by the editor's having substituted his "&" for the poet's "And" with its stressed initial capital? – as if Hopkins were responding to the substitute ampersand: "Dammit – can't you SEE the word is stressed?"'[61]

Hopkins's poetry can be intensely deliberate, giving in the eyes of his detractors an 'excessive weight ... to the idea of mastery' over language and experience.[62] Even taken as a whole, however, it still differs from the 'scientific works' he latterly believed were required of him.[63] Part of the danger of believing otherwise is that we expect the faith of his poems to be somehow perfect, regularising what may be strange or contingent in their meaning. To see only poise and exactness in Hopkins is to mirror the doubts some have held about his importance as a poet. One main objection to Hopkins has been that his highly unfamiliar manner is 'adopted to compensate by strangeness for the lack of pure merit' (as A. E. Housman complained); another is that his writing has limited scope.[64] T. S. Eliot is the most prominent of those who have taken against Hopkins on the latter basis, writing in relation to Hopkins that 'To be a "devotional poet" is a limitation: a saint limits himself by writing poetry, and a poet who confines himself to even this subject matter is limiting himself too.'[65] The complaint chimes with Eliot's remark about it being generally understood that 'the religious poet is not a poet who is treating the whole subject matter of poetry in a religious spirit, but a poet who is dealing with a confined part of this subject matter'; it also echoes with Eliot's further (albeit in this case more positive) classification of 'devotional poetry' as 'religious poetry which falls within an exact faith and has precise objects for contemplation'.[66]

The word 'exact' has to take an impossible weight here, as does the word 'achieved' in Morris Dickstein's recent renewal of hostilities with the idea of religious poetry. Dickstein writes: 'There is an unavoidable conflict between any achieved faith – the confidence of being saved, of having found a single, all-embracing truth – and the tentative, exploratory nature of the literary imagination.'[67] This prizing of unfettered creative impulse is of course not new, but the way it is here opposed to religious belief involves extreme simplification. Hopkins shows that we need a more generous sense of the possibilities of religious poetry. First: although poetic and religious conviction are not identical for Hopkins, part of why they are able to exist in harmony as well as in conflict is that the faith which takes shape in his writing is not a single unchanging entity but can instead be seen to shift its position on the wide spectrum of belief. Second: Dickstein assumes a sharp separation between theological precepts and actual lives of faith that misconceives the nature of much religious adherence, and with it the variety feasible within religious poetry. What he more precisely means by 'achieved faith' is doctrinal faith, and his article goes on to enlist Hopkins's later poetry in making his case that 'the poetry we most value is personal and resistant to dogma': 'Hopkins, like other post-Romantic writers, negotiates the precipices of his mind rather than finessing them with abstract theology or facile moral casuistry.'[68] One senses here what the contemporary poet Michael Symmons Roberts, writing of the reputation of religious poetry, calls 'a terror of the imagination in thrall to a belief'.[69] Hopkins's poems have always provoked resistance in some readers, especially, perhaps, when at their most determinedly synoptic and proclamatory – as in 'The Wreck', disliked enough to be excluded from the leading anthology *The Penguin Book of Victorian Verse* (1997) despite its status as a major work ('The Wreck' is 'a poem which I cannot stomach,' the volume's editor, Daniel Karlin, later remarked, 'but which I now regret not forcing myself to include').[70] From this perspective, it can be consoling to think that Hopkins becomes almost a new poet when he turns to contemplate the mental 'precipices' of individual religious experience in his later, less declarative and synthesising poetry. Yet in reality his poems about individual struggles of faith always have communal and doctrinal significance. It could hardly be otherwise. As Brian Cummings says of the literary culture of an earlier period, the assumption that 'theology is an activity separate from the personal and psychological sphere of religious experience ... mistakes the way that spiritual life is invested in theological language': 'Any experience, any psychology, is inseparable from the language in which it operates and by which it is identified.'[71] Recognising the truth of this for Hopkins in turn requires an attention to his immediate spiritual and theological contexts.

Contexts for Religious Experience

Having come up to Oxford as an undergraduate in 1863, Hopkins was drawn into an atmosphere of religious controversy still shaped by the Tractarian or Oxford Movement that had arisen there three decades earlier with the aim of recalling the Church of England to Catholic principles and practices. He would quickly come under the influence of what we now know as Anglican ritualism or early Anglo-Catholicism, which held strong affinities with the catholicising ambitions of the earlier Tractarians. As time went on, however, Hopkins began to have doubts about the Church of England, worrying that the authentic Catholic Church in England was not Anglican, but Roman. Eventually, in October 1866, he joined the Roman Catholic Church. Much changed for Hopkins upon his conversion, but most of his fundamental religious beliefs remained constant. A good example is the doctrine of the real presence of Christ in the Eucharist, to which Hopkins already fully subscribed when an Anglican. Indeed, what John Henry Newman wrote generally of converts to Rome is true for Hopkins: 'They come, not so much to lose what they have, as to gain what they have not; and in order that, by means of what they have, more may be given to them.'[72] (Newman was himself a convert from Anglicanism, and the person who received Hopkins into the Roman Catholic communion.)

In the years following his conversion, Hopkins developed the sacramental understanding of the created world which is so integral to his poetry. This understanding is likely to have been influenced by the Tractarian interest in patristic writings Hopkins knew in his Anglican years, which would have introduced him to a sacramental view of nature.[73] It ran counter, however, to dominant trends in the Roman Catholic thought of Hopkins's period. Indeed, parts of the training Hopkins received as a Jesuit went profoundly against his instinct for discerning God's energising presence in natural forms. The curriculum followed in his Jesuit studies in philosophy, including what Hopkins called a 'hard course of scholastic logic', was Thomist in foundation and dominated by sixteenth-century commentaries on Aquinas, headed by that of the Jesuit Francisco Suárez.[74] Students participated in frequent disputations, in which they were required to defend particular theses; such 'defensive-minded training', as T. E. Muir observes, 'was fully in accord with the attitudes of a Tridentine Church, for the object was not the development of new ideas, but knowing how to out-argue disputatious laymen, especially Protestants, in what was perceived to be an increasingly secular-minded and even atheistic world'.[75] That God's existence can be known subjectively as well as objectively, and that he is an object that can be contemplated immediately in our life, was here made the subject of dry argument, when for Hopkins it was a passion and a conviction.[76]

The academic formation Hopkins received at Oxford occurred in an atmosphere of vigorous philosophical discussion and had encouraged considerable intellectual freedom. His 1868 notes on Greek philosophy at one

point reflect on the way Parmenides and others, faced with the problem of
how a common nature can determine many particular things (the problem of the one and the many), 'argued in abstractions without referring
to the concrete', contrasting this with the scientism of his own period in
its 'elaborated knowledge of the concrete'. Hopkins implies the need for
a middle way between these approaches: 'for no doubt, taking the Idea
[i.e. ultimate or essential nature] for a hand and the name for its glove
left behind, then although to handle it by the concrete may leave it a dry
crumpled piece of skin, abstraction may as injuriously blow it out into a
graceless bladdery animation; in either case the charm is gone.'[77] These
highly unusual metaphors convey something of the liveliness Hopkins
sought in intellectual life. His undergraduate studies clearly met this
demand: one of his Oxford essays, again reflecting on the problem of the
one and the many, notes that the 'always recurring coexistence of contra-
ries is highly exciting to thought'.[78]

Hopkins sought similar dynamism in his religious understanding.
Remarks he made to Bridges on the mystery of the Trinity describe an alter-
native to scholastic methods similar to instress in the way the mystery of the
Trinity is seen to take hovering grasp of its beholder's intellect and feeling:

> There are three persons, each God and each the same, the one, the only
> God: to some people this is a 'dogma', a word they almost chew, that is an
> equation in theology, the dull algebra of Schoolmen; to others it is news of
> their dearest friend or friends, leaving them all their lives balancing whether
> they have three heavenly friends or one – not that they have any doubt on
> the subject, but that their knowledge leaves their minds swinging; poised,
> but on the quiver.[79]

Hopkins was wholly of the second camp he describes. Behind his later
interest in writing a commentary on Newman's *Grammar of Assent* (1870),
with its distinction between 'notional' and 'real' assent, can be sensed
a desire to move beyond the drearily inferential methods he had earlier
encountered in his Jesuit training.[80] Underlying such methods was the perception that human discourse about God must proceed by analogy, not
equivalence, since God exists beyond human understanding. This was also
antithetical to Hopkins's own feeling that the same language is applicable
to created being as to God's being, for all the manifest difference he saw
existed between them.

Hopkins's lifetime saw the beginnings of the revival of Thomistic philosophy, in what we now know as Neo-Scholasticism, a revival given offi-
cial sanction and new momentum by Pope Leo XIII in his 1879 encyclical
Aeterni Patris. Hopkins's philosophy professors, however, appear to have

clung to the established textbooks. His later studies in theology may have
been shaped more by Neo-Scholastic calls to make Aquinas his own inter-
preter, but the manner of its teaching proved equally wearisome: the dominant figure in Hopkins's theological training is said to have 'buttressed
his stolid neo-Thomism with a particularly uninspiring classroom manner'.[81] It was in this unhappy intellectual context that Hopkins became
an enthusiast for the philosophy and theology of the thirteenth-century
Franciscan John Duns Scotus, having discovered a copy of Scotus's commentary on the *Sentences* of Peter Lombard in the library at Stonyhurst
in 1872.[82] Thereafter Scotus became for Hopkins (in the words of a later
sonnet) he 'who of all men most sways my spirits to peace' ('Duns Scotus's
Oxford', l. 11).

A great deal has been made of Scotus's influence on Hopkins, yet it
is difficult to establish precisely what Hopkins took from Scotus – or
even how much he was able to read of the texts of Scotus to which we
know he did have access.[83] The critical essay which has done most to
shape interest in Hopkins and Scotus admits that 'Documentarily speaking, there are only four significant places in GMH's spiritual writings
where he certainly refers to Scotus. From these, as from four small bones
of a prehistoric monster, must be reconstructed the skeletal outline of
the undoubted relations between the two men.'[84] It is a necessary but
also a highly speculative activity. What is apparent is that the discovery of Scotus provided a telling moment in Hopkins's own experience
of faith. He had sought since his Oxford days for a theory of knowledge attuned at once to the binding individuality of things and to their
ultimate essence and unity; in Scotus, he found crucial support for his
belief that a grasp of particularity was integral to the search for essential
nature, a search that might involve (rather than cast off) direct sensory
apprehension. The 'new stroke of enthusiasm' he felt upon the discovery
of Scotus in 1872 was hoped to be 'a mercy from God' for appearing to
confirm Hopkins's own metaphysical scheme: 'just then when I took in
any inscape of the sky or sea I thought of Scotus'.[85]

It has long been thought that Scotus was seen as suspect by Hopkins's
teachers (Hopkins's championing of Scotus is suggested to have been in
large part responsible for his later failure to progress to a fourth year of
theological study).[86] However, a recent revisionist account of Hopkins's
theology argues precisely the opposite: 'Scotism was in the air, so much
so that it would have been quite impossible for Hopkins not to have
caught a whiff of it, or even inhaled large quantities of the stuff.'[87]
This would render puzzling Hopkins's sense, also shared by his Jesuit

contemporaries, that he was in a minority in championing Scotus; it would mean, for example, that there was no cause for his surprise at by chance making 'the acquaintance of two and I suppose the only two Scotists in England in one week' when visiting the London Oratory in 1874.[88] Rightly or wrongly, Hopkins evidently perceived Scotus to be peripheral to the dominant tradition. Indeed, this was for Hopkins a likely part of Scotus's appeal, and as vital as the specific ideas Hopkins took from Scotus may be what, for him, Scotus could be defined against: the dry, syllogistic Thomism which asserted 'a clear and deep line of cleavage' between created and divine orders.[89] Hopkins intuited differently, seeing the world as 'word, expression, news of God', and arriving at the sacramental view of nature that led him on one occasion to remark of the beauty of a bluebell: 'I know the beauty of our Lord by it.'[90] He drew inspiration from the unfamiliar idea that Christ's Incarnation had always been part of God's plan, and thus it was more than a contingency faced with Adam and Eve's sin and humanity's fall: 'The love of the Son for the Father leads him to take a created nature and in that to offer him sacrifice', Hopkins observed in his Dublin notebook of 1884–85, 'The sacrifice might have been unbloody; by the Fall it became a bloody one.'[91] This logic allowed Hopkins to believe that creation is for Christ, lending the natural order a special dignity. Christ in his person and being provided the vital core of the poet's faith.

The scholasticism Hopkins encountered in his formal studies was by contrast more occupied with how Christ saved a fallen creation. Related to this emphasis was the tendency of much theology of the period constantly to recall humankind's sinful nature and moral weakness.[92] Hopkins shared the concern with the miraculous and prophetic in God's action that was the corollary to the distancing of nature from grace in his formal studies. The impulse manifest from his Anglican High Church days onwards, to see in doctrine and tradition the objective deposit of revealed truth, remains conspicuous in all of his poetry. These provided his stability faced with what an Oxford letter describes as 'the sordidness of things, wh. one is compelled perpetually to feel ... the most unmixedly painful thing one knows of'.[93] Hopkins's awareness of human corruption and sin was brought to new pitch by his later witnessing of urban squalor in his parish work in Liverpool and elsewhere. Many of his poems share what has been identified as the perception of 'an awesomely absent God, and the created world in alienation from his grace'.[94] At the same time, Hopkins also clung to the opposite sense, of a world indwelt by God, in which grace was not occasional or temporary, but vitally present to actual everyday existence, and visible in what he described in 'Pied Beauty' (1877) as the 'dappled things' of creation (l. 1).

This was a sense easier to sustain amid the beauty of North Wales, where Hopkins studied theology, than in the life of 'gingerbread permanence' endured in his subsequent pastoral ministry, or, later still, amid the frustration known in his final years in Dublin.[95] Even so, the concern with the created order as representing sacramentally the mystery of God continues to be a prominent feature of Hopkins's later poetry. Indeed, part of the struggle of that later poetry is to continue to conceive of the immediacy of God's presence beyond the ecstatic celebration of nature's variety. 'Brothers' (1880), a poem written in admiration of the affection shared between two brothers, ends by drawing the following moral:

> Ah Nature, framed in fault,
> There's comfort then, there's salt!
> Náture, bad, base, and blind,
> Déarly thou canst be kind;
> There déarly thén, déarly,
> Dearly thou canst be kind.   (ll. 38–43)

The dearness the poem recognises in the brothers is the more precious for being hard won; Hopkins's delight is in what has been overcome, namely, the disposition to sin. The clash of human goodness and corruption is here set up as a direct competition, in which goodness only just prevails (four 'déarlys' meeting the triple designation of nature's fault, 'bad, base, and blind'). In this confrontation, we see something of the difficulty Hopkins had in extending his sense of the goodness of the physical world to human nature. It is a difficulty characteristic of many of the poems with which this book is concerned.

'Brothers' is based upon an encounter Hopkins had while teaching in Chesterfield in the late 1870s. Many of Hopkins's poems are drawn from incidents and feelings known in his own life, even if they are never straightforward psychological self-portraits ('I do not think that they are Hopkins's selfies', as Hill memorably remarks).[96] A recent suggestion in respect of Hopkins's own spiritual experience is that he was influenced by new, highly emotional and florid forms of continental piety, much of it 'ultramontane' in character, which appeared in England from the mid-century.[97] What evidence survives of the extent of his encounter with such piety is mixed. Certainly Hopkins found himself greatly affected by the ecstatic visions of Anne Catherine Emmerich and Marie Lataste recorded earlier in the century, though the notice books from the various churches to which Hopkins was posted as a priest suggest that traditional forms – especially public Rosary and Benediction – continued to dominate the forms of Roman Catholic devotion he would have known, and it also seems likely (as Joseph Pizza has argued) that the 'conservative, even reactionary vein in Hopkins' thought … is rooted more in his inveterate English patriotism than his supposed Ultramontanism'.[98] Whatever the truth of Hopkins's encounter with exotic Italianate piety, its recent prominence in accounts of his work reveals a tension in commentary on the poet, the same tension Jonathan Z. Smith recognises within the study of religion generally: that 'between religion imagined as an *exotic* category of human experience and expression, and religion imagined as an *ordinary* category of human expression and activity'.[99] There are good reasons why Hopkins is known as a poet of spiritual extremity. Yet it is possible to see in his writing a concern with the immediacy as well as the exceptionality of God's presence, especially when it addresses religious experience. These two senses of God do not wholly accord, and we ought not to be surprised that Hopkins's poetry ultimately does not attempt to resolve their relation. In common with a penetrating recent essay by Simon Humphries, this book 'takes contradiction to constitute part of the richness of his response to existence'.[100] The tension between the asceticism prominent in Hopkins's youthful verse and the sacramental awareness of creation which characterises his poetic maturity is not always settled when Hopkins turns to religious experience, but nor should we expect it to be. The lack of resolution is frequently an element of his poetry's theological and spiritual expressiveness.

Chapters 1 and 2 of this book are concerned with 'forms' of spiritual life, examining the connection of Hopkins's poetry to his reading of the Bible, and to prayer. The first of these chapters argues that attending to a range of biblical texts and translations in connection with Hopkins's work yields important insights into the nature of the religious commitment signalled by biblical language in his poetry. The second begins by entering a caution about the influence of Ignatius's Spiritual Exercises on Hopkins before moving to consider the place of prayer in his poetry more generally, highlighting contrasts and connections between the different phases of his writing. In both these chapters, I present the innovativeness of Hopkins's attention to religious experience in spiritual knowledge. Later chapters focus on the tension between sacramental and ascetical impulses that this attention to religious experience serves to reveal. Chapters 3 and 4 consider two 'models' of faith that recur in Hopkins, that of the soldier and of the martyr. In Hopkins's several soldier poems, I argue, can be seen the variability in his sense of how God relates to human experience. The chapter on the figure of the martyr in his writing posits that 'The Wreck' is distinct from Hopkins's other poems on martyrs in its avoidance of details of individual history; elsewhere, the effort is to remain proximate to the situation of the lives and deaths with which he is concerned. Finally, in Chapters 5 and 6, I turn to evocations of death and the future life more generally in Hopkins's poetry, arguing that the impression given of the last things in Hopkins marks the limit of the unusual dignity he ascribed to the natural order, appearing more often as the defeat of experience than as its culmination.

PART I

Forms of Devotion

CHAPTER I

Bibles

Hopkins knew difficulty in his preaching. A chronicle of disappointment, often sadly comical in bearing, is to be found in his sermon book, recalling among other things the penitent who admitted in the confessional to having slept through parts of one of his homilies, and, most excruciatingly, the occasion Hopkins believed he had moved his congregation to the extent 'that I even saw some wiping their tears, but when the same thing happened next week I perceived that it was hot and that it was sweat they were wiping away'.[1] Such letdowns were familiar to this most unpredictable of preachers. If on occasion Hopkins enjoyed speaking 'very plainly and strongly' from the pulpit ('for I dearly like calling a spade a spade'), his more usual practice was to do otherwise.[2] A willingness to depart from expectation knew some success: the panegyric on St Stanislaus he preached as a novice was recalled in his obituary to be 'as brilliant and beautiful as it was out of the usual routine of pulpit deliveries'.[3] More often, though, Hopkins's originality was not well appreciated. The trio of elaborate sermons he delivered on the subject of 'God's Kingdom' in Liverpool in 1880 is a case in point, with the planned title of the final of his addresses – 'On the Fall of God's First Kingdom' – having at the behest of his superiors to be pasted over with blank paper on the printed handbills which listed preachers and sermon titles because it was believed to hint of unorthodoxy.[4] This would not be the only occasion in Liverpool when Hopkins faced objections to his preaching. Later in his time there, it was even proposed that his sermons should be vetted in advance of delivery to ensure they did not contain too much out of the ordinary; this came after Hopkins told a congregation that God 'takes more interest in a lover's sweetheart than the lover': 'In consequence of this word *sweetheart* I was in a manner suspended and at all events forbidden (it was some time after) to preach without having my sermon revised. However when I was going to take the next sermon I had to give after this to Fr. Clare for revision he poohpoohed the matter and would not look at it.'[5]

Joseph J. Feeney suggests of Hopkins's sermons that 'His contests are, as it were, with the over-familiarity of Gospel stories, with the dull sermons his congregations have suffered through.'[6] The danger here was that uncommonness in the pulpit would be taken as evidence of singularity, a trait considered by a Jesuit contemporary to be 'diametrically opposed to the spirit of the Society [of Jesus, i.e. the Jesuits]', and one that Hopkins himself would eventually tire of being reproached with ('You give me a long jobation about eccentricities', he told Bridges in 1881, 'Alas, I have heard so much about and suffered so much for and in fact been so completely ruined for life by my alleged singularities that they are a sore subject').[7] It was a risk Hopkins in his sermons appears to have been willing to take, most especially in the act of drawing surprising or peculiar analogies between religious truth and ordinary circumstance. The famous story told about the occasion when Hopkins in a sermon compared the munificence of the Roman Catholic Church to a milk cow whose seven teats are like the seven sacraments is of doubtful provenance, but one cannot argue with the likelihood of its fiction.[8] Hopkins once told his congregation that the sending of the Paraclete to the apostles at Pentecost was akin to 'when one of the batsmen at the wicket' in a cricket match 'has made a hit and wants to score a run, the other doubts, hangs back, or is ready to run in again, how eagerly the first will cry / Come on, come on!'[9] This conception of the Holy Spirit is more quaint than strange, as is finding the way two miracles are interlaced within the same Gospel story comparable to 'when you drive a quill or straw or knitting needle through an egg, it pierces first the white, then the yolk, then the white again'.[10] The same cannot be said for a training sermon Hopkins gave at his Jesuit seminary in North Wales in 1877. Taking for his subject the miracle of the feeding of the five thousand, Hopkins gave special notice to Christ's seemingly unremarkable instruction to his disciples in advance of the meal to 'Make the men sit down' (Luke 9.14).[11] 'People laughed at it prodigiously', Hopkins observed in a note written at the end of the sermon, 'I saw some of them roll on their chairs with laughter', with the oddity of the sermon's laboured repetition of 'Make the men sit down' causing the congregation to 'roll more than ever', and eventually forcing Hopkins to cut short his planned discourse.[12]

All this is evidence of the strangeness Hopkins acknowledged others saw in him, even if he struggled to see it in himself. But is it anything more? At the risk of embellishing simple ingenuousness, there is, I suggest, a way in which these apparent foibles might be the outworking of something more profound, namely an assurance about the expansiveness of the Gospel. No doubt making Hopkins's fellow students laugh all the harder at the training sermon was the fact that Christ's instruction to 'Make the men sit down' was given by Hopkins not only in the sacred languages of Greek and Latin, but, more improbably for his otherwise resolutely Anglophone fellow students, also rendered into Welsh.[13] This perhaps confirmed the preacher's growing reputation for eccentricity, but, to judge from the rest of the sermon, what Hopkins may have hoped to illustrate, if only in a small way, is that Christ's message speaks anew in every circumstance. Analogy is again important here. The sermon observes that the Sea of Galilee is not only 'shaped something like a bean or a man's left ear' but can also be compared – as Hopkins proceeded to do at some length – with the topography of the Vale of Clwyd.[14] Evidently this was an attempt to bring familiar understanding to bear upon an unfamiliar geographical location. Given the earlier translation into Welsh of 'Make the men sit down', however, the incongruity of the comparison, again seeking to associate the Gospel with the contemporary circumstance in which it is preached, may also have served an additional purpose: it may have served to imply that the Word of God was as original and vital in nineteenth-century North Wales as it had been in first-century Israel. Perhaps Hopkins's manner of illustration was unlikely because he wished to demonstrate that disparate languages and locations can be united in Gospel truth. Taken in isolation this sermon is undoubtedly strange, but when put alongside other far-fetched moments in Hopkins's preaching, its oddities begin to seem part of a decided attitude to the nature of the biblical message. Indeed, it is possible that those sermons of Hopkins in which inaptness seems almost to be cultivated were not wholly the product of pulpit naiveté; they may also have been tokens of a trust that there is nowhere the divine Word cannot speak. If this is the case, the sadness of Hopkins's preaching career must be that such confidence was itself frequently obscured and misunderstood.

In one way the multitude of critics of Hopkins's poetry who confine themselves to a single version of the Bible in discussions of his work – often a modern translation – seem to display the same confidence in an alternative form. To compare (as does Justus George Lawler) biblical references in a Victorian poem with the New American Bible, first published in 1970, is as much as to say that Scripture exceeds its particular conditions of reception.[15] Yet this attitude is in reality quite different from Hopkins's own. Hopkins did learn some Hebrew and was proficient in Greek, but the King James Version and, later, the Latin Vulgate, always had priority. Having acquired a personal copy of the Vulgate after his reception as a Roman Catholic, Hopkins subsequently returned his Anglican Bible to his father.[16] The variation between these translations mattered to him poetically. Following his conversion, Hopkins found it necessary to revise a poem so that it no longer echoed the King James Version: 'the Douay is of course an inferior version', he told a friend, and 'the differences wd. most likely be unimportant', but he wanted 'the thing to be correct'.[17] To describe the Douay-Rheims as 'an inferior version' may appear surprisingly critical, but Roman Catholic controversialists of this period were wont to flaunt their denominational colours by insisting that fluency in translation was in any case delusive, so that being 'prepared to sacrifice the graces of style' associated with the King James Version could actually serve as a badge of allegiance.[18] More important to Hopkins than 'graces of style' would have been the Roman Catholic insistence on the canonical status of biblical books Hopkins prior to his conversion would have known as non-canonical, and also the authority of the Latin Vulgate, which provided the sole version of the Bible from which Roman Catholic translations (such as the Douay-Rheims) were permitted to be made.

Victorian converts to Roman Catholicism were brought more often than most to a realisation of the associations held by particular biblical versions. John Henry Newman, who received Hopkins into the Roman Catholic Church, was a fellow convert who tended to carry a Roman Catholic Bible with him into the pulpit so that he could be certain he was quoting from the correct version.[19] This was not over-caution, for echoes of the King James Version abound in Newman's post-conversion writings – a fact which piqued certain of his fellow Roman Catholics.[20] Hopkins faced an identical difficulty to Newman but does not appear to have exercised the same level of vigilance over his use of biblical versions. If Hopkins's letters give ample evidence of how easily the words of the Vulgate came to hand, made available to all manner of situations and contexts, knowledge of the Roman Catholic versions did not remove the influence of the King James Version or of the Prayer Book (the latter follows the King James in most respects but retains Coverdale's Psalter, from the 'Great Bible' of 1549). This much is obvious from Hopkins's sermons. In broad terms, when Hopkins quotes from lesser-known passages of Scripture in his sermons, and, one senses, has cause to refer to the text itself, he follows the Roman Catholic versions – most likely transliterating from the Latin Vulgate, in a manner close to that of the English Douay-Rheims Bible (itself a translation of the Vulgate). When the passage in question is well known, however and, it seems likely, is quoted from memory, the resonances with the King James Version are unmistakable. Thus in quoting John's Gospel, Hopkins told his congregation that Christ promises '*to finish his work*' (4.34) and not to 'perfect' it, as in the Douay-Rheims Bible; in citing Deuteronomy Hopkins observed that 'The Scripture says *the blood is the life*' (12.23) and not (as in the Douay-Rheims Bible) 'the blood is for the soul'; the fleeing disciples at Gethsemane who abandoned Christ to his fate, rather than 'leaving him', as the Douay-Rheims Bible has it, '*forsook him*' (Matthew 26.56); Christ warns '*Repent, for the kingdom of heaven is at hand*' (Matthew 4.17) and not the Douay-Rheims Bible's 'Do penance, for the kingdom of heaven is at hand'.[21]

This is also a feature of Hopkins's letters, which throughout evince an intimacy with biblical language that allowed for its familiar use beyond religious subjects. More than a decade into his life as a Roman Catholic, Hopkins could voice to Bridges a wish to see more of a mutual Oxford friend with an allusion to the King James Version of Acts 26.29.[22] Equally, his later complaint that Tennyson was in thrall to the Broad Church party of the Church of England invokes the King James Version of the Letter to the Galatians (2.13): 'Tennyson in his later works has been "carried away with their dissimulation"' (the Douay-Rheims Bible, by contrast, has 'led by them into that dissimulation').[23]

The purpose of citing these instances is not to suggest that something was held back from Hopkins's conversion to Roman Catholicism. Few of Hopkins's choices in any case engage specific doctrinal differences. Even the one which is most striking, the preference for 'repent' over 'do penance', long a crux of disputes between Roman Catholic and Protestant translators, is probably not as significant as might first appear, for this was an issue approached with new freedom by nineteenth-century interpreters. The Roman Catholic historian John Lingard, for instance, opted for 'repent' in his 1836 translation of the Gospels on the grounds that 'though there can be no true repentance which produces not reformation, there is often a reformation which is not produced by repentance'.[24]

What can be extrapolated from the persistence of the forms of the King James Version in Hopkins's letters and sermons is the way that familiarity with a given version of the Bible lends a particular colouring to spiritual apprehension, setting in train patterns of thought and recurring motivations. Thus when in 'The Wreck of the Deutschland' Hopkins addresses God with the idea that the victims of the shipwreck he is describing were 'not under thy feathers' (l. 93), it is significant not only that the image of God's protection that most readily comes to mind is that of Psalm 91, 'He shall defend thee under his wings, and thou shalt be safe under his feathers' (*Book of Common Prayer*), but also that intimacy with the psalm frames a particular way of thinking about God's protection. Had Hopkins known only the Roman Catholic version of this psalm, which has 'overshadow thee with his shoulders' (as in the Vulgate's *scapulis*'), his poem might have had a different supposition in respect of this covenant, perhaps somewhat more hard wearing and a little less soothing.[25] What is involved here is more than simply a question of variant phrasing.

These biblical nuances are harder to appreciate in Hopkins than in many of his poetic contemporaries, including Christina Rossetti, in whose work can be found frequent and overt echoes of particular biblical versions. Would the maxim from Proverbs (13.12) which reverberates through so many of Rossetti's lyrics – 'Hope deferred maketh the heart sick' – have enjoyed such prominence had it been encountered in its Roman Catholic form, 'Hope that is deferred afflicteth the soul'? And would this have altered her poetry's feeling for 'Hope deferred'? When poetry is so evidently laced with biblical echo, it becomes easier to perceive not only the way in which knowledge of a version of Scripture lends a particular texture to writing and thought but also something of the tussle between professing poet and biblical source. To give one example: Diane D'Amico nicely brings out the way in which Rossetti's 'The Heart Knoweth Its Own Bitterness' (1857), its title (taken from Proverbs 14.10) already dropping the heart's masculine identification found in the King James Version, wrestles with the gender characterisation found in its biblical inspirations. Choosing to have one line – 'I will not lean on child of man' – follow the Prayer Book version of Psalm 146, 'O put not your trust in princes, nor in any child of man', rather than the King James, which has 'nor in the son of man', registers a small but important shift in emphasis.[26]

That little of the kind of analysis undertaken by D'Amico appears in commentary on Hopkins, even as much attention is given to biblical influence generally, is likely because echoes of biblical language are more difficult to isolate in his poetry.[27] The conspicuousness of the word '*Ípse*' in a famous stanza of 'The Wreck' has his editors reaching for help from the Vulgate in explaining its meaning ('he himself') in a way rare with any of the versions of the Bible that Hopkins knew.[28] Yet the scarcity of clear and precise biblical reference in Hopkins's poetry may itself be what is significant. It suggests that we need to move beyond simply adducing potential scriptural sources for Hopkins's allusions to the Bible and instead consider how biblical language and echo mix with other elements in his diction. This in turn requires attention to the specific contours and contexts of the biblical texts and translations Hopkins himself knew.

Biblical Echo in 'That Nature is a Heraclitean Fire'

The codas of 'That Nature is a Heraclitean Fire and of the comfort of the Resurrection' (1888) provide an extraordinary moment in Hopkins's poetry. This was not the first occasion on which he had 'felt forced to exceed the beaten bounds' of his favourite poetic form; 'Harry Ploughman' and 'Tom's Garland' (1887) both extend the sonnet beyond its usual fourteen lines.[29] Yet the inclusion of three codas in 'That Nature is a Heraclitean Fire', each a half-line plus couplet, the first of which is enjambed from the fourteenth line, with the further addition of a half-line to close the poem, goes beyond anything Hopkins had attempted previously or that he knew in the precedent of John Milton's experiments with the caudate sonnet. It is a remarkable change of direction for a poet who had earlier employed the sonnet's brevity to achieve intensely deliberate effects and had gone as far as to condense an already short form to lend it new forcefulness in his invention of the ten-and-a-half line curtal sonnet. 'That Nature is a Heraclitean Fire', in contrast to these earlier experiments, gathers dramatic intensity from the stretching of formal constraints. Early in the sonnet's 'tails' occurs a sudden shift of feeling. Here the dissolution of matter in 'nature's bonfire' (l. 9) described earlier in the poem finds abrupt reversal:

>   … Enough! the Resurrection,
> A héart's-clarion! Awáy grief's gásping, || joyless days, dejection.
>   Across my foundering deck shone
> A beacon, an eternal beam. || Flesh fade, and mortal trash
> Fáll to the resíduary worm; || world's wildfire, leave but ash:
>   In a flash, at a trumpet crash,
> I am all at once what Christ is, || since he was what I am, and
> Thís Jack, jóke, poor pótsherd, || patch, matchwood, immortal diamond,
>   Is immortal diamond.   (ll. 16–24)

These lines have the muscularity of style that is distinctively Hopkins's own, licensed by his conviction that breaking out of the usual repetitions of patterns of metrical feet to achieve newly 'stressy' form would render back to poetry its true nature as 'emphatically speech, speech purged of dross like gold in the furnace'.[30] This was not an easy ambition to fulfil, since what Hopkins called 'the inflections and intonations of the speaking voice' are hard to direct consistently or accurately; Hopkins himself recognised that 'the art [of speech] depends entirely on living tradition' and that 'The phonograph may give us one, but hitherto there could be no record of fine spoken utterance.'[31] Yet for all the problems inherent to attempts to follow Hopkins's instructions to give voice to his verse (which have been criticised for the assumption that 'we have a powerful ability ... to imagine accurately what those sounds that Hopkins intended would have been'), it is at least clear that the conviction that his poems should be performed frames the way in which they are constructed.[32] As David Nowell Smith has said of Hopkins, 'One does not need to posit a single hypostasised performance to suggest that the poetry's diverse prosodic effects are predicated on the possibility of performance.'[33] Here, Hopkins indicated that in the penultimate line 'This' but not 'Jack' should receive stress, continuing a habit of leaving nouns, adjectives, and verbs 'unstressed in favour of prepositions, conjunctions, and pronouns', and thereby yielding the intense 'markedness of rhythm' he believed was 'rhythm's self' (given the similarity between the two words, the stress on 'This' also prepares for another surprising strong emphasis on 'Is' in the following line).[34]

Even at its most individual, however, Hopkins's poetry also taps a communal idiom. 'Flesh fade, and mortal trash | Fáll to the resíduary worm', in particular, has been thought by James Finn Cotter to echo a passage in the Book of Job well known for its prominence in the Prayer Book Burial Service: 'For I know that my redeemer liveth, and that he shall stand at the latter day upon the earth: And though after my skin worms destroy this body, yet in my flesh shall I see God' (19.25–26).[35] If Cotter is right, the allusion is specific to the Anglican version of Job. Although the authority for considering Job's declaration an anticipation of personal salvation is ancient, Hopkins would not have caught any reference to worms in the Roman Catholic versions, as they were added by the translators of the King James Version (the Hebrew does not identify a particular agent striking at the body). The traditional interpretation of the Anglican Burial Service passage as presaging corporeal resurrection was as a result much contested in the period. James Anthony Froude was among those complaining that words such as 'worms' 'have nothing answering to them in the original, – they were all added by the translators to fill out their interpretation ... If there is any doctrine of a resurrection here, it is a resurrection precisely *not* of the body, but of the spirit.'[36]

An allusion to the Anglican Burial Service more than twenty years after Hopkins had left the Church of England behind would seem evidence for continuity in the inspiration the poet took from the Bible. Yet while the Book of Job is likely to be important to 'That Nature is a Heraclitean Fire', the poem's reference to the Bible is far from straightforward. In line 23, for instance, 'poor pótsherd' hints at an affinity with the beleaguered Job, who had taken 'a potsherd and scraped the corrupt matter, sitting on a dunghill' (2.8; Douay-Rheims). The same line also echoes a familiar image from the Psalms, as for instance in Psalm 22 (21 in the Vulgate numbering), which complains that 'My strength is dryed up like a potsherd' (22.14; *Book of Common Prayer*); this Psalm, which is often associated with the sufferings of Christ, also includes the lament 'I am a worm, and no man' (22.6).

Such phrases may well be echoed by 'That Nature is a Heraclitean Fire', but they remain hard to isolate from the concentrated sound matter of the final lines, as 'poor pótsherd' and 'patch' are combined in 'matchwood', this last a distinctly modern usage (the first definite instance in the *OED* comes from 1838 and probably owes something to the invention of the friction match a decade earlier). 'Jack', 'jóke', 'patch', and 'matchwood' are common words, but in the context of the poem they still represent a type of poetic diction: Hopkins did not advocate the abandonment of a special language of poetry but instead looked to renew such language by having his poems refine and exalt patterns of speech, describing in one letter his decision to 'cut myself off from the use of <u>ere</u>, <u>o'er</u>, <u>wellnigh</u>, <u>what time</u>, <u>say not</u> (for <u>do not say</u>), because, though dignified, they neither belong to nor ever cd. rise from, or be the elevation of, ordinary modern speech'.[37] The implications for biblical echo and allusion in his work are strange and surprising. We are far from the 'gradualist' approach to biblical allusion of Wordsworth, as described by Eleanor Cook, in which 'Biblical words approach, enter, become part of everyday language almost imperceptibly sometimes.'[38] 'That Nature is a Heraclitean Fire', for instance, is a poem that labours at its idiosyncratic dictional blend. The acoustic progression from 'patch, matchwood' to 'immortal diamond' is not smooth, the affricatives grating on the sonorants, even as the line attempts to elide the difference between its categories. 'Blend' remains the right word to describe the effect created, however, for the biblical here does not stand apart from the whole. The way the poem mixes its registers, encompassing biblical echo, Latinate legalism ('residuary'), and earthy colloquialism ('Jack', 'patch'), in fact works to create an apt incongruity: this is a very individual poem about the transformation and elevation of ordinary experience.

The incongruity extends beyond the poem's language. There is an ungainly quality to this extraordinarily long sonnet, not least in the structure of its lines. 'I am all at once what Christ is, ‖ since he was what I am' parallels syntactically and semantically Christ's declaration in John's Gospel: 'He that eateth my flesh, and drinketh my blood, dwelleth in me, and I in him' (6.57; King James). By contrast, the lines which follow shun chiastic movement for more laboured progression. Daniel Brown writes that 'The rhyme of the phrase "I am, and" with "diamond" expresses the greatness that each mortal embodies by being not just a fragmentary part, a "potsherd" or "patch", but an integral part of a whole that is greater than the sum of such parts.'[39] It is important that the arrival at this sense of a greater whole is effortful. The strain in rhyming 'I am, and' with 'diamond' is easy to exaggerate, for not all the rhyme's parts are equal ('and' has a lesser place for the absence of stress and for its reliance for sense on what follows over the line-break, meaning that 'diamond' would likely not need to stretch to become trisyllabic, as might first appear). However, other elements in the poem's closing lines are clearly taxing. With 'Thís Jack, jóke, poor pótsherd, ‖ patch, matchwood, immortal diamond, | Is immortal diamond', we encounter what is essentially a list. A common tendency of lists is to establish 'an implicit hierarchy by the order of listing',[40] but 'That Nature is a Heraclitean Fire' works from the opposite tendency, collapsing customary ascendancies by a feat of classification. For all the claim of equivalence, if Hopkins had declared 'Thís Jack, jóke, poor pótsherd, ‖ patch, matchwood, | Is immortal diamond', we would still detect a scale of improvement. He instead risks stating what is by itself obvious – that 'immortal diamond, | Is immortal diamond' – so as to assert an astounding parity.

The closing lines are concerned not with the maladroit becoming progressively graceful, but with how, in the aftermath of the 'trumpet crash' of the Resurrection, it *is* graceful. That verb – 'Is' – may be unobtrusive syntactically, but it takes on an unlikely semantic burden in the abrupt return of the final line. Where fluency would have risked making familiar a remarkable and perplexing redemption, the poem instead cultivates more encumbered expression, in which awkwardnesses are not shed but instead used to reveal the unexpectedness of God's mercy. Scriptural echoes in 'That Nature is a Heraclitean Fire' may be too fragmentary for their provenance to be beyond doubt, even if the Book of Job seems a plausible inspiration for the poem as a whole. But in disrupting the accustomed sound of biblical reference, the poem also manages to bring its textual inspirations to new sense.

What survives of Hopkins's private spiritual meditations on the Bible occur in a similar pattern, conducted by means of an Ignatian method that strongly emphasises the personal and ongoing contact of heart and mind with biblical revelation. In the 'Dublin Notebook' of 1884–85, a meditation on the Transfiguration (Matthew 17.1–9; Mark 9.2–8; Luke 9.28–36) yields the resolution to 'practise what you did at Roehampton in the tertianship [from 1881–82, a time for Hopkins of great 'calm of mind'],[41] entering into the joy of our Lord, not his joys but the joys of him'. Another from the same notebook, this time on the Three Kings (Matthew 2.1–12), determines to 'Pray to be on the watch for God's providence, not determining where or when but only sure that it will come' and to 'apply this to all your troubles

and hopes, to England and Ireland, to growth in virtue', something especially necessary for the fact that 'it seems a spirit of fear I live by'. A third
meditation, focusing on the story of the woman taken in adultery (John
7.53–8.11), causes Hopkins to note: 'Let him that is without sin etc – Pray
to keep to this spirit and as far as possible rule in speaking of Mr. Gladstone
for instance'.[42] The turn to find Scripture's specific relevance to the present
moment may be the same in each of these cases, but the results are diverse
enough to suggest that an aspect of Scripture's vitality for Hopkins's life of
prayer was that it allowed sense to be made of the miscellaneousness of his
lived experience.

The same point can be made about Hopkins's sermons. As I have suggested, part of the strangeness of his pulpit manner seems to have been
rooted in a desire to signal the amplitude of God's message – its practical
benefit for disparate moments of life – by coupling the biblical with the
mundane and the homely. Addressing a congregation at Bedford Leigh,
Lancashire, in 1879, on the subject of Romans 13.12 ('The night is passed,
and the day is at hand. Let us therefore cast off the works of darkness, and
put on the armour of light'; Douay-Rheims), Hopkins was concerned to
lend tangible form to scriptural reasoning:

> The Scripture in one place calls life night and in another calls it day. But these
> do not disagree. In respect of truth and the clearness we see it with / life is
> night and what comes after life is day; in respect of doing work in God's ser-
> vice and earning a reward hereafter life is day and what comes after is night.
> But you yourselves, brethren, are some of you well aware of this: to most men
> the daylight is the place to work in but those that work in the pit go where
> all is darker than night and work by candlelight and when they see the light
> of day again their work is over, as if day were night to them and night day, so
> then this life is dark, a pit, but we work in it; death will shew us daylight, but
> all our work will then be done.[43]

This passage has been read with great sympathy by Eric Griffiths, who calls
it 'magnificent': 'It brings together the persuasive fluency of the pulpit –
"death will shew us daylight, but all our work will then be done" – with an
awareness of the divisions in working practice even within his working-class
audience.'[44] Such admiration would likely be increased by knowing that the
passage is an insertion, added on reflection, especially when it is seen against
the analogy with which Hopkins had originally toyed, and which he eventually deleted: 'For the same thing is light in one light and dark in another;
compared with a dark moonless night moonlight is like day, compared with
sunlight it is seen to be but night.'[45] In this earlier version of the sermon, the
example does not function personally. The force of Hopkins's revisions is to

bring the Gospel closer to ordinary experience, even while retaining what Griffiths calls 'an elevated intellectual level'.[46]

It is done in a manner comparable in feeling to the conviction of Henry Parry Liddon, Hopkins's sometime spiritual mentor at Oxford, about the impact of the Gospel upon its first hearers, as described by Liddon in an 1863 sermon: 'The Gospel comes home to them; it comes home to their hearts and thoughts. It comes to them wrapped in swaddling-clothes; it appeals to their daily wants and to their deepest sympathies ... The Gospel is eminently the property of the people.'[47] The poetry written when Hopkins was directly under Liddon's influence, before his conversion to Rome, and at a time when he sought in Liddon's mode of belief 'an intellectual haven from the threatening liberalism at Oxford', does not risk anything like the startling juxtaposition of biblical and colloquial idioms seen at the end of 'That Nature is a Heraclitean Fire'.[48] It is only later that biblical language is brought into contact with commonplace experience, the ordinariness of 'Jack' and 'patch'. The tissue of biblical quotation and paraphrase seen in early poems such as 'Barnfloor and Winepress', 'The Half-way House', or 'New Readings' (all 1864–65), in fact imply a different awareness of Scripture. For example, the phrase 'broken reed' is now proverbial, but without observing an allusion to its source in the thirty-sixth chapter of Isaiah ('Lo, thou trustest in the staff of this broken reed, on Egypt'; King James), one could not make much of two lines from 'The Half-way House': 'My national old Egyptian reed gave way; | I took of vine a cross-barred rod or rood' (ll. 7–8). The specialness of biblical reference is here insisted upon as part of the poem's earnest piety.

The biblical texture of 'That Nature is a Heraclitean Fire' is not so deliberate. Nor does the later poem have the explicitness of 'The Wreck of the Deutschland', written at the opening of Hopkins's poetic maturity, in its many allusions to the Bible. When Hopkins calls upon the 'Lord of living and dead' (l. 4) in the first stanza of 'The Wreck', he is clearly recalling Romans 14.19, where St Paul asserts that 'Christ both died, and rose, and revived, that he might be Lord both of the dead and living' (King James). The same stanza later addresses God in terms that conceive of the stress of individual being as a fluid and volatile energy, saying 'Thou hast bóund bónes and véins in me, fástened me flésh, | And áfter it álmost únmade, what with dréad, | Thy doing' (ll. 5–7); this is a sure allusion to Job 10.8–11: 'Thine hands have made me and fashioned me together round about; yet thou dost destroy me ... Thou hast clothed me with skin and flesh, and hast fenced me with bones and sinews' (King James). Biblical echoes in Hopkins's later poetry tend to be more scattered and fragmented, constituting one variety of language among many. The intensity of the encounter between biblical echo and patterns of common speech makes source hunting difficult: few unambiguous references can be extracted. Yet it is not so much that the biblical texture of Hopkins's earlier verse has been supplanted as that it has become more interspersed with other idioms. Hopkins once stated his objections to Swinburne's diction: 'essentially archaic, biblical a good deal, and so on: now that is a thing that can never last; a perfect style must be of its age'.[49] He had earlier told Bridges that 'it seems to me that the poetical language of an age shd. be the current language heightened, to any degree heightened and unlike itself, but not (I mean normally: passing freaks and graces are another thing) an obsolete one.'[50] By 'heightening' the patterns and idioms of quotidian speech, Hopkins wished to force attention to the acoustic texture of common words such as 'Jack', 'joke', or 'patch' and so gather to his own poetry the muscular strength he praised in Dryden, the poet whose rhythms Hopkins believed 'lay the strongest stress of all our literature on the naked thew and sinew of the English language'.[51]

This aspect of his work has been widely discussed. But if there exists a great deal of critical commentary on Hopkins's language, only rarely has this been related to his use of biblical allusion and echo, which was very far from the biblical manner he noticed in Swinburne.[52] My claim is that what James Milroy names as Hopkins's feeling that a poem's language 'must be intimate and close to ordinary life' has in the case of biblical echo and allusion a spiritual as well as a linguistic importance.[53] The poet's priestly ministry enabled a close encounter with dialect and common speech, and that these elements coexist with biblical echo in his later poetry may be seen as an attempt to discover scriptural afterlife true to his own experience, to discover a biblical style 'of its age'.

The Varnish of Biblical Words: 'Felix Randal' and *'Justus quidem tu es, Domine'*

On 21 April 1880, one of Hopkins's parishioners in Liverpool, a blacksmith named Felix Spencer, died of tuberculosis. Hopkins had ministered to Spencer in his illness and entered his death into the church notice book.[54] A week later he composed a sonnet which may have been sparked by Spencer's memory, 'Felix Randal':

Félix Rándal the fárrier, O is he déad then? my dúty all énded,
Who have watched his mould of man, big-bóned and hardy-handsome
Pining, píning, till time when reason rámbled in it and some
Fatal four disorders, fléshed there, all contended?

Síckness bróke him. Impatient, he cursed at first, but mended
Being anointed and all; though a heavenlier heart began some
Mónths éarlier, since Í had our swéet repríeve and ránsom
Téndered to him. Áh well, God rést him áll road éver he offénded!

This séeing the síck endéars them tó us, us tóo it endéars.
My tongue had taught thee comfort, touch had quenched thy tears,
Thy tears that touched my heart, child, Félix, poor Felix Randal;

How far from then forethought of, all thy more boisterous years,
When thou at the random grím fórge, pówerful amídst péers,
Didst fettle for the great grey drayhorse his bright and battering sandal!

Straining for monumental effect, the poem's final lines are at risk of appearing exaggerated. The risk is largest in the case of 'sandal', which according
to one editor's gloss is 'the technical name for a particular type of horseshoe', but whose appearance in this context feels unlikely, a feeling only
increased by its prominence as the final word of the poem and by virtue of
its rhyme with 'Randal'.[55] The word's associations seem curiously to lean
towards the Homeric rather than the homely.

One way to make sense of the final lines is to say that their inspiration is biblical. The critic who first revealed the existence of Felix Spencer
believed Hopkins was indebted for these lines to a passage in Ecclesiasticus
(38.29–39; Douay-Rheims) on the exercise of craft:

> So doth the smith sitting by the anvil and considering the iron work. The
> vapour of the fire wasteth his flesh, and he fighteth with the heat of the fur-
> nace: The noise of the hammer is always in his ears, and his eye is upon the
> pattern of the vessel he maketh. He settleth his mind to finish his work, and
> his watching to polish *them* to perfection ... All these trust to their hands,
> and every one is wise in his own art ... [T]heir prayer shall be in the work of
> their craft, applying their soul, and searching in the law of the most High.[56]

The Thirty-Nine Articles declare Ecclesiasticus deuterocanonical or outside the primary biblical canon, meaning that Hopkins was more likely to
have encountered this passage in a Roman Catholic than in an Anglican
setting (it does figure in the Roman Catholic biblical canon). But while
the biblical precedent is certainly plausible given the passage's fame and the
poet's fondness for this particular biblical book, it has to be said that the
poem's relation to Ecclesiasticus is far from straightforward. For one thing,
parts of its language do not sound especially ecclesiastical. The alignments
the sonnet countenances are instead more disconcerting. 'Áh well, God
rést him áll road éver he offénded!' has been glossed by an editor as 'God
forgive him for whatever (sins) he committed'.[57] 'Felix Randal' has this

type of affectionate colloquialism meet with the language of priestly duty in the 'swéet repriéve and ránsom' brought to Felix in the sacraments. It is a combination of registers that recalls an earlier sermon in which Hopkins told his congregation, 'There is a crowd of you, brethren, and amidst that crowd some must be in this road – I mean are out of your duty, out of God's grace, and in mortal sin', and which is also close to the sense of 'road' that appears in the earlier poem 'The Handsome Heart', figuring the journey of life which decides eternal fate: Hopkins's hope for the boy admired in one version of 'The Handsome Heart' is for 'all your road your race | To match and more than match || its sweet forestalling strain' (ll. 13–14).[58]

It seems hard to distinguish Ecclesiasticus in all of this, but that should not be a cause for discounting the biblical precedent altogether. Difficulties with extracting precise biblical references from 'Felix Randal' may instead result from a conviction that there should be no rupture between the Word and the world. The poem's language toils, struggling to combine disparate elements, but this lack of fluency is itself poignant. The blacksmith, Hopkins writes, 'Didst fettle' his horseshoe, and 'fettle', as the best-selling of the Victorian self-education manuals noted in 1853, 'is in the genuine Lancashire dialect a very expressive word, giving rise to the general idea of ranking a thing good, excellent, delicious; and occurring in such instances as to *fettle* a *horse*, means to restore him to soundness'.[59] Hopkins's poem has the blacksmith make ready a horseshoe rather than restore the horse 'to soundness', but the appearance of the word is traced with the expressiveness of its varied usages.[60] Compare this to the blacksmith in Ecclesiasticus who 'settleth his mind to finish his work, and his watching to polish *them* to perfection'. '[R]estore him to soundness'; Ecclesiasticus's 'polish *them* to perfection': the sense is akin, but if we take 'fettle' in 'Felix Randal' to be the Lancashire dialect word, we can say that in Hopkins's poem there is an attempt to return the sound of virtuous craftwork to concrete circumstance.

In the case of this sonnet, it may not seem much to matter which of the biblical versions is cited alongside Hopkins's poetry. The scriptural echo appears too faint for there to be any pressing need to attend to those biblical texts the poet himself would have known. Yet not to do so would be to go against the grain of how the Bible stands to Hopkins's poetry, in the sense that his poems have a large stake in what accrues to biblical texts over time, as they become involved in the conventions of human living. Prior to his conversion, Hopkins had known the High Church emphasis on personal holiness, which lent itself to a heightened awareness of the practical application of Scripture to one's life. His later use of Ignatian methods of

prayer – discussed further in the next chapter – fostered a similar awareness. By contrast, the theology Hopkins was taught as a Jesuit distanced
the natural from the supernatural realm in a way common to much Roman
Catholic thought of his period. This gave the impression that divine revelation occurred outside human experience and could best be approached via
dialectical reasoning, the timelessness of religious enquiry guaranteed by
the fact that it was siphoned off from the ordinary and everyday. Such an
attitude also shaped predominant modes of Roman Catholic biblical interpretation, making it often a matter of buttressing syllogistic arguments
about God that were quite removed from the lived experience of faith.[61]

Hopkins lived in a period which saw great controversy over the nature
and status of the Bible, but he seems to have been largely unmoved by the
Higher Criticism, with its systematic attention to historical content and
context in relation to biblical texts. This was not for lack of acquaintance
with contemporary debates: Hopkins was tutored at Oxford by Benjamin
Jowett, whose piece in *Essays and Reviews* (1860) had caused a sensation
with its precept to '*Interpret the Scripture like any other book*'; he also knew
something (if possibly only by report) of Ernest Renan's *La Vie de Jésus*
(1863), which dared to treat the life of Christ as if it belonged to a historical and not a divine personage.[62] There is even a suggestion from his close
friend William Addis that early in his time at Oxford, Hopkins, being 'at
first a little tinged with the liberalism prevalent among reading men', had
told Addis that '"I never can believe that the Song of Solomon is more
than an ordinary love song".'[63] Yet in the main the anxieties about the
Bible that appear to have afflicted Hopkins's father, whose private notes
include an attempt to prove by mathematical calculation that Abraham
could be father to many nations in the time frame allowed by biblical
chronology, do not seem to have troubled Hopkins himself.[64]

What is clear is that Hopkins was influenced by accounts of the literary
structure of the Bible and stimulated in particular by Robert Lowth's discovery that Hebrew poetry was structured through parallelism, a theory
advanced in Lowth's 1741 *Lectures on the Sacred Poetry of the Hebrews*.[65]
As Stephen Prickett has argued, the potential for aesthetic appreciation of
the Bible revealed by Lowth, along with his Romantic counterpart Johann
Gottfried Herder, was to a large extent obscured by the inexorable advance
of historical-critical readings in the nineteenth century, as well as by the
rupture between biblical studies and the study of classical and modern
literatures enforced by university reform in Germany and elsewhere.[66] It
was partly through his reading and admiration for Lowth that Hopkins
was able to retain an interest in the literary construction of biblical writing

despite its relative neglect in Roman Catholic biblical scholarship, so that, for instance, we find him in a letter of 1883 comparing and contrasting the methods of Greek lyric art with the 'principle of composition' at work in the Epistles of James, Peter, and Jude.[67]

Lowth was interested in biblical style primarily as the expression of a historical people, in which questions of technique could yield a unique insight into the culture inhabited by biblical writers. This is the impulse followed by most modern inheritors of Lowth's tradition of interpretation, notably those who participate in the movement to reflect on the Bible as literature, for whom literary construction gives the temper of a historical people and place.[68] The ambition of this movement is to set the Bible stylistically within the context in which it was written, largely foregoing consideration of its later reception. Harold Bloom is more tenacious than most such interpreters, but his feeling that 'we need to begin by scrubbing away the varnish' from biblical texts, the varnish given by centuries of religious and theological debate, is not untypical.[69] That is why critics of the Bible as literature have been relatively indifferent to the question of translation: faithfulness to the original is, for their purposes, the only thing that counts, and since the original was not composed by the familiar means of European poetry, having no traffic with rhythm and rhyme, literary attention has to be focused on questions of structure – most obviously that of narrative – for which translation is not seen to hold much importance.[70] This is an approach to the Bible that Lowth to some extent made possible, for by his showing that Hebrew poetry worked by parallelism rather than by verbal sound, 'it could be appreciated for the first time how *little* of the Hebrew poetry was in fact lost through the normal processes of translation'.[71]

If, as I want to suggest, Hopkins in his poetry is by contrast much engaged with the varnish accrued by biblical texts over time, especially in translation, this is because his stylistic awareness of the Bible is primarily spiritual rather than focused on the historical origins of biblical texts. I wish to focus on the late sonnet '*Justus quidem tu es, Domine*' (1889), which provides a rare instance of direct quotation from the Bible, taking as its epigraph a verse from the Latin Vulgate: '*Justus quidem tu es, Domine, si disputem tecum; verumtamen justa loquar ad te: quare via impiorum prosperatur? etc*' (Jeremiah 12.1).[72] The body of the poem interprets and develops this complaint:

> Thou art indeed just, Lord, if I contend
> With thee; but, sir, so what I plead is just.
> Whý do sínners' ways prosper? and why must
> Dísappóintment all I endeavour end?

Wert thou my enemy, O thou my friend,
How wouldst thou worse, I wonder, than thou dost
Defeat, thwart me? Oh, the sots and thralls of lust
Do in spare hours more thrive than I that spend,

Sir, life upon thy cause. See, banks and brakes
Now, leavèd how thick! lacèd they are again
With fretty chervil, look, and fresh wind shakes

Them; birds build – but not I build; no, but strain,
Time's eunuch, and not breed one work that wakes.
Mine, O thou lord of life, send my roots rain.

By virtue of its controlled ferocity, '*Justus quidem tu es, Domine*' stands out from most other sonnets Hopkins wrote in Dublin during the last years of his life. Whereas other late sonnets are remarkable for their dramatic inversions and collisions of word and phrase, being formed in the characteristic abrasiveness of Hopkins's style, '*Justus quidem tu es, Domine*' is poignant in restraint. One of its quiet effects is the inversion in the fourth line needed to provide the end-rhyme, which also allows for 'endeavour' to shrink into 'end', shadowing the curtailment of which the poem complains. In the rest of the poem, the syntactic dislocations are no less numerous than elsewhere in late Hopkins ('leavèd how thick'; 'lacèd they'; 'not I build'), but they are in a lower key, more archaic than arduous. A particular dignity accrues to the sonnet's combination of outspokenness and restraint, in a discourse which seems chastened by years of sterility, unable to 'breed one work that wakes', but which is resolute in the conviction that an injustice has been committed and that the case offered will stand up in God's Court of Appeal.

In all of this, the epigraph is crucial. The sonnet is tasked with both confrontation and petition; it has to achieve a delicate balance between objecting to unfair treatment and continuing to hope in a future reversal of misfortune. One has only to turn to Tractarian poems of spiritual aridity – to the half-hearted grumblings of Isaac Williams's 'Despondency', say – to see how easily in religious poetry expectant trust can overshadow feelings of despair. Unanswered prayer in Williams's poem ('And is this all? and what avail | These cloistral watchings pale?') soon finds answer: 'These to His presence chamber bring, | Where, as an abject thing, | In that true light for evermore, | We should ourselves deplore.'[73] Hopkins's '*Justus quidem tu es, Domine*' risks an appeal to God's mercy ('Mine, O thou lord of life, send my roots rain'), but this does not seem to undercut the preceding accusation of ill treatment. On the contrary, it is apposite to end the poem with petition, a defiant claim of possession following from a measured display of anger at dispossession. Here '*Justus quidem tu es, Domine*' leans on its epigraph. Placed in relation to the tradition of prophetic complaint, it becomes easier to see how the sonnet manages to be at once authentically antagonistic and yet also devotional. The turn from accusation to appeal has an established precedent: as it was for Jeremiah, the source of the affliction the poem describes is identical with the source of possible relief.

Hopkins rarely used biblical epigraphs. A presentation piece, 'May Lines' (c. 1873), is prefaced with a verse from Ecclesiasticus, and some versions of 'Ribblesdale' have an epigraph from the Letter to the Romans. Leaving aside these poems and '*Justus quidem tu es, Domine*', the only other substantial instances occur in 'Barnfloor and Winepress' and '*Nondum*', pieces written before Hopkins had crossed to Rome.[74] Between their composition and '*Justus quidem tu es, Domine*', Hopkins would become familiar with the Bible in its Roman Catholic forms – a fact not only reflected in the quotation from the Vulgate but also in the manner of the adaptation of Jeremiah in the body of the poem. The verse from Jeremiah is translated in the Douay-Rheims Bible as 'Thou indeed, O Lord, art just, if I plead with thee, but yet I will speak what is just to thee: Why doth the way of the wicked prosper: why is it well with all them that transgress, and do wickedly?' The King James Version, by contrast, renders the verse as 'Righteous art thou, O Lord, when I plead with thee: yet let me talk with thee of thy judgments: Wherefore doth the way of the wicked prosper? wherefore are all they happy that deal very treacherously?' Another potential source for these lines shows the same distinction seen here between 'just' and 'righteous': 'Righteous art thou, O Lord, and upright are thy judgments' (Psalm 119.137; King James) or 'Righteous art thou, O Lord: and true is thy judgment' (*Book of Common Prayer*), as against 'Thou art just, O Lord: and thy judgment is right' (Psalm 118.137; Douay-Rheims).

The difference between these biblical versions shadows a large doctrinal variance. The semantic connection between *iustitia* and *iustificatio* is fundamental to the doctrine of justification, and whether God is considered 'righteous' or 'just' is a crucial dividing line in the debate over whether justification is imputed or imparted.[75] It marks a major difference between the Protestant and Roman Catholic Churches from the time of Luther onwards concerning the nature of God's action. Does God's redemption come from outside human initiative or – as Hopkins believed – does it rather amend human nature without overriding it? To put this another way: is the sinner declared holy by God or is she or he made holy by God? The Roman Catholic complaint is that 'righteous', when the word is applied to human nature, does away with any emphasis on inward transformation: as a famous document of Roman Catholic controversy Hopkins could have encountered puts it, 'by their translating righteous, instead of just, [the Protestants] bring it, that Joseph was a righteous man, rather than a just man; and Zachary and Elizabeth were both righteous before God, rather than just; because when a man is called just, it sounds that he is so indeed, and not by imputation only.'[76] Evidently Hopkins's poem does not enter into this confessional controversy. But in a poem which complains that the divine presence does not make itself felt in the life of the believer, and of an inability to 'breed one work that wakes', it seems fitting that God should not be understood to act forensically, in a manner extrinsic to human nature. A 'just' plea in '*Justus quidem tu es, Domine*' is directed to the 'just' God. It is a choice of words which might suggest both claim (a 'just' God will answer a 'just' plea) and accusation (a 'just' God should have dealt justly with his own).[77]

The adaptation of the epigraph, then, follows Roman Catholic modes of biblical translation; it is also likely that it has a Roman Catholic liturgical source, given the prominence of Jeremiah in the Lenten readings which Hopkins encountered in the Mass at the time of year at which he wrote '*Justus quidem tu es, Domine*'. The other biblical source proposed for the poem, the previously quoted verse from Psalm 118, would also have been known in liturgy, for it featured each week in the prayer of the Church, the Divine Office, which Hopkins was obliged to follow daily in his Breviary as a priest. In retreat notes of 1889, feeling 'loathing and hopelessness', and struggling to meditate successfully, he found he could 'do no more than repeat *Justus es, Domine, et rectum judicium tuum* and the like, and then being tired I nodded and woke with a start'. 'What is my wretched life?' the notes continue, 'All my undertakings miscarry: I am like a straining eunuch.'[78] A familiar text to which Hopkins resorted when at the limit of his energies, it is plausible that the same psalm is in the background of a poem written just a few months later, which complains of being 'Time's eunuch', and of the failure to 'breed one work that wakes'.

Given these likely contexts for '*Justus quidem tu es, Domine*', it is regrettable that the editors of the Oxford anthology *Chapters into Verse: Poetry in English Inspired by The Bible* (1993) have seen fit to preface the poem with the King James Version of Jeremiah and omit the Vulgate, as if English poetry could only be inspired by a Bible in English, and the dominance of the King James was total in this respect.[79] It is unfortunately all too familiar an error.[80] The neglect of the Roman Catholic versions in connection with '*Justus quidem tu es, Domine*' can sometimes appear wilful, as when Donald Davie focuses on a doubtful connection between 'justly famous lines' in '*Justus quidem tu es, Domine*' and one of Coverdale's versions of the Psalms in his excellent anthology *The Psalms in English* (1996), ignoring other, more obvious connections with the Vulgate and the Douay-Rheims (the awkwardness of the probably unintended echo – the poem's 'just', Davie's 'justly famous' – perhaps indicates the problems with his method).[81]

However, even if Roman Catholic versions of the Bible are important to '*Justus quidem tu es, Domine*', the body of the poem hardly constitutes a straightforward transcription from these sources. Indeed, the difference that exists between the poem and its biblical epigraph is nearly as important as their more obvious similarity. Jonathan Z. Smith writes that 'it is precisely the juxtaposition, the incongruity between the expectation and the actuality that serves as a vehicle of religious experience'.[82] Hopkins's poem deals in this kind of incongruity. Among other things, it shows itself in a slight departure from the syntax of the biblical epigraph. Hopkins writes 'Thou art indeed just, Lord, if I contend | With thee; but, sir, so what I plead is just.' In this he is in the pattern of Douay-Rheims Bible in departing from the Vulgate and having the subject ('Thou') precede the verb and the complement. The King James and *Book of Common Prayer* versions, by contrast, persist with a complement-verb-subject construction ('Righteous art thou'), a syntactic fronting which brings the quality of righteousness to the fore. These versions sound more like a straightforward affirmation than the preface to a complaint. The Douay-Rheims compensates through its Vulgate-derived adverb and in having the vocative split the clause: 'Thou indeed, O Lord, art just.' By contrast, the poem's placement of the adverb so that it no longer precedes the verb affords it significantly less prominence than either the Vulgate or the Douay-Rheims Bible, shifting the emphasis subtly from the designation ('Thou art indeed just, Lord') to the contention ('if I contend | With thee'), thereby making the acknowledgement of God's justice appear a touch more grudging.

Where the poem instead pauses is over the justice of the complaint, exchanging the colon which appears in both the Vulgate and the Douay-Rheims Bible for a full stop: 'so what I plead is just.' The expressiveness of the change rests on its being slight; the sonnet neither revokes nor assimilates itself to biblical lament but is instead engaged in its renewal. The poem's juxtaposition of formality and familiarity in address (from 'sir' to 'my friend' and back again to 'Sir') issues from the same imperative. God in '*Justus quidem tu es, Domine*' is at once the recipient of earnest petition,

arbitrating as in a courtroom between competing claims, and also an inti-
mate foe, akin to 'an enemy' who 'dost | Defeat, thwart me'. All of this
works to make the poem's biblical reference appear highly individual. That
the poem is engaged with a tradition of lament does not prevent Hopkins's
jeremiad from being very much his own.

Walter J. Ong comments of Hopkins's theological and spiritual writing
that despite Hopkins's awareness of the Latin academic theological tradition, his prose has 'its roots sunk directly and deeply into living vernacular
English'.[83] A similar point can be made in respect of his poetry. Nowhere is
its strenuous combination of elevated and colloquial idioms more pointed
than in Hopkins's manner with biblical allusion and echo. It is a manner,
we can say finally, encapsulated by the feebleness and promise of 'Felix
Randal', labouring in the heat of the smithy:

> How far from then forethought of, all thy more boisterous years,
> When thou at the random grím fórge, pówerful amídst péers,
> Didst fettle for the great grey drayhorse his bright and battering sandal!

If Ecclesiasticus is somewhere in these lines, then biblical language has
passed through the crucible of personal suffering to find individual voice.
Yet that fact does not remove the need to think of the poem in relation to
the specifics of biblical language. '*Didst* fettle', '*thy* more boisterous years',
'*thou* at the random grím fórge': no doubt Hopkins is attempting here
to replicate dialect speech, for he felt – as he told Coventry Patmore in
1884 – that it was 'a lamentable thing that the educated have lost the thou
and thee', even as 'Here in Lancashire one constantly hears it.'[84] Given
the morphological bearings of a later poem such as '*Justus quidem tu es,
Domine*', however, it is also possible that the language of 'Felix Randal',
in enlisting words such as 'Didst', 'thy', and 'thou', equally partakes of the
elevated music of religious English, familiar to Hopkins from Prayer Book
and Bible. The combination of biblical and colloquial would be typical of
his mature poetry.

We are entitled to ask about the appropriateness of this type of elevated
language to what 'Felix Randal' describes, given that the poem was likely
inspired by a death from consumption in a notorious Liverpool slum district, the experience of ministering to which, in Hopkins's own words,

> laid upon my mind a conviction, a truly crushing conviction, of the misery
> of town life to the poor and more than to the poor, of the misery of the
> poor in general, of the degradation even of our race, of the hollowness of
> this century's civilisation: it made life a burden to me to have daily thrust
> upon me the things I saw.[85]

According to Philip Endean, Hopkins in 'Felix Randal' is 'moved by an almost embarrassing tenderness towards the man', but 'fails wholly to come to terms with him': 'All he can do is to blow him up into some sort of elemental presence, as we see in the last line, while the attempt at the common touch in the use of Lancashire dialect comes over as merely patronising.'[86]

I wonder if the failure 'to come to terms' with Felix is actually what is poignant. There is little doubt that 'Felix Randal' does not achieve the fluency and confidence of Hopkins's great nature sonnets, but a lack of fluency seems essential to its effect, not least in the curious blend of elevated and colloquial language which Hopkins attempts. This is a poem that conveys the strain as well as the tenderness that it sees to exist between priest and people. It is awkward in a manner akin to the difficulty Hopkins knew in his own ministry, of overcoming the remoteness sensed by his Liverpool parishioners of their priest, 'little Father Hopkins': the perception, as one parishioner would later recall, that he was too much above the people of the parish, 'too vasty for us'.[87] Indeed, the maladroitness of 'Felix Randal' is very like that of the highly cerebral priest who yet sought to speak of God in comparison with 'a lover's sweetheart' in one of his sermons, and who also, much earlier in his career, had attempted to bring alive for his hearers the miracle of the feeding of the five thousand by drawing improbable analogies between the Sea of Galilee and the Vale of Clwyd. To recoil from this type of discordance in Hopkins would be to disdain a fundamental aspect of his biblical thought. It would be to miss the way that for Hopkins the language of the Gospel was nowhere out of place, with its amplitude proved by locating it where others found it strange.

CHAPTER 2

Prayer

Hopkins's late sonnet '*Justus quidem tu es, Domine*' ends with a prayer: 'Mine, O thou lord of life, send my roots rain' (l. 14). The form of this ending is unusual, for Hopkins rarely has the final line of his sonnets form an independent sentence. He worked over the last line of '*Justus quidem tu es, Domine*' in revision, with earlier drafts having 'Then send, thou Lord of life, these roots their rain', more roundabout phrasing which seeks to establish what the final version of the poem leaves as obvious: that the poem's closing request follows from its earlier complaint.[1] In its final version, the last line is newly assertive and exclamatory. The fierce placement of 'Mine' is now what distinguishes the poem's ending, in a possessiveness which not only suggests a certainty of being in the right, as against the unfairness of God's neglect, but also indicates the recognition of a unique relation, a confession from emphatically personal conviction. The poem's speech exists unshaded by anxiety about the 'long success of sin' ('My prayers must meet a brazen heaven', l. 8) seen in Hopkins's early poems, several of which are distressed by God's seeming distance from individual life. The manner of '*Justus quidem tu es, Domine*' is instead close to that of a psalm of lament, which likewise addresses in prayer to God a complaint against God, with the poem's cry of despair at the same time an act of faith, engaging what the Old Testament scholar Walter Brueggemann describes in psalms of lament as 'a radical discernment of [a] God who is capable of and willing to be respondent and not only initiator'.[2]

'*Justus quidem tu es, Domine*' was written later than the series of 'dark' or 'terrible' sonnets Hopkins composed in the mid-1880s, but it has sometimes been appended to this group of poems because it shares in their feeling of spiritual dryness and difficulty.[3] Some interpretations of the 'terrible sonnets' claim they show an image of spiritual 'paralysis'.[4] '*Justus quidem tu es, Domine*' is clearly not this. It is instead a poem of prayer, both in its closing petition and in its likeness to the form of meditation Hopkins knew in St Ignatius of Loyola's Spiritual Exercises. The Spiritual

Exercises frame the spirituality of the Jesuits; they provided the pattern for Hopkins's daily life of prayer as well as for the retreat that he, in common with all Jesuits, made annually. One of the principal features of the Spiritual Exercises is the prayer of 'colloquy' with God, which, as Hopkins noted from Ignatius, 'is made properly by speaking as a friend speaks to a friend, or as a servant to his master, at one time asking for some favour, at another accusing oneself of some evil done, at another informing him of one's affairs and seeking counsel concerning them'.[5] '*Justus quidem tu es, Domine*' may not have the same quality of exchange Ignatius describes, and it deals more in accusation than in self-accusation; yet the expression of the poem's grievance can still be seen to rest upon the kind of intimacy and directness in speech with divine persons that Ignatius sought to inspire. This affinity provides another reason to notice confidence as well as desperation in the poem's feeling.

The affinity is a familiar one. Much has been made of the connection of Hopkins's poetry with Ignatian meditation, to the extent in one case of proposing that 'Hopkins made over the sonnet form into an Ignatian form of the sonnet' by employing the threefold structure of the Spiritual Exercises, a movement between the traditional 'powers of the soul': memory, understanding, and will.[6] What is usually overlooked in this argument is the history of the religious texts and methods said to have influenced Hopkins's writing.[7] 'Spirituality is never pure in form', comments the theologian Philip Sheldrake, for '"Context" is not a "something" that may be added to or subtracted from spiritual experiences or traditions but is the very element within which these find expression.'[8] Critics who discover connections between the Spiritual Exercises and Hopkins's poetry frequently restrict themselves to a modern translation of Ignatius's text for the Exercises in putting their case, as if Ignatian influence were received pure and unmediated by the poet, despite the long passage of time between the sixteenth and nineteenth centuries. In fact, as Sheldrake has elsewhere observed, the period following Ignatius's founding of the Jesuit Order saw 'a move towards a greater rigidity, both with regard to life-style and specifically with regard to the interpretation of *The Spiritual Exercises* and approaches to prayer, and involving substantial departures from what seems to have been Ignatius's original intention and insight'.[9] Such rigidity is manifest in the schematising impulse shown by many of Hopkins's Jesuit contemporaries in their approach to the Spiritual Exercises, which proves difficult to reconcile with the idealised, threefold pattern taken by a number of Hopkins scholars to characterise the Ignatian method of prayer. The 'three powers of the soul' are always prominent in nineteenth-century Jesuit treatises on the Spiritual Exercises, but the numerous additional divisions and subdivisions familiar to these texts indicate a desire closely to delineate further stages in meditation. In the title of one such treatise, they are attempts to elaborate a *Science of Spiritual Life*.[10]

Behind this local difficulty with critical approaches to Hopkins and the Spiritual Exercises lie larger questions about the general connection between Hopkins's poems and prayer, questions that are at once poetic and religious. '*Justus quidem tu es, Domine*', for instance, is certainly a poem of prayer. But is it a poem made in the image of prayer, and thus mimetic and fictional in the way we have come to expect from lyric poetry – or should we think of it actually as a prayer, even as Hopkins's own personal prayer? Studies of Hopkins's use of an Ignatian model rarely address such questions, but implied in their approach to the 'terrible sonnets' is the notion that these poems are barely, if at all, fictional. Whilst they frequently adhere to the convention of discussing poetic 'speakers', such studies tend either to take the 'terrible sonnets' as simulating directly the feelings of their author or else leave invention out entirely and establish the poems as true acts of Hopkins's spiritual life. In his book-length study of the 'terrible sonnets', for example, Daniel A. Harris is careful to insist that his commentary does not constitute 'a partial biography of Hopkins's last years', but then he proceeds to investigate the 'terrible sonnets' for what they reveal of Hopkins's spiritual life, as poems whose religious and poetic 'incompleteness … is telling evidence of Hopkins's inability to wrest free of the "fell of dark" that enshrouded him'.[11] Other accounts which highlight the Ignatian character of the 'terrible sonnets' find them more hopeful, on the grounds that taken as a series they follow 'the classical descent and ascent of the Ignatian Exercises'. Here too, however, the interest of these sonnets is taken to be highly individual and very little mimetic: 'The sonnet … becomes more and more a prayer form, a personal talk between the priest and his God.'[12]

The belief that the 'terrible sonnets' are true acts of speech made by the poet in his own personal and unalienated voice may seem surprising given the consensus in twentieth-century thinking about poetry that the lyric speaker represents a 'fictional person of all times and all places'.[13] Yet from its early beginnings, Hopkins criticism has favoured the idea that his poems constituted a form of self-expression for their author. The critical moment in which he first came to wide prominence emphasised the mental and emotional significance of complex meanings in poetry. The aptness of Hopkins's work to this interest was part of what made him seem a contemporary to his early critics. Thus Laura Riding and Robert Graves could begin their pages on Hopkins in *A Survey of Modernist Poetry* (1927) by declaring him to be 'One of the first modernist poets to feel the need of a clearness and accuracy in feelings and their expression so minute, so more than scientific, as to make of poetry a higher sort of psychology'; and F. R. Leavis, whose praise for Hopkins in writings of the 1930s and 1940s did much to shape the poet's initial reputation, could prefer 'The Windhover' to 'The Wreck of the Deutschland' on the basis that technical skill 'is most unmistakably that of a great poet when it is at the service of a more immediately personal urgency, when it expresses not religious exaltation, but inner debate'.[14]

The poet's early critical champions were also not constrained by the orthodoxy about the fictional status of the poem's speaker that typified the later American New Criticism. Instead, I. A. Richards, in his influential 1926 article on Hopkins in the *Dial*, could claim that two of the 'terrible sonnets' 'represent the poet's inner conflict'; and William Empson, for all that his famous account of 'The Windhover' in *Seven Types of Ambiguity* (1930) emphasises how tensions in the poem might 'pierce to the regions that underlie the whole structure of our thought' and 'tap the energies of the very depths of mind', could comment later that 'I think the poem is about training and about the doubt in Hopkins's mind, expressed with painful force in later sonnets, as to whether the severe Jesuit training had only crippled him.'[15] In retrospect, it seems obvious that 'The Windhover', and not, say, 'Pied Beauty' or the poem which begins 'As kingfishers catch fire, dragonflies draw flame', would become exemplary for early Hopkins criticism. A poem not just tense and dense but also formed of highly individual and personal speech was perfectly suited to the new method of close reading then emerging.

Successive early readings of Hopkins which concentrated on 'The Windhover' helped establish a view of the poet as having – in the words of Michael Roberts, who opened his influential anthology *The Faber Book of Modern Verse* (1936) with Hopkins – 'moulded a style which expressed the tension and disorder that he found inside himself'.[16] Later studies have likewise made little distinction between poetic expression and real-world speech act. This is especially true of criticism that imagines these poems to be prayers – as for instance when the 'heart-wrenched prayers' of the 'terrible sonnets' are held by Maria R. Lichtmann to 'embody direct and honest colloquies' addressed to God, thus giving us transparent access to the poet's 'tortuous journey of self-examination'.[17]

This approach has important merits, but in practice it has worked to narrow our appreciation of the 'terrible sonnets'. No doubt the special nature of the addressee of these poems should make their discourse more than hypothetical, since a belief in God's omniscience has him present to human expression in all of its forms: God as recipient of these poems presumably cannot be abstractly addressed in the manner familiar to one of Hopkins's main influences, the Petrarchan tradition of lyric love poetry, for in Hopkins's system of belief there is never a moment in which God is absent. There are also good reasons to reflect hard on the convention of describing 'speakers' in Hopkins's poems. More problematic, though, is the tendency to restrict the significance of the 'terrible sonnets' to Hopkins's individual history. Taken as an attempt at real communication with God, the 'terrible sonnets' are assessed for what is imagined to be their spiritual efficacy or, at the opposite pole of argument, for their supposed inability to reach God and consequent helplessness. Where more than personal significance has been attributed to these poems, it is usually to make an individual case representative of the larger religious dilemmas of the period, as when J. Hillis Miller concludes that 'like so many of his contemporaries, [Hopkins] believes in God, but is unable to reach him', or when Isobel Armstrong finds in Hopkins 'an isolated modern subjectivity': 'Hopkins, stranded on his "cliffs of fall", is unable to leap from them to God.'[18]

What is missed by back-and-forth arguments over whether these poems show religious faith deepening or disappearing is the idea of God's relation to human experience from which they begin. In particular, the dominant focus on what the 'terrible sonnets' reveal of the poet's own life has tended to obscure the larger theological and spiritual force of their addresses to the divine. These addresses mediate questions of doctrine, for, as Donald Davie observes, 'when a poet chooses a style, or chooses *between* styles, he is making a choice in which his whole self is involved – including, if he is a Christian poet, that part of himself which is most earnestly and devoutly Christian': 'The question is, for him: what sort of language is most appropriate when I would speak of, or to, my God?'[19] Thinking in these terms allows us to see that the prominence given to inward experience in Hopkins's later work alters rather than ends his poetry's thought. We need to take seriously what the 'terrible sonnets' say of God as well as what they say of the state of Hopkins's faith. My effort here is to show that Hopkins's later poems conceive an understanding of God by the manner in which they attempt to encounter him.

Occasions for Prayer

Before turning in detail to the 'terrible sonnets', it is worth first of all surveying the range of devotional expression to be found in Hopkins's poetry. Kirstie Blair remarks that for a variety of Victorian religious poets, 'the poetics of the liturgy and the liturgical aspects of religious poetry acted in harmony together and to the same ends'.[20] For Hopkins, too, poetry and formal worship were able to be allied. The manuscript albums in which his poems are preserved contain several translations of medieval Eucharistic hymns, including multiple versions of a hymn traditionally ascribed to Thomas Aquinas, '*Adoro Te Devote*', which Hopkins appears to have worked on at intervals over several years, from 1876 to 1882. Medieval Latin hymns were enthusiastically revived by Tractarians such as John Mason Neale, who also translated '*Adore Te Devote*'; the same hymn was also translated by Hopkins's fellow Jesuits Henry Coleridge and George Tyrrell, who like Hopkins had their versions of '*Adoro Te Devote*' published in the Catholic magazine the *Irish Monthly*. Part of the importance of '*Adoro Te Devote*' to Hopkins and his fellow Jesuits would have been derived from the fact that it is one of the hymns habitually sung at the (extra-liturgical) service of Benediction, a mainstay of Victorian Roman Catholic devotion, as well as at the outdoor procession on the Feast of Corpus Christi, for which the hymn is supposed originally to have been composed. Writing to Robert Bridges of one such Corpus Christi procession, which Bridges had attended at his invitation, Hopkins regretted that Bridges 'had not a book to follow the words sung', for Aquinas's hymns, 'though they have the imperfect rhetoric and weakness in idiom of all medieval Latin verse ... are nevertheless remarkable works of genius and would have given meaning to the whole, even to the music, much more to the rite'.[21]

Hopkins's hymn translations form part of a share of his poetry that was composed in proximity to the Roman Catholic devotions, even if not intended for liturgical use. Alongside the hymn translations we should place Hopkins's several Marian presentation pieces, which were also written as devotional exercises, this time in honour of Mary's month, May, and intended for display in the Jesuit houses in which Hopkins lived. Most of these date from the period when Hopkins was still determined to write no poetry as a Jesuit unless it was requested for specific occasions; a later and more remarkable Marian work, 'The Blessed Virgin compared to the Air we Breathe' (1883), was likewise written for event as another of his 'May verses'.

Prayer is prominent in these poems. Of the earlier poems, '*Ad Mariam*' (1873) and '*Rosa Mystica*' (c. 1873–74) both experiment with Swinburnean rhythms, with 'Rosa Mystica' taking up that of the famous chorus of Swinburne's *Atalanta in Calydon* (1865), 'When the hounds of spring are on winter's traces', and turning Swinburne's measure to the praise of the May Virgin:

> The rose in a mystery, where is it found?
> Is it anything true? Does it grow upon ground? –
> It was made of earth's mould but it went from men's eyes
> And its place is a secret and shut in the skies.
> Refrain –
> *In the gardens of God, in the daylight divine*
> *Find me a place by thee, mother of mine.* (ll. 1–7)

The poem draws on Mary's traditional conception as the Mystical Rose, given famous expression in the best known of the Marian litanies, the Litany of Loreto, which, like '*Adoro Te Devote*', is also used at the service of Benediction. The words of the refrain of Hopkins's poem change, so that its final version reads '*To thy breast, to thy rest, to thy glory divine* | *Draw me by charity, mother of mine*' (ll. 47–48), but Hopkins's object remains constant: an appeal to Mary that, for all the energy with which Hopkins applies his conceit, is conventional for a period in which Marian piety tended to conceive of her intercession as above all an expression of maternal solicitude.[22]

The conceit of the later poem 'The Blessed Virgin compared to the Air we Breathe' is greatly more elaborate, not least in being fashioned partly from Hopkins's interest in optical theory.[23] Its final lines also have recourse to petition as a natural end to the poem's praise of Mary, but in less conventional manner than the earlier Marian pieces:

> Be thou then, O thou dear
> Mother, my atmosphere;
> My happier world, wherein
> To wend and meet no sin;
> Above me, round me lie
> Fronting my froward eye
> With sweet and scarless sky;
> Stir in my eyes, speak there
> Of God's love, O live air,
> Of patience, penance, prayer:
> World-mothering air, air wild,
> Wound with thee, in thee isled,
> Fold home, fast fold thy child. (ll. 113–26)

There are hints here of a familiar manner of invocation. Compare the Mary prayers in the *Raccolta*, among the most popular of the Roman Catholic prayer books in Hopkins's lifetime: 'Men say thou art the refuge of the sinner, the hope of the desperate, the aid of the lost: be thou, then, my refuge, hope, and aid'; 'Mother, be thou mine aid; standing beneath my shelter, make me victorious over the common foe of our eternal welfare'; 'Mary! be thou our Mary, and may we feel the saving power of thy sweetest name.'[24] Hopkins's closing petition in 'The Blessed Virgin compared to the Air we Breathe' begins similarly, but its arrival at 'atmosphere' represents an early mark of the difference from conventional addresses to Mary that later lines will go on to confirm. The petition moves the poem from elaborate simile – the conception, as it is put earlier in the poem, that 'men are meant to share | Her life as life does air' – into metaphor ('Be … my atmosphere').[25] Thereafter, the faintly archaic turn taken by 'wend' and 'froward' is not quite that habitual to formal religious language, even if the latter word does have biblical precedent (the *OED* in its definition of 'frowarde' cites from Coverdale's version of Psalm 18: 'With the frowarde thou shalt be frowarde').

As it proceeds, Hopkins's petition gathers distance from the manner of formal prayer. The demand that Mary 'Stir in my eyes, speak there | Of God's love, O live air, | Of patience, penance, prayer' echoes an earlier poem, 'The Starlight Night' (1877), which in raptures at the night sky at one point exclaims: 'Buy then! bid then! – What? – Prayer, pátience, alms, vows' (l. 9). Unlike 'The Blessed Virgin compared to the Air we Breathe', however, 'The Starlight Night' calls its readers to spiritual observance without the poem itself constituting an act of prayer. 'Prayer, pátience, alms, vows' are works of devotion that the earlier poem makes urgent but which are clearly hoped to occur beyond its confines. The final stanza of 'The Blessed Virgin compared to the Air we Breathe', by contrast, is itself a prayer; but a prayer that includes within it an appeal to be reminded to pray, as if at this point in the closing address, the poem was not quite sure of itself *as* a prayer. This is a doubt which is only eclipsed by what follows in the final three lines. For all that their language is rare (the American poet and critic Yvor Winters found Hopkins's distinctive use of 'wild' to be 'very curiously in discord with the subject of Mary'), these lines have a chiastic neatness which makes the poem's final plea to Mary newly direct, especially once the short trimeter lines are refined of any but monosyllabic words.[26]

Hopkins offered a disclaimer to Bridges in respect of 'The Blessed Virgin compared to the Air we Breathe': 'It is partly a compromise with popular

taste, and it is too true that the highest subjects are not those on which
it is easy to reach one's highest.'[27] Bridges, to the contrary, told Hopkins
that he thought the poem 'admirable'.[28] Compiling his edition of Hopkins
in 1918, however, he supplied a general dismissal of Hopkins's occasional
pieces on the same basis as Hopkins had entered a caution about 'The
Blessed Virgin compared to the Air we Breathe' specifically: 'they were
efforts to please a taste with which [Hopkins] had artistically no sympathy,
and no doubt his wish to make use of his talent in practical influence persuaded him to write them'.[29] The remark has a share of truth as well as of
churlishness, but it also exaggerates the issue. Seen in the context of prayer,
the distance between Hopkins's poems written for occasion and his other
work is significant but not absolute. Consider 'Pied Beauty':

> Glóry be to God for dappled things –
>   For skies of couple-colour as a brinded cow;
>   For rose-moles all in stipple upon trout that swim;
> Fresh-fírecoal chestnut-fálls; fínches' wings;
>   Lándscape plotted and pieced – fold, fallow, and plough;
>   And áll trádes, their gear and tackle and trim.
>
> Áll things counter, original, spáre, stránge;
>   Whatever is fickle, frecklèd (who knows how?)
>   With swíft, slów; sweet, sóur; adázzle, dím;
> He fathers-forth whose beauty is pást chánge:
>   Práise hím.

'Pied Beauty' is shaped according to Hopkins's personal metaphysic and
answers to his poetic theory. The poem celebrates the variegated unity
Hopkins sought by his formulation of 'inscape', in which the sensory perception of natural diversity affords access to an ultimate principle of order
capable of unifying discrete particulars. It equally shows an intense effort
to weigh the distinctiveness of individual words and evinces his fascination
'with the way a single word opens up a precise area of the world, and gives
him a way to seize it'.[30] What results is intensely deliberate, particularly
because of the way Hopkins condenses the sonnet form. He tended to
think of the sonnet as like a device or mechanism. His arrival, in one place,
at an equation for the 'best sonnet' – which is given as '$(4+4) + (3+3) =
2.4 + 2.3 = 2 (4+3) = 2.7 = 14$' – indicates a preoccupation with the math-
ematical ratios of poetic forms that also prompted his experiments with a
shorter sonnet length, as in this ten-and-a-half line poem, which Hopkins
described as a 'curtal-sonnet'.[31] Length is crucial to its effect, and part of
what helps align the poem with prayer. 'Pied Beauty' accumulates natural

detail in a way similar to Hopkins's other sonnets of this period, especially 'The Starlight Night' and the poem which begins 'As kingfishers catch fire, dragonflies draw flame', but the variation provided by the final half-line ensures an ending that brings 'Pied Beauty' close to his poetry written for occasion. The previous ten lines hum with activity, copiously diverse in range, and in constant progression. They describe items or attributes ('fold', 'fallow', 'plough', 'gear', 'tackle', 'trim') that might also be actions, putting one in mind of Gillian Beer's remark that 'In Hopkins's poetry all parts of speech incline to verbs.'[32] 'Práise hím', coming at the end of 'Pied Beauty', brings this motion up short, to what, in the poem's forceful logic, is its rightful end in exhortation.

The balance between fulsome and stark expression in the poem suggests an effort to forestall what Hopkins once alleged were Wordsworth's faults in handling the sonnet: 'dulness, superfluity, aimlessness, poverty of plan'.[33] Proclamation in 'Pied Beauty' is artfully conceived, enabling what has been called 'a smooth and lucid track of feeling', with the design of the sonnet made prominent by having its two halves as a grammatically inverted pair, bookended by imperatives.[34] These imperatives, 'Glóry be to God for dappled things' and 'Práise hím', are not far from the two Jesuit mottoes, *Ad Majorem Dei Gloriam* ('For the greater glory of God') and *Laus Deo Semper* ('Praise always to God'), mottoes which are traditionally written at the head and foot of written exercises in Jesuit schools, as well as being a convention of writing undertaken by Jesuits themselves. Hopkins's hymn for display, '*Ad Matrem Virginem*' (probably dating from 1870), has the mottoes, as do several other of his presentation pieces. If Hopkins in his major poetry does not hold to the same convention, he lends the dedication the mottoes express fresh life in 'Pied Beauty', with the difference that 'Glóry be to God for dappled things' and 'Práise hím' are not appendages, but instead main elements, committing the sonnet's admiration for natural beauty to the honour of God.

Can 'Pied Beauty' then be called a prayer? A Jesuit using the mottoes *Ad Majorem Dei Gloriam* and *Laus Deo Semper* indicates that he is offering his best effort to God; as with a book dedication, the presence of the mottoes does not decide the content of what he writes. 'Glóry be to God for dappled things' and 'Práise hím' similarly align 'Pied Beauty' with the traditional idea that committing work to God makes of it a type of prayer. But that they appear within rather than outside the poem also makes prayer into the poem's substance. In Hopkins's manuscript 'Práise hím', as Randall McLeod notices, 'indents to an unprecedented depth for a *c* rhyme, far beyond the axis of the page', a positioning ignored by several twentieth-century editions of Hopkins, but which is crucial, McLeod observes, for placing 'Práise hím' as something like a concluding Amen.[35] The dash that appears at the end of the first line, as if to signal that 'Glóry be to God for dappled things' stands as a preface to the main declaration of the poem, likewise makes this line analogous to the invocation which is prayer's traditional opening. In addition is the fact that 'Glóry be to God for dappled things' and 'Práise hím' are both exhortations and acts of praise, meaning the lines actually are that which they recommend.

The poem's joy in nature's variety is deeply felt but occurs at a remove from any single experience or individual history. This is not to deny, as Susan Chambers has said, that 'Even when [Hopkins's] work is least self-regarding … it shows the touch of a man who has felt, described, and discriminated his own inner world acutely.'[36] The effort of 'Pied Beauty' is to retain the immediacy and freshness of particular observations even in the assertion of laws of nature, resulting in a poem which at every point seeks to 'counter' familiar impressions of natural variety through the aggressive newness of its description. Even so, 'Pied Beauty' finally does not insist upon the specialness of its perceptions, aiming instead at a more universal pronouncement. Its singularities – who else but Hopkins could envisage 'Fresh-firecoal chestnut-falls'? – bear repeating at other times, and in other lives, than his own. The poem finds a place in modern anthologies of prayer, where its devotion is seen to be open to a variety of circumstances, as are set forms of prayer or hymns.[37] Able to be detached from unique individual history in a way that encourages its reading as part of a systematic intellectual venture, it also has the quality sometimes held to be the special preserve of lyric poetry when lyric is seen as 'intended to be voiceable by anyone reading it' – with the important difference that Hopkins's original expression need not be thought fictional for it later to be reprised by others.[38]

Such uses of the poem require us to think of 'Pied Beauty' similarly to Hopkins's poems of occasion. Both share in what Jonathan Culler, intervening in recent debates about lyric, identifies as its 'ritualistic' quality, involving 'the presentation of assertions or judgments that are not relativized to a particular speaker or fictional situation but offered as truths about the world' and in which 'the present of discourse or articulation cannot be reduced to the narrating of past events; on the contrary, the narrated events seem to be subsumed by, trumped by, the present of lyric enunciation'.[39]

Culler's emphasis on lyric as 'memorable writing to be received, reactivated, and repeated by readers' provides a means of bringing poetry and prayer into closer proximity than most existing accounts of the subject are willing to countenance.[40] Along with fictiveness, one recent discussion of poetry and prayer lists as further marks of poetry's distinction from prayer its prizing of verbal invention ('a private prayer that seemed to revel too much in its verbal and formal ingenuity might seem to strain against prayerful norms'), its self-consciousness (as against prayer's 'self-forgetfulness'), and its 'weighting of signifier and signified' ('To a greater extent than in prayer, the medium of poetry is its message').[41] These are distinctions owed to a particular idea of lyric as the preserve of 'idiosyncratic individualism' that is currently the subject of much debate; they also hinge on the idea that prayer can have little or no art.[42]

Hopkins himself was well acquainted with the idea that ordinary private prayer should be humble and uncomplicated. One of the main books of instruction on the spiritual life used in his training is keen that Jesuit novices should guard against mystical ecstasies, insisting that meditation as a form of prayer 'is not singular, nor is it like others filled with such inventions and novelties as savour of illusion' but instead 'is a very common method, ... more easy, more secure, and more profitable than any other'.[43] However, Hopkins also evidently prized the elegance of formal public prayers, naming 'glowing prayers' as one of the attractions of 'the Catholic system' in a letter to his parents defending his decision to convert, and later describing St Patrick's 'Breastplate' or prayer, dating from the eighth century, as 'one of the most remarkable compositions of man'.[44] The long formal prayer Hopkins drafted for publication in 1883 may not be so remarkable, but it too is composed in a manner that renders problematic the notion that the 'message' of prayer can be separated from its 'medium'. Here is the middle section of Hopkins's prayer:

> But thou, O God, madest us to serve thee, in our thoughts to reverence, and with our lips or by our deeds to praise thee; and with sorrow we own against ourselves that whereas we should have glorified thy majesty we have grievously come short of thy glory; nay, worse, that we have been thy rebels and many many times in small things and in great broken thy holy law and not kept thy commandments. We are ashamed, we look at ourselves and thee and are confounded. We wither at thy rebuke, we faint at thy frown, we tremble at thy power and threatened punishments. To offence we have added ingratitude, because for these same sins thy son had died; therefore we have despised his death. But have mercy, O Lord, have mercy on us sinners. We repent of our sins, we wish they were undone; they cannot be undone, but thou canst pardon them; we humbly hope to be forgiven. And though we cannot ask for ever to be free from all the

faults which, daily, human frailty falls into, yet we do hope and, with thy seasonable help afforded, earnestly purpose never wilfully and with full malice to offend thee; and, that in this we may not mock thee with our promises, we add this promise too, not without necessity to venture into those occasions which either we forsee or sad experience has taught us will to us be fatal or dangerous. Yet if, which do thou forbid, these promises of ours were to be broken, however deeply and however often, still we should hope for fresh grace to repent and be forgiven. For thou desirest not the sinner's death, but that he should be converted and live. Our better hope, built on the promise of thy availing help, is never more to sin against thee, but henceforth to live as in thy sight and in the doing of thy service, the end that we were made for and our bounden duty; living thus, at our deaths to hear thy sentence of mercy; and, meeting with thy mercy, to see thy face for ever.[45]

The notion that prayer always transcends ordinary language use will not get us far here. Instead, we need to acknowledge the way in which (as one recent study puts it) 'prayer abstracts and amplifies aspects of discourse constitutive of all communication.'[46] Hopkins's prayer is an elaborate and stylised act of penitence, highly aware of itself as an instrument of the reverence extolled at the opening to this passage ('But thou, O God, madest us to serve thee, in our thoughts to reverence, and with our lips or by our deeds to praise thee'). To be derivative is a mark of the prayer's orthodoxy, and the reason it depends heavily on biblical echo, as well as on existing spiritual formulas (the statement 'we have grievously come short of thy glory' harks back to the *Confiteor*, the confession of sins made at the beginning of the Roman Catholic Mass: 'I have sinned exceedingly in thought, word, and deed, through my fault, through my most grievous fault').[47] The prayer may be less bold with such formulas than is Hopkins's poetry, but this is an aspect of its design, not the result of any obligation for prayer to have greater plainness, or to be less studied, than other forms of expression. To think otherwise requires that we conceive of religious writing and speech as subsequent to spiritual life, as if patterns of belief were somehow able to float free from language.

Commentaries on poetry and prayer, from Henri Bremond's classic 1926 study *Prière et poésie* onwards, usually want to maintain that these are close but distinct forms. For Bremond, poetry moves towards but does not reach the heights of prayer, with the poet 'a broken-down mystic'; the contributors to a 2015 volume on the same topic are likewise led predominantly to speak of 'strong affinities' and 'shared concern' between poetry and prayer rather than anything more entire.[48] Hopkins is a poet who complicates the desire to distinguish poetry from prayer, for there are occasions in his writing when it is not enough to describe his poetry as only prayer-like, borrowing prayer's manner of invocation, or to say that it imitates prayer, and so is mimetic rather than real. This is the case with 'Pied Beauty'; it is also true of the final stanza of 'The Wreck':

> Dáme, at óur dóor
> Drówned, and among óur shóals,
> Remémber us in the róads, the heaven-háven of the
> rewárd:
> Our kíng back, Oh, upon Énglish sóuls!
> Let him éaster in us, be a dáyspring to the dímness of us,
> be a crímson-cresseted east,
> More bríghtening her, ráre-dear Brítain, as his réign rólls,
> Príde, rose, prínce, hero of us, hígh-príest,
> Oür héart's charity's héarth's fíre, oür thóughts' chivalry's
> thróng's Lórd.
>
> (ll. 273–80)

This address is not apostrophic; its speech is more than a pretence. The poet's plea is directed to the tall nun, who is remote from Hopkins but not absent, in the sense that he believed she had been raised to the communion of saints by her act of martyrdom, which allowed her intercession to be demanded on behalf of all England (and, later in the stanza, all Britain).[49] Coming in a poem as much occupied by Hopkins's own faith and situation as by the destiny of the German nuns in whose memory it is written, this is an appeal forged out of personal feeling, whose directness is prepared for in the way poet and tall nun are juxtaposed in earlier passages, most notably in stanza 24 ('I was under a roof here, I was at rest, | ... She to the black-about air, to the breaker, the thickly | Falling flakes, to the throng that catches and quails, | Was cálling "O Chríst, Chríst, come quíckly"'). Yet significantly the plea is not private. Indeed, its manner befits a poem that Hopkins probably from the outset intended to make public, hoping that it would appear in a Jesuit journal.[50] The effortful formality of this address combines with the stanza's insistent return to the collective pronouns 'our' and 'us' to ensure that the weight of 'The Wreck' at its close is communal, not individual. This is especially the case in the final line: Hopkins indicated by his diacritical marks that the diphthong in the 'oür' of 'oür thóughts"' should be split further than is normal in reading and consequently dragged out for emphasis; the preference in the more reliable of the two extant transcripts of the poem for 'Oür héart's' over the second transcript's 'Our héarts"' likewise stresses the collective nature of the appeal.

One of the puzzles of 'The Wreck' concerns the relationship between its two parts: why does Hopkins preface 'Part the second' with 'Part the first', none of whose eighty lines have explicitly to do with the subject announced in the poem's title? Probably there is no complete explanation for their combination, but we can at least say that 'Part the first' signals that telling the details of the story of the *Deutschland* tragedy will not be the poem's main purpose ('The Deutschland would be more generally interesting if there were more wreck and less discourse, I know', Hopkins told Bridges, 'but still it is an ode and not primarily a narrative'; Hopkins in this letter cancelled 'lyric' in favour of 'ode', which suggests he was clearer in terms of categories about what 'The Wreck' was not than about what it was).[51] We realise immediately from the opening lines of 'Part the first' ('Thou mastering me | God! giver of breath and bread') that the poem's object is to declare God's truth and goodness, and only secondarily to provide an account of the shipwreck. This determination also frames the structural unity which exists between the poem's two parts. They are organised to be mirror images of each other. Each moves from the acclaim of God's action in particular circumstance to the contemplation of divine reality at large; each also culminates in prayer. 'Part the first' ends with the following two stanzas:

> Be adored among men,
> God, three-numberèd form;
> Wring thy rebel, dogged in den,
> Man's malice, with wrecking and storm.
> Beyónd sáying swéet, past télling of tóngue,
> Thou art lightning and love, I found it, a winter and warm;
> Father and fondler of heart thou hast wrung:
> Hast thy dark descending and most art merciful then.

> With an anvil-ding
> And with fire in him forge thy will
> Or rather, rather then, stealing as Spring
> Through him, melt him but master him still:
> Whether át ónce, as ónce at a crásh Pául,
> Or as Áustin, a língering-óut swéet skíll,
> Make mercy in all of us, out of us all
> Mástery, bút be adóred, bút be adóred Kíng.   (ll. 65–80)

The alteration in pronouns is again revealing here. Until this moment, the action and address of 'Part the first' had lain between the poet and his God. 'Part the first' had even occasionally moved away from address to declare admiration of God without seeming to speak directly to him, reprising the manner Hopkins had adopted in a cancelled version of the first lines of the poem: 'God mastering me: | Giver of breath and bread'. Here, though, the poem discovers a collective voice and moves from the contemplation of Hopkins's personal encounter with God as an individual experience to tell of broader paradigms of spiritual history. There is a turn to the variety in the way in which God's grace becomes known, in which the contrast is between gradual arrivals at religious truth – for which the exemplar is the 'língering-óut swéet skíll' with which developed St Augustine's faith in God – and the 'át ónce, as ónce at a crásh' Damascene conversion.

The individual history described earlier in 'Part the first' lies more in the second of these camps. Hopkins told Bridges that 'what refers to myself in the poem is all strictly and literally true and did all occur; nothing is added for poetical padding', an avowal felt to be necessary presumably because the spiritual tumult recounted in 'Part the first' is so intense and dramatic.[52] In what refers to Hopkins in 'Part the first', we encounter the extremity of relation between an individual and God for which 'The Wreck' is known ('The God of *The Wreck of the Deutschland* is a being who can be refused, wrestled with or surrendered to', comments Elizabeth Jennings: 'He is a person whom the poet knows through the confrontation of personalities').[53] The first stanza describes being 'álmost únmade, what with dréad, | Thy doing' (ll. 6–7); the second recalls an occasion when 'Thou heardst me, truer than tongue, confess | Thy terror, O Christ, O God' (ll. 11–12). The foundation of spiritual intimacy in both cases is the perception of a God who, faced with his own, moves to overwhelm and subdue.

At the end of 'Part the first', however, Hopkins makes greater allowance for a gentler encounter with the divine, preparing the way for its closing prayer, which is open to varieties of relationship with God (the 'bút' of 'Mástery, bút be adóred, bút be adóred Kíng' is the counterpart to that of 'melt him, but master him still' of earlier in the stanza; both indicate the wish for a rounded and multiple knowledge of God). The effort to balance alternatives here anticipates the turn taken at the close of 'Part the second'. Here, too, there is a determination that the poem's spiritual confidence should be more than individual. As in his poems of occasion, Hopkins in 'The Wreck' turns to prayer conscious of the need to make allowance for others to adopt the poem's sentiment. The closing stanzas of each of its two parts are rendered in such a way that their speech might have reality in lives beyond Hopkins's own.

This is writing which is at once a form of individual self-expression and at the same time capable of being repeated and reiterated as a type of ritual. Unlikely though it might appear, this double function is replicated in the poems traditionally seen as Hopkins's most personal and private works: the 'terrible sonnets'. Realising this enables us to see that the 'terrible sonnets' are poems which in dramatising personal processes of belief also hold to a distinct conception of God's relation to ordinary human experience.

The 'Terrible Sonnets'

That the 'terrible sonnets' might have truth in lives other than Hopkins's own is not immediately obvious. Indeed, in some ways it is curious to find Hopkins's later poems 'My own heart let me more have pity on', 'I wake and feel the fell of dark, not day', and *'Justus quidem tu es, Domine'* appearing alongside 'Pied Beauty' in the poetry appendix to the current Roman Catholic Breviary, a revised version of the book from which Hopkins himself daily prayed the Divine Office, the Liturgy of the Hours.[54] 'My own heart let me more have pity on', 'I wake and feel the fell of dark, not day', and *'Justus quidem tu es, Domine'* all have an ostensible situation and require to be understood with reference to an apparent pragmatic context. Their speech appears private, which risks making the access of later readers to these poems seem awkward when the poems are thought of not simply as representational, or as the dramatisation of a real situation, but rather as actual or attempted forms of communication to God on Hopkins's part.

'My own heart let me more have pity on' and 'I wake and feel the fell of dark, not day' were only discovered posthumously; it appears to have been Hopkins's intention to send these and other 'terrible sonnets' to Bridges, but he had not yet done so before his death.[55] Hopkins famously wrote that certain of his late poems arrived as 'inspirations unbidden', and commented in 1885 of two unidentified poems, likely to be 'terrible sonnets', that 'I have after long silence written two sonnets, which I am touching: if ever anything was written in blood one of these was.'[56] Together with their intimacy of feeling, such remarks encourage Hopkins's critics to cast the 'terrible sonnets' as the poet's own prayers. There is support for this view from the editors of Hopkins's 'Dublin Notebook', who find evidence which 'suggests that he may have abandoned contemplative prayer altogether, with the exception of his required annual retreat, sometime in the spring of 1885, a period of extreme emotional stress and distress', making it plausible that he turned to poetry as its substitute: 'Perhaps most especially after he found he could no longer tolerate the emotional exigencies of regular meditative prayer, Hopkins's religious life was not merely chronicled in his Dublin poems, but rather was often enacted in and through them, albeit sometimes obliquely.'[57]

As the several caveats indicate, this can only ever be speculation about what is finally unknowable. It might seem safer to align the 'terrible sonnets' with the dominant conception of lyric poetry as fiction or mimesis, and thus consider their addresses to God and self to be figurative – a notion of lyric that, in having the lyric poem transcend social reality, enables a reader to identify with the speaker of the poem and take ownership of its words. We could then say of Hopkins what A. D. Nuttall insists of George Herbert: that his 'prayers in poetic form are really poems which imitate or represent prayer ... from first to last dramatic fictions ... pictures of the way a man might pray.'[58] Either way, the point to register would seem to be that made by Nuttall in respect of Herbert: 'Even if Herbert were giving us not prayers, but pictures of prayers, some mimetic fidelity to the real conditions of prayer must presumably be required.'[59] Thinking of the 'terrible sonnets' in this way provides an opening to the much-discussed question of what kind of spiritual state or process these poems imagine or inhabit. It also allows us to probe the more neglected idea of God from which they begin. Take the first lines of the untitled poem which begins thus:

> No worst, there is none. Pitched past pitch of grief,
> More pangs will, schooled at forepangs, wilder wring.
> Comforter, where, where is your comforting?
> Mary, mother of us, where is your relief?   (ll. 1–4)

The inwardness of the first two lines makes it hard to think of the poem as speech intended to draw answer. The opening statement, 'No worst, there is none' is startlingly emphatic but leaves us guessing as to its context; thereafter, 'Pitched past pitch of grief, | More pangs will, schooled at forepangs, wilder wring' is a sentence turned in upon itself, tied into an almost impossible grammatical knot that leaves still obscure the poem's circumstance.

Afterwards, the subsequent address made to the Holy Ghost in 'No worst' seems to turn the poem outwards, and yet this is done in a manner so stifled as to again make external speech doubtful. 'Comforter, where, where is your comforting?' appears less to play on words than to be unable to move on from them. The repetition of 'where' looks exasperated rather than expectant; to have 'comforting' succeed 'Comforter' likewise seems a token of frustration rather than a happy symmetry. Compare a Liverpool sermon, in which Hopkins observed that 'Comforter' is only an approximate translation of 'Paraclete' in designating the Holy Ghost:

> The word [Paraclete] is Greek; there is no one English word for it and no one Latin word, *Comforter* is not enough. A Paraclete is someone who

comforts, who cheers, who encourages, who persuades, who exhorts, who stirs up, who urges forwards, who calls on; what the spur and word of command is to a horse, what clapping of hands is to a speaker, what a trumpet is to the soldier, that a Paraclete is to the soul: *one who calls us on*, that is what it means, a Paraclete calls us on to good.[60]

Hopkins's description here answers to the nature of what it describes, and the contrast this presents with 'No worst' is telling: 'Paraclete' proliferates in definition in the sermon, whereas 'Comforter' cannot get past itself in the poem, with 'Comforter, where, where is th your comforting?' insisting on the terms of this designation as if to pinpoint a failure of duty.

William Waters proposes that 'doubts about the effectiveness of poetic address may become … integral to the quality of that address.'[61] So it is in 'No worst': the question asked of the Holy Ghost is allowed to be fierce partly, it seems, because of the feeling that it is unlikely to be answered. Such ferocity is especially evident in Hopkins's choice of pronouns, with the only surviving autograph copy of this poem revealing that he first contemplated an alternative to 'your' for line 3. The manuscript reads 'Comforter, where, where is th your comforting?'[62] Perhaps the deleted word if complete would have been 'this' or even 'the', but it is most likely to have been 'thy', in which case Hopkins decided in the end to depart from the custom of his own poetry as well as from the conventions of religious language with which he was familiar. This decision makes it harder to think of the address as a true petition, as it does also in what follows ('Mary, mother of us, where is your relief?'), a succession from the previous line which has something of the aspect of a litany, especially given the familiar communal weight of 'mother of us', but which then departs markedly from habit in asking 'where is th *your* relief?'[63] In contrast to '*Justus quidem tu es, Domine*', where the adoption of the pronoun familiar to religious language ('Mine, O thou lord of life, send my roots rain') instils a measure of confidence in the poem's appeal to God, the particular quality of the speech of 'No worst' appears determined by its being sceptical of a hearing from its addressees. Indeed, even allowing for the belief that God knows each petition before it is asked, the questions of 'No worst' still sail close to apostrophe, turning what Jonathan Culler identifies as the danger in a poem's address 'turning away' from any actual hearer – 'that this figure which seems to establish relations between the self and the other can be read as an act of radical interiorization and solipsism' – into a strong element of this poem's meaning.[64]

To make a demand of God (or of another object of spiritual petition) without the expectation of a response would be an inversion of prayer as

Hopkins understood it. According to notes on prayer made by Matthew Russell, an Irish Jesuit who was Hopkins's colleague in Dublin, 'The mere fact that God bids us to pray … involves a sort of correlative obligation and engagement on God's part that He will give heed to our prayer. To bid us pray unless He meant to listen to our prayer is not consistent with an idea of His goodness and love.'[65] The same would apply to prayers to the Virgin Mary. In a favourite prayer to Mary of Hopkins's period, the *Memorare* prayer, the profuse meekness of the petition stands as a counterpart to trust in Mary's generosity of feeling:

> Remember, Mary, tenderest-hearted Virgin, how from of old the ear hath never heard that he who ran to thee for refuge, implored thy help, and sought thy prayers, was forsaken of God. Virgin of virgins, Mother, emboldened by this confidence I fly to thee, to thee I come, and in thy presence I a weeping sinner stand. Mother of the Word Incarnate, O cast not away my prayer; but in thy pity hear and answer. Amen.[66]

This is a declaration of unworthiness made in the expectation of a sympathetic response. The historian Mary Heimann observes of the *Memorare* prayer in Victorian Roman Catholic devotion that 'Open to the most spiritual of interpretations, it was above all the prayer's immediacy, its concrete offer of tangible results, which no doubt accounted for the breadth of its popularity.'[67] To this the addresses of 'No worst' seem remote, as petitions instead shaped by the unlikelihood of their being answered. The poem borrows from the style of prayer only to depart pointedly from its expectation of a response.

What in consequence surprises about the poem's sestet is the extent to which it leaves behind the inwardness of the octave, drawing out general truths from a particular situation whose nature remains unclear. I quote the sestet with its uncancelled variant in the second line:

> O the mind, mind has mountains; cliffs of fall
> Frightful, sheer, $\begin{cases} \text{not man's fathoming. Hold them cheap} \\ \text{no-man-fathomed.} \end{cases}$
> May who ne'er hung there. Nor does long our small
> Durance deal with that steep or deep. Here! creep,
> Wretch, under a comfort serves in a whirlwind: all
> Life death does end and each day dies with sleep.   (ll. 9–14)

The universal reach of these lines has allowed them to become widely known, with 'O the mind, mind has mountains' recently adapted as a title for items as various as a volume on psychiatric practice, a cultural history of mountaineering, and an episode of the British television crime drama

Lewis. It is not that Hopkins's poem in its sestet necessarily becomes dia-logic, for 'Hold them cheap | May who ne'er hung there' and the 'our' of 'Nor does long our small | Durance deal with that steep or deep' could still be internally directed, but that the perspective of 'No worst' has shifted. A situation that in the octave had appeared darkly private and individual is made representative of common experience.

Writing in the late 1940s, Yvor Winters complained that the poem's com-bination of obscurely personal feeling with general pronouncement was unsatisfying: 'One is inclined to ask: "What do you know of these matters? Why are you so secretive? And above all, why are you so self-righteous in your secretiveness?"' For Winters, the personal situation of 'No worst' is too inde-terminate, meaning that 'the mind cannot organize itself to share Hopkins' experience with any real feeling of security'.[68] Here Winters was at one with New Critical assessments of Hopkins in measuring the success of the poems by their internal coherence. For a number of early critics of Hopkins asso-ciated with the New Criticism, his poems are to be taken in isolation from relations external to the text itself. Thus R. P. Blackmur, in a 1939 review of an edition of Hopkins's letters, was careful to divide the correspondence from the poetry: 'the more life or mind, the more extraneous material of any sort, you introduce into the study of a poem as belonging to it, the more you violate the poem as such, and the more you render it a mere document of personal expression'; similarly Austin Warren, faced several years later with a recently published life of Hopkins, was relieved to say that 'Hopkins is not … a poet suitably approached through biography': 'With the possible excep-tion of the late sonnets, his poems are devotional and rhetorical, not self-ex-pressive.'[69] There is a striking difference here with early British commentary on Hopkins, in which – from Richards's essay in the *Dial* onwards – refer-ence to the poet's own inner struggle helps unlock poetic meaning. It is this that allows C. Day Lewis, in a book of 1934, to identify 'No worst' as 'the greatest poem to my mind that [Hopkins] ever wrote', having first observed that Hopkins's 'intense faith and his violent spiritual agonies are experiences which few of us to-day – happily or unhappily – are able to share'.[70]

Faced with the 'terrible sonnets', later Hopkins criticism has in general sided more with the biographical emphasis of his early British proponents than with the determination towards fictional speech typical of American New Criticism. Studies treating these poems without reference to the poet's life are rare indeed. Conversely, the association of the 'terrible son-nets' with Hopkins's private and personal struggle is probably why they are often overlooked by synthesising accounts of his theology and philosophy, which are instead drawn to the proclamatory clarity of 'The Wreck' and the Welsh nature sonnets.[71] These last are also personal poems, of course.

The difference is that their ambition is seen to extend beyond the circumstances of Hopkins's own life in a way rarely allowed to the 'terrible sonnets'. Implicit here is the idea that the inwardness of Hopkins's later poetry involves a retreat from the ambition of 'The Wreck' and the nature sonnets to declare general truths about the world – an assumption also widely in evidence in accounts of Hopkins that do dwell on the 'terrible sonnets'.

Hopkins's attempt to couple the reiterable with the personal in 'No worst' gives cause to rethink this assumption. Even if the effect is strange, as Winters believed, this is a poem whose situation is at once intensely particular and yet also made available for common utterance. There is no necessary opposition between its possible reality for Hopkins and its potential replication in the lives of later readers: the ritualistic quality of his earlier verse has not been abandoned in this poem, but rather refigured. That the poem allows of such replication may appear unlikely when it closes with violent self-address: 'Here! creep, | Wretch, under a comfort serves in a whirlwind: all | Life death does end and each day dies with sleep' (ll. 12–14). Leaving behind the general pronouncement of earlier in the sestet, the poem becomes once again close and personal, returning to the manner of the octave. Even in this resolution, however, Hopkins engages a kind of shared sentiment, for the way these lines recall *King Lear*, alluding to the storm scenes in Shakespeare's play, when Lear takes shelter in a hovel, enables a moment of intimate self-address to hold broader resemblance.[72] In addition, and like much else in the poem, the deixis 'Here!' manages at once to intimate a particular context for the poem's speech and to leave details of that context unspecified. The situation of the poem may be Hopkins's own, but it is also made available to others by virtue of its lack of specificity.

Thinking about the poem in this way, one notices anew its difference from the piety of Hopkins's own period. Seen against the *Memorare* prayer in particular, what is striking about the distress of 'No worst' is how little it is accounted for by way of inevitable human failings, even as the poem presumes to speak of the human condition at large. There is not here the emphasis on the individual's progress in overcoming sin that featured so largely in Catholic spirituality of Hopkins's time. Even the poet's near contemporary George Tyrrell, whose theological unorthodoxy was such that in 1906 he was expelled from the Jesuits, could remark conventionally that in periods of spiritual dryness, 'A steady, unbroken gaze on our sinfulness and wilfulness, will provide us with a sombre background against which the mercy and loving kindness of God will shine out more brightly.' According to Tyrrell, 'The more one grows in intimacy with Christ, the deeper is the sense of sin and our regret that, even to some extent unwittingly, we should have offended Him, and must daily and hourly pain Him by our gross

ways and ignorant inconsideration.'[73] 'No worst' is differently attuned to
the nature of relations between the individual and God. It is true that the
poem senses the poverty of human awareness and comprehension in the
situation it describes. Line 10 began as 'Frightful, sheer down, not fath-
omed' before Hopkins altered it to read 'Frightful, sheer, no man's fathoming', and then 'not man's fathoming' and 'no-man-fathomed': the effect of
these changes is to hint that what is impenetrable to humankind may not
be so generally. Perhaps God knows better, in which case the succeeding
declaration of pitifulness – 'Here! creep, | Wretch' – is implicitly contrasted
to God's sufficiency. That said, this last self-abasement seems not to be
an act of mortification, and it is also moderated by the grand image of
mental tribulation that appears in earlier lines ('O the mind, mind has
mountains'). Above all, and even if the poem's earlier questions to the Holy
Spirit and Virgin Mary are apostrophic, their directness bespeaks the same
assurance of being in the right – as against the injustice of leaving this
'Wretch' without relief – also seen in '*Justus quidem tu es, Domine*'. Solace
is deserved and ought to have come.

This is a notable aspect of the 'terrible sonnets' more generally. Behind
their drama of feeling stands a strong expectation of the naturalness of
God's presence, against which these poems measure their frustration and
despondency. Take 'I wake and feel the fell of dark, not day', which also
includes uncancelled variants:

> I wake and feel the fell of dark, not day.
> What hours, O what black hŏurs we have spent
> This night! what sights you, heart, saw, ways you went!
> And more must, in yet longer light's delay.
>
> With witness I speak this. But where I say
> Hours I mean years, mean life. And my lament
> Is cries countless, cries like dead letters sent
> To dearest him that lives alas! away.
>
> I am gall, I am heartburn. God's most deep decree
> Bitter would have me taste: my taste was me;
> Bones built in me, flesh filled, blood brimmed the curse.
>
>   ⌜a dull dough
> Selfyeast of spirit ⌊my selfstuff sours. I see
>   ⌜scourge
> The lost are like this, and their ⌊loss   to be
> ⌜As I am mine, their sweating selves;
> ⌊Their sweating selves as I am mine, but worse.

'I wake and feel' combines extreme convolution in syntax (most obviously 'Selfyeast of spirit a dull dough sours') with constructions that surprise by their plainness. One of these plainer constructions – 'With witness I speak this. But where I say | Hours I mean years, mean life' – makes reference to the event of speech ('where I say') in a way that suggests the poem is in the image of a talk between persons. This suggestion of course proves deceptive. Indeed, it is one of the effects of 'I wake and feel' to first create and then undo the impression that the poem goes beyond the self. In the opening quatrain, the shift in pronouns from 'I' to 'we' between the first and second lines raises the possibility that the experience described is at least not solitary. Distressingly, this seeming companionship turns out to be another form of self-address. What is more, the conceit of speaking to one's heart is only partially sustained: it is 'I', 'me', and 'my', and not 'we' that resounds through the rest of the poem, conveying a suffocating introversion, with what should be the delight of selfhood become 'gall' and 'heartburn'.

Like other 'terrible sonnets', 'I wake and feel' depends upon a contextual situation (ostensible or otherwise) whose circumstances are obscure and multiple. This is part of what animates arguments familiar to Hopkins criticism about the nature of the spiritual state the 'terrible sonnets' represent. What rests more neglected is the basic idea of God's action against which these poems weigh their discontent. Of course it is important to reflect on the state of belief this poem imagines. But we should also notice the conception of the individual's relationship with God from which it begins. The second quatrain of 'I wake and feel' follows two terse statements ('With witness I speak this. But where I say | Hours, I mean years, mean life') with a figurative flourish. Here, lament to God is imagined as 'cries countless', cries which are themselves 'like dead letters' unsuccessfully posted to a distant deity. The simile 'like dead letters' is contemporary: the Dead Letter Office 'handled letters that were mis-sent, uncollected (or unpaid), and hence undeliverable … Returning letters became profitable when, beginning in 1811, the Post Office charged the sender the cost of receiving an undeliverable letter back.'[74] All of these details have relevance to Hopkins's poem, in which blame for miscommunication may lie with the intended recipient of the complaint, who perhaps unfairly has made himself distant, but also with its sender, whose addresses may not be rightly directed given the state of life the poem describes.

Either way, the poem's upset is at the distance of a God ordinarily capable of being known within everyday realities. The upset is extreme: Hopkins's

choice of the sonnet form, known for its facility for antithesis and resolution, allows him to draw effect from the meagreness of the sonnet's final
turn in feeling, in which the comparison with the worse fate of lost souls
provides only a dark consolation. Yet what is significant here is not just the
poem's despondency but also its confidence that analogies from human
discourse are appropriate to the workings of divine grace. We are close
to the spirit of the Ignatian instruction cited earlier, in which the prayer
of colloquy (as Hopkins noted) 'is made properly by speaking as a friend
speaks to a friend, or as a servant to his master, at one time asking for some
favour, at another accusing oneself of some evil done, at another informing him of one's affairs and seeking counsel concerning them'. As I have
suggested, much has been made of the influence of the Ignatian tradition
on Hopkins's poetry, but often without much attention to how this tradition was understood and interpreted in the poet's own period. The crucial
point to observe in this respect is that the mystical possibilities of Ignatius's
emphasis on direct communication between the individual and God were
overshadowed in Hopkins's lifetime by 'the trend that saw in the *Spiritual
Exercises* (and hence in Jesuit spirituality) a recipe only for "strengthening
the will" in order to achieve moral rectitude'.[75] This trend went alongside
an understanding of the Spiritual Exercises as providing standard norms
for Jesuit life, the influence of which is largely apparent in the writings of
Hopkins's Jesuit contemporaries – as when a Jesuit of Hopkins's period,
not identified, desired in notes on the Spiritual Exercises 'To draw on
principles from the Exercises & traditions of the society, thus to avoid all
singularity[,] all over-reliance on one's own judgment'.[76] Hopkins's near
contemporary George Tyrrell 'was convinced that the order as a whole had
systematized its approach to Ignatian spirituality and government to the
extent of obliterating the mystical element in Ignatius's teaching'.[77]

'I wake and feel', by contrast, has the expectation of a quality of experiential encounter with God that was not recognised as more than the
most remarkable possibility in the Roman Catholic thought of Hopkins's
period. The tendency in his time was to understand grace 'as purely extrinsic to human experience'.[78] Hopkins's poem is closer to earlier and later
conceptions of individual history as a site for God's self-communication.
The poem is not wholly consistent on this score: like 'No worst', 'I wake
and feel' fluctuates in spiritual feeling, with 'God's most deep decree |
Bitter would have me taste' suggesting a lack of receptivity which seems
not to be imagined as the fault of God alone. The possibility is left open
that sin is a barrier to communication with God in the situation the poem

describes. Yet even if not unambiguous, or capable of being raised to the type of systematic insight favoured in recent accounts of Hopkins, there is enough here to suggest an expectation of divine presence in quotidian life strikingly different from the predominant understanding of nature and the supernatural seen in the poet's immediate contexts.

This is a feature of the 'terrible sonnets' generally. In the manner in which they decry God's absence, these poems imply the conviction that God should be known in lived history, revealed to the ordinary world in the day-to-day interior life of the individual. This was not a conviction much shared by nineteenth-century Roman Catholic theology, which tended to secure immutable religious truth by emphasising its distance from historical conditions. It involves a departure, too, from the tradition of Tractarian devotional poetry with which Hopkins has often, if loosely, been associated, and to which he is sometimes cited as the 'natural heir'.[79] The influence of Tractarianism on Hopkins's poetry was of course large, perhaps especially in that Tractarian efforts to renew interest in the writings of the Church Fathers provided him with a strong awareness of patristic thought. Hopkins knew here an alternative to the opposition between nature and grace seen in the scholasticism he would later encounter when a Roman Catholic. But this influence was not received from Tractarian poetry, which has relatively little in common with the works Hopkins produced in his creative maturity. Tractarian poetry rarely has the intensely personal quality seen in 'No Worst': in the work of John Keble, as an 1867 article in the *Quarterly Review* commented, 'We do not see, we are not permitted to see, the manifold intricate movements of an individual soul. While certain phases of thought and emotion are carefully and accurately described, there is a vague generality about them.'[80] Generality served a purpose for Tractarian poets. The enormous popularity of Keble's *The Christian Year* (1827) was secured by the way its devotion could be taken up by all manner of people, in all manner of contexts.[81] The devotion of Hopkins's poetry also often finds expression general enough to be taken up in different situations. What is remarkable about the 'terrible sonnets' is that this goes alongside a concern with 'the manifold movements of an individual soul' which is unsparingly particular.

This choice of focus hinges on a theological judgement. It assumes that God's presence should be known intimately in ordinary and everyday experience. That the focus is unsparingly particular is true not only of expressions of inner torment in the 'terrible sonnets' but also of moments of self-possession. Take the untitled poem which begins thus:

> Not, I'll not, carrion comfort, Despair, not feast on thee;
> Not untwist – slack they may be – these last strands of man
> In me ór, most weary, cry *I can no more*. I can;
> Can something, hope, wish day come, not choose not to be.
>
> (ll. 1–4)

The confidence expressed here is immensely hard won. Hopkins's lines are categorical in their rejection of desolation, yet also able to take in that the matter is desperately close run. In line 3, 'I can' comes so hard upon '*I can no more*' as to be shaded by its opposite, a proximity also exposed when the final clause returns us to negation just at the moment when the stanza seems finally to have been released into affirmation.

'Not, I'll not, carrion comfort' is most often read as a drama of the private and inward self. Commentators assess the strength or weakness of its spiritual confidence according to what they judge to be the extent of its unity or disunity, as if it represented a statement of belief in God rather than evoking the believer's shifting experience of God.[82] To set the poem in the context of prayer allows us once again to notice the idea of God's dealings with the individual person upon which this spiritual confidence (or its absence) is predicated. In another work of this period, 'Thee, God, I come from, to thee go' (probably dating from 1885), described by one of Hopkins's editors as 'a hymn for communal worship',[83] such confidence is accompanied by a familiar emphasis on human sinfulness and unworthiness before God:

> Once I turned from thee and hid,
> Bound on what thou hadst forbid;
> Sow the wind I would; I sinned:
> I repent of what I did.
>
> Bad I am, but yet thy child.
> Father, be thou reconciled.
> Spare thou me, since I see
> With thy might that thou art mild.   (ll. 9–16)

Human alienation from grace is made to appear obdurate, requiring to be perfected from without by God. In 'Not, I'll not, carrion comfort', by contrast, the struggle with a divine adversary is imagined to be more than simply the reflection of sinfulness or self-deception. The poem continues:

> But ah, but O thou terrible, why wouldst thou rude on me
>   {wring-world}
> Thy{wring-earth }right foot rock? lay a lionlimb against me? scan
> With darksome devouring eyes my bruisèd bones? and fan,
> O in turns of tempest, me heaped there; me frantic to avoïd thee and flee?

Why? That my chaff might fly; my grain lie, sheer and clear.
Nay in all that toil, that coil, since (seems) I kissed the rod,
Hand rather, my heart lo! lapped strength, stole joy, would laugh, cheer.
Cheer whóm though? The héro whose héaven-handling flúng me, fóot tród
Me? or mé that fóught hím? O whích óne? is it eách óne? That níght, that yéar
Of now done darkness I wretch lay wrestling with (my God!) my God.

(ll. 5–14)

'Not, I'll not, carrion comfort' is a difficult poem, partly for the lack of clarity about the nature of its addressee, who may at various points be 'Despair', the self, and God. However, that its ferocious questions hold to the familiar pronouns of religious English suggests a proximity to prayer that is also borne out by the sonnet's many biblical allusions, several of which relate to speech to God: 'lay a lionlimb against me', for example, recalls Job's protest to God that 'Thou huntest me as a fierce lion' (10.16; King James). As it was for Job, the poem's complaint is at suffering that initially appears unwarranted. As too for Job, such suffering turns out actually to have purpose: 'That my chaff might fly; my grain lie, sheer and clear.'

Unlike for Job, however, this realisation yields further questions ('Cheer whóm though?' and so on), darkening the comfort it is seen to afford. Of course, the poem does eventually come to a kind of settlement, working with rather than against what Michael Hurley calls 'the sonnet's promise, established through convention, to resolve the problem that is its occasion for being'; there is here the trust identified by Hurley in Hopkins in the capacity of poetry – and particularly the sonnet – to make sense of individual struggles of faith.[84] Yet the sense made of the situation is fragile. In particular, Hopkins's complicated way with tense inhibits any complacency that might be seen to derive from a position of retrospection. Even the belated acknowledgement in the final line that the sonnet is spoken from a position of recovery finds a counterpoint in the sudden shock registered by '(my God!) my God'. This exclamation runs the risk of appearing affected, but it is at the same time daringly multiple in implication, traced with the suggestion at once of profane curse, angry confrontation, and shout of recognition. We encounter here what Geoffrey Hill describes as 'the expletive of a potentially filthy bare forked animal ("I wretch", "carrion") and the bare word of faith'.[85] This provides a striking contrast with another of the poem's biblical inspirations. For Jacob in the Old Testament, mysteriously wrestling with God at Peniel, a willingness to enter into such conflict was a heroic act which brought divine blessing (Genesis 32.22–32). Hopkins's poem knows something of the same blessing, lapping strength and stealing joy from spiritual toil, yet the starkness of the appositional construction of the final line – 'I wretch' – suppresses in the way it is echoed by 'wrestling' any potential honour to be derived from defiance. It is another of the poem's steadfast refusals of easy compensation.

The basis this poem has in individual history – whether real or imagined – is surely the cause of its absence from recent studies of Hopkins's poetry as a systematic project of intellectual understanding.[86] Yet there is more than personal significance to be drawn from the expectation seen in 'Not, I'll not, carrion comfort' that God should be known intimately in subjective experience. Again, this expectation is not wholly consistent in the poem, with the words 'I wretch' in the final line signalling human alienation from the supernatural order and a feeling of profound unworthiness before God. Clearly the process of purgation and renewal described earlier in the sestet is far from complete. The sense of shame glimpsed in the closing self-ad-dress of 'No worst' – 'Here! creep, | Wretch' – is present at the end of this poem too. That said, the potential for this same final line of 'Not, I'll not, carrion comfort' to verge on prayer manages at the same time to imply the existence of an innate human longing for God and the expectation that his revelation will be apparent in individual history. According to Geoffrey Hill, short words in Hopkins can comprise both 'the most elemental mate-rial' and 'the abrupt selving of prayer': '(my God!) my God' is one of his main examples.[87] Developing Hill's argument, Ian Ker relates '(my God!) my God' to forms of ejaculatory prayer familiar to Roman Catholic devo-tion, noting that 'Nineteenth-century Catholic prayer books were full of these kind of prayers (to which indulgences were attached), such as, at their simplest, "My Jesus, mercy!", "Jesus, Mary!"'[88] He finds that here and elsewhere in his poetry Hopkins has 'the demotic sound of Catholic ver-nacular piety ringing in his ear'.[89] Given what comes before it in the poem, '(my God!) my God' may appear more exasperated than pious. Its relation to the tradition described by Ker is indirect, to say the least. Yet if we do think of it as a prayer, this cry will appear not only as one of recognition but also of the possession of faith in God, akin to the 'Mine' that appears in the final line of '*Justus quidem tu es, Domine*' ('Mine, O thou lord of life, send my roots rain'). It will be seen to derive from an assurance that the transcendent is capable of being experienced in ordinary life.

What is remarkable here is the nearness of seemingly irreconcilable modes of religious awareness. In one way the poem seems to privilege an interior response to God grounded in human experience, at least if we think of '(my God!)' as a type of ejaculatory prayer of hope and trust. When seen as the shock of recognition of a 'wretch' who did not expect to encounter the divine so closely, however, '(my God!)' serves to reveal the profound limitations of experience in knowledge of the divine. The inner life the poem presents is able to be seen equally as a site of grace and as acutely alienated from God.

Such incongruity in meaning has implications that extend well beyond only the personal and psychological sphere of religious experience. Those implications are not stable or consistent, which is the likely cause of their absence from synthesising accounts of Hopkins's poetry as a project of conceptual understanding, but neither are they only individual and local, as those studies tracing the influence of the Spiritual Exercises on Hopkins have sometimes assumed. The prominence given to individual experience in his later work is itself of larger relevance, since it implies the perception, however partially and incompletely rendered in the poems themselves, that divine grace ordinarily permeates everyday human exist-ence. Contrary to the divided priorities suggested by Hopkins criticism, then, the importance of prayer to both the earlier and later phases of his poetry reveals what they hold in common. Both offer expressions of faith able to be taken up in lives other than Hopkins's own; both are at once of individual and communal significance. The turn to particular individual experience made in the later phase represents an alteration in the manner of his poetry's thought, and not a retreat into a purely private realm of personal feeling.

'Not, I'll not, carrion comfort' shows this well. In his tract on prayer, Alphonsus Liguori, the eighteenth-century saint who exerted a large influence on continental Roman Catholic devotion in Hopkins's period, emphasises that humility and confidence 'are indispensably necessary for the efficacy of prayer', as an act in which 'each one should consider that he is, as it were, on the top of a lofty mountain, suspended over the abyss of all sins, and supported only by the thread of God's grace; if this thread gives way he shall infallibly fall into the abyss, and shall perpetuate the most enormous crimes.'[90] There is here the twin emphasis André de Bovis detects in Roman Catholic writing on prayer from the sixteenth to nineteenth centuries: 'the sense of God, of adoration, of the infinite respect due to the "Divine Majesty" in the act of prayer', and at the same time a stress on 'the misery of the sinful man, his "corruption"'.[91] The '(my God!)' of 'Not, I'll not, carrion comfort' seems at once to attach to the same emphasis on sin, as the word of a 'wretch' astonished by a distant God come close, and yet also to turn this emphasis inside out, bespeaking a confidence (whether exasperated or pious) that grace should be known in individual life as more than a desperate rope thrown from above. The poem's word of faith is at once a prayer of its time, aligning with the often ascetical Roman Catholic spirituality of the period, and also looks beyond it, in the expectation that God should indwell the lived experience of faith at every ordinary moment.

PART II

Models of Faith

CHAPTER 3

The Soldier

Seldom published in his lifetime, Hopkins's poetry only came to prominence long after his death, first attracting significant interest in the period of the First World War. Some had their initial encounter with Hopkins whilst actually at war. These included the poet Ivor Gurney, who read Hopkins in Robert Bridges's anthology *The Spirit of Man* (1916) when stationed on the Western Front in 1916. Gurney described with hollow wryness in a letter of August of that year how his recent loan of the anthology had since become a permanent acquisition: 'My best friend [F. W. Harvey, Gurney's fellow Gloucester poet] went out on patrol some weeks back, and has never returned. I am glad to say that we accidentally met on that morning and he lent me R. B.'s *Spirit of Man*. Mine for always I suppose now. Unless that event occurs which will dissolve rights of ownership, or desire.'[1] A store of neo-Platonic consolation intended to afford relief in wartime, Bridges's anthology included several of Hopkins's poems, among them 'Spring and Fall', the opening stanza of 'The Wreck of the Deutschland', 'The Candle Indoors', and 'In the Valley of the Elwy'. Gurney thought it 'a good book, though very far below what it might be': 'Why all that Shelley and Dixon, and Hopkins or what's his names of the crazy precious diction? … Where is Wordsworth, Stevenson, Whitman, Browning? And why not more Tolstoi?'[2]

The Spirit of Man provided many with their first meeting with Hopkins, among them F. R. Leavis, then working as an orderly serving ambulance trains, who (as he later recalled) 'picked it up somewhere or other in wartime France, and, since no one else wanted it, got to know its contents pretty well'.[3] Leavis would think it inevitable that Hopkins had to wait so long for recognition; he was one of a number of the poet's early critical champions to conceive of Hopkins as an advance party in the modernist effort to renew and revitalise forms of poetic expression.[4] Many years on Leavis was able to recall his support of Hopkins in martial terms, as part of a battle against 'taste and critical orthodoxy': 'Hopkins in fact gave one a good military opportunity', he wrote, for 'an effective attack in that sector could tell in the campaign to get recognition for a greater poet – [T. S.] Eliot'.[5] It was also Hopkins's innovativeness that attracted the notice of a fellow Cambridge critic I. A. Richards: Richards's influential 1926 essay in the *Dial* notes of Hopkins that 'It is an important fact that he is so often most himself when he is most experimental.'[6] Richards was another who seems to have first come across Hopkins in Bridges's wartime anthology, and he would go on to use its version of 'Spring and Fall' in the exercises in practical criticism he held at Cambridge in the 1920s. Wartime interest in his friend's poetry was also what finally persuaded Bridges to press ahead with the full edition of Hopkins's poetry eventually published in December 1918, a month after the armistice, its appearance having been slowed by 'war conditions'.[7] The prefatory sonnet Bridges himself wrote for the 1918 edition notices the coincidence, observing that

> Hell wars without; but, dear, the while my hands
> Gather'd thy book, I heard, this wintry day,
> Thy spirit thank me, in his young delight
> Stepping again upon the yellow sands.[8]

'I have had lately some very authoritative appeals for the publication of all Gerard's poetical remains', Bridges had earlier told Kate Hopkins, the poet's mother, in 1917:

> The other day Sir Walter Raleigh, whose judgment is very highly esteemed, said to me that Gerard's poems in the Spirit of Man were the only ones among the comparatively unknown writers whom I had introduced, which stood up alongside of the greater writers. And this afternoon I met a man who had just come from Petrograd, who said much the same thing. He was very urgent about having a complete edition.[9]

The complete edition, when it finally appeared, revealed that the poet who had first come to prominence in wartime was also a poet of war. Hopkins composed several poems which take a soldier for their hero. These poems are evidence at once of nationalistic fervour and of the appeal of soldierly physique: for Hopkins to picture the muscular body put to work in honourable cause allowed for patriotic feeling to be aligned with an attraction to male bodies. Their significance is also theological and spiritual. In the only previous assessment of the religious meaning of war to Hopkins, Bernadette Waterman Ward observes that Hopkins's poems often turn on an idea of spiritual warfare. She finds that in his poems actually about war, 'the courage war demands is only an outward manifestation of the virtue of fortitude', and that, more generally, war stands in imitation of God's justice, the justice 'wrested from a world under occupation by a spirit of lovelessness'.[10] This chapter offers a different interpretation of the religious virtue Hopkins saw in war – and of his perception of the spiritual life as a type of war – by revealing how his soldier poems carry varied senses of how God relates to the world and to ordinary human lives. These are poems which grapple with the promise and the uncertainty of religious experience. When allowed more than private significance, we see in these poems a hesitant and conflicted side to Hopkins's ideas about God and faith all but absent from recent accounts of his thought as a complete edifice. The tussle in these poems between ascetical and sacramental impulses might in turn cause us to look again at a much greater work which shares the attraction to chivalry seen in Hopkins's writing on soldiers: 'The Windhover'.

A Practical Christ: 'The Soldier'

Severn and Somme (1917), Ivor Gurney's first book of poems, offers what John Lucas calls 'an innocent response to war', imagined as an opportunity for heroism and sacrifice.[11] Hopkins knew an earlier form of such innocence and did not live to see it reversed. Bridges's 1918 edition of Hopkins's poetry brought into print a sonnet from 1885, to which Bridges gave the title 'The Soldier':

> Yes. Whý do we áll, séeing of a ‖ sóldier, bléss him? bléss
> Our rédcoats, óur tars? Bóth ‖ thêse béing, the gréater párt,
> But frail clay, nay but foul clay. Hére it ís: the héart,
> Since, proud, it calls the calling ‖ manly, gives a guess
> That, hopes that, mákesbelieve, ‖ the men must be no less;
> It fáncies; ít deems; déars the ártist áfter his árt;
> So feigns it finds as sterling ‖ all as all is smart
> And scárlet wéar the spírit of wár thére expréss.
> Mark Christ our King. He knows war, served this soldiering through;
> He of all can reeve a rope best. ‖ There he bides in bliss
> Now, and séeing somewhére some mán ‖ do all that man can do,
> For lóve he léans forth, néeds ‖ his néck must fáll on, kíss,
> And cry 'O Christ-done deed! So God-made-flesh does too:
> Were I come o'er again' cries ‖ Christ 'it should be this'.[12]

'The Soldier' is familiarly mid-Victorian both in the anxiety that soldierly appearances may deceive and in its quieting by means of religious analogy. Coming of age after the end of the Crimean War, Hopkins knew the old suspicion of the professional army as rough and dissolute, and also the slow reversal of that perception, as imperial fervour combined with manly

Christianity to arrive at 'the cult of the heroic-warrior'.[13] 'The Soldier' stages this reappraisal of martial values. As Matthew Bevis remarks, 'The journey of "foul clay" in this sonnet is the rite of passage of the soldier in Victoria's reign: from dens of prostitution to stages of pilgrimage, from inebriation to incarnation.'[14] In tracing this rise in status, Hopkins concludes that 'the spirit of war' mirrors the spirit of Christ.

The poem also partakes of apprehensions over the want of military heroism seen amidst imperial misadventure, such as that which befell British troops in the battle of Majuba Hill in 1881, during the First Boer War, an event Hopkins lamented to Bridges as an 'unredeemed disgrace', and to his mother as 'a deep disgrace, a stain upon our arms ... The effect will, I am afraid, be felt all over the empire.'[15] The pain of defeat can be felt more locally in the worry harboured by 'The Soldier' that customary admiration for soldiers is mere custom only (Hopkins had been reading Cicero's *De Officis*, with its observation that 'The very fact that the statues we look upon are usually in military dress bears witness to our devotion to military glory').[16] Trying different verbs to describe acts of admiration ('calls the calling', 'gives a guess', 'hopes', 'mákesbelieve', 'fáncies', 'deems', 'déars', 'feigns'), the poem implies the extent to which a high estimation of soldiers is prized. Yet none of this is enough to remove the sense that the question with which the poem opens – 'Whý do we áll, séeing of a ‖ sóldier, bléss him?' – has been asked because this estimation is susceptible to reversal. The worry is that guesswork about soldiers may actually be a form of wish-fulfilment.

It is the sestet's recourse to Christ's example that relieves the poem's unease. The example Christ offers is strikingly material, given by one who 'knows war, served this soldiering through'. Here Hopkins shares ground with a tradition of religious thought with which he would otherwise appear to have little in common. Thinking of poems including 'The Soldier', Joseph Bristow writes about Hopkins's attempt to comprehend 'how male strength might be invested with a glory that unites man and God, dissolves class differences, and, what is more, enables same-sex desire'.[17] According to Bristow, '[Hopkins's] poetry signals an altogether new male-male eroticism that largely stems from an idealisation of the fighting fit body praised by F. D. Maurice, Thomas Hughes, and especially Charles Kingsley',[18] theological liberals whose muscular Christianity was an expression of trust in the goodness of human nature.[19] Hopkins's religious formation was largely opposite, steeped in disciplines of self-denial and unworldly reserve Kingsley so detested in Hopkins's mentor John Henry Newman.[20] (The test of Christian manhood, according to one of Newman's Tractarian sermons, is 'to break with the world, and make religion our first concern', an ideal Hopkins's early confessional notes show him tortuously attempting to live out in the face of myriad distractions and temptations, notably those provided by male bodies.[21])

Hopkins's early sonnet 'Easter Communion' (1865), written whilst an undergraduate at Oxford, hymns self-mortification in a manner that Kingsley would doubtless have thought 'unmanly':

> Pure fasted faces draw unto this feast:
> God comes all sweetness to your Lenten lips.
> You striped in secret with breath-taking whips,
> Those crookèd rough-scored chequers may be pieced
> To crosses meant for Jesu's; you whom the East
> With draught of thin and pursuant cold so nips
> Breathe Easter now; you sergèd fellowships,
> You vigil-keepers with low flames decreased,
>
> God shall o'er-brim the measures you have spent
> With oil of gladness, for sackcloth and frieze
> And the ever-fretting shirt of punishment
> Give myrrhy-threaded golden folds of ease.
> Your scarce-sheathed bones are weary of being bent:
> Lo, God shall strengthen all the feeble knees.

The product of this marriage of religious and poetic enthusiasms is certainly unlikely: we have here a Keatsian sonnet about fasting. Julia F. Saville claims that in Hopkins's poetry 'ascetic practices that appear to mortify the flesh in the interests of spiritual invigoration may paradoxically prove sensually and erotically satisfying too'.[22] So it is in 'Easter Communion': the poem's breathless praise for 'breath-taking', a true meeting of 'lips' and 'whips', takes obvious pleasure in austerity and self-punishment. It is not hard to see why Hopkins later made a record in his confessional notes that 'In looking over the above poem [likely to be 'Easter Communion'] an evil thought seemed to rise from the line before.'[23] The precise nature of this 'evil thought' may be unknowable. What is apparent, however, is that the Lenten discipline admired in 'Easter Communion' has a masochistic charge that paradoxically is a function of the poem's piety.

Such piety is very far from 'The Soldier', and not only in the sense that what is lauded in 'Easter Communion' is bodily meekness and self-denial rather than strength. Whilst the later poem marks out the sacredness of secular military discipline, 'Easter Communion' conceives of a retirement from the world for privileged initiates (the 'sergèd fellowships'). It

is thoroughly in the High Church spirit, as befits a poem Hopkins gave
to a friend at Oxford with whom he shared similar religious inclinations.[24]
Newman's 1829 essay on poetry opposes 'virtues peculiarly Christian' and
'especially poetical' to 'ruder and more ordinary feelings', placing in the
first category 'meekness, gentleness, compassion, contentment, modesty',
and in the second, 'anger, indignation, emulation, martial spirit, and love
of independence'.[25] Perceptions of martial spirit had begun to shift by
the time Hopkins wrote 'Easter Communion' in 1865 (this was also the
year of Sabine Baring-Gould's hymn 'Onward, Christian Soldiers'), yet
the poem gives every indication that he held to the same ideal of sanctity
Newman meant to indicate by opposing military attitudes to the Christian
virtues. Hopkins's letters of this period speak of the necessity of Catholic
belief when confronted by 'the sordidness of things', and of 'the incredible
condescension of the Incarnation' amid 'the mean and trivial accidents of
humanity'.[26] In its praise for forms of devotion secluded from everyday
life, the spiritual temperament of 'Easter Communion' is of a piece with
these pronouncements.

The piety of 'The Soldier' is more inclined to see how grace permeates experience as well as rescues it, and so closer to Bristow's notion of
Hopkins as sharing an ideal of Christian manliness widely promoted in the
culture he inhabited. The poem deals in a venerable motif, of the spiritual
life imagined as a field of battle, applying it with unusual literalness. 'He
knows war, served this soldiering through' is a metaphor trying hard to
be otherwise, with the Incarnation made to sound more like a matter of
professional discipline than of awesome exploit ('He of all can reeve a
rope best' adds a dose of practical know-how for good measure). There
is something precious and extravagant about this claim which serves to
show how vitally Hopkins's poetry cherishes Christ's humanity, in sharp
contrast to elements of the theology he was taught, in which (as James
Finn Cotter remarks) this aspect 'was either ignored or treated as a fixed
quantity known only to men in its exterior accidents'.[27]

The poem's admiration for human achievement has surprising culmination in its final lines:

> For lóve he lěans forth, néeds || his néck must fáll on, kíss,
> And cry 'O Christ-done deed! So God-made-flesh does too:
> Were I come o'er again' cries || Christ 'it should be this'.

This is not a holy kiss of peace, but one of tender spontaneity, in some ways
the mirror image of the heavenward-directed kiss offered in 'The Wreck of
the Deutschland': 'I kiss my hand | To the stars, lovely asunder … Kiss my

hand to the dappled-with-damson west' (ll. 33; 37). Unlike in 'The Wreck', however, the kiss of 'The Soldier' is given, not sent, and its main echoes are biblical, most obviously recalling the father's delight at his son's return in the New Testament parable of the prodigal son: 'And when he was yet a great way off, his father saw him, and was moved with compassion, and running to him fell upon his neck, and kissed him' (Luke 15.20; Douay-Rheims). This parable 'is only addrest to *sinners*', remarks Newman in one of his Anglican sermons, and 'if therefore a man thinks himself harmless and naturally excellent and acceptable to God, such an one Christ does not invite'.[28] Hopkins's poem appears more to stress the proximity of God to man, and man to God, marking the natural orientation of one towards the other. As Matthew Campbell says, 'The Soldier' is 'a Catholic disquisition on metaphor or analogy, of the uniform expressing the man, and the reality, not mere idealism, of God made flesh'.[29] Here too, though, it remains important that the matter is close run. If the difference of 'The Soldier' from 'Easter Communion' signals the change in Hopkins's idea of holiness from his early, earnest, High Church years, the trace of a reservation about military honour in the opening lines suggests that the transformation in his attitude was not entire. Christ's delight in the poem is at a show of human vigour that cannot be assumed, born of the relief that 'frail clay' has been rescued from turning 'foul'.

The return conjectured at the close of 'The Soldier' is not, as in the New Testament parable, that of sinful man to ever-forgiving God, but rather of Christ's own to the world. Norman MacKenzie suggests that Hopkins may be thinking of the apocalypse, and of the return of Christ at the head of a heavenly army described in the Book of Revelation (19.11–16; Douay-Rheims):

> And I saw heaven opened, and behold a white horse; and he that sat upon him was called faithful and true, and with justice doth he judge and fight. And his eyes were as a flame of fire, and on his head were many diadems, and he had a name written, which no man knoweth but himself. And he was clothed with a garment sprinkled with blood; and his name is called, THE WORD OF GOD. And the armies that are in heaven followed him on white horses, clothed in fine linen, white and clean. And out of his mouth proceedeth a sharp two edged sword; that with it he may strike the nations. And he shall rule them with a rod of iron; and he treadeth the winepress of the fierceness of the wrath of God the Almighty.[30]

The parallel is interesting as much for the contrast it presents with Hopkins's poem as for any noticeable similarity. 'Warriors of this world wage *unjust* wars, but our Almighty Leader fights for a heavenly cause and with heavenly weapons', wrote Newman in a meditation on this same biblical passage.[31] The implication of Hopkins's poem is starkly different. 'Were I come o'er again' appears hypothetical, in the past subjunctive, and so concerned with the manner of Christ's Incarnation rather than with the forecast of his Second Coming: should Christ have his time on earth over again, he would, according to Hopkins's scenario, be wearing scarlet, not white. That may sound unlikely in its daring, but then this is – at least in its spiritual implications – a notably daring poem. The final lines of 'The Soldier' represent the only place in his poetry where Hopkins puts words into God's mouth. Those words are brief, and as also often happens in Hopkins's nature sonnets, concision works to funnel argument. 'O Christ-done deed! || So God-made-flesh does too' is a piece of reasoning so neatly syllogistic that we do not startle at the order of thought, in which usual priorities are reversed. To say that the action of God is imaged in man may be no different doctrinally from stating that man acts in the image of God, but it is a less obvious formulation of the same truth and serves to reinforce the poem's emphasis on Christ's humanity. (A deleted revision of the sestet does not involve the use of compounds and is consequently less taut: 'If Christ, that our world's warfare once went through | And knows what soldiering is, now, being in bliss | Sees where some man does all that man can do, | He needs must fall around his neck and kiss | And cries "O good deed done! So God does too: | Could Christ come o'er again I should be this."'[32])

Hopkins gave a sermon in 1880 in which Christ is said to encourage 'by his own example: he led the way, went before his troops, was himself the vanguard, was the forlorn hope, bore the brunt of battle alone, died upon the field, on Calvary hill, and bought the victory by his blood'.[33] The example Christ gives in 'The Soldier' is notably less singular, empha-sising diligence above exploit. He is the skilled fastener of ropes, not the self-sacrificing hero. Of course, the poem's more general admiration is for virtues not attained in civilian life, for that which exists beyond ordinary experience, yet it is also the case that this doing of 'all that man can do' is, by the poem's measure, hardly unique, for the soldier admired here is 'a || sóldier', any soldier, actually any type of military, given that 'reeve a rope' is nautical, and that the poem considers admiration for 'tars' as well as 'redcoats' (Hopkins, as is obvious from his 1878 poem 'The Loss of the Eurydice', also greatly admired sailors).

Perhaps there is not the equanimity here of Hopkins's late sonnet on the Jesuit laybrother 'St. Alphonsus Rodriguez' (1888), a poem which discov-ers that the 'world without event' (l. 13) can itself be a kind of martyrdom.

In that sonnet, the humdrum work of the hall porter gives no outward sign of glory, for 'where war is within, what sword we wield | Not seen, the heroic breast not outward-steeled, | Earth hears no hurtle then from fiercest fray' (ll. 6–8).[34] The saint simply 'watched the door' (l. 14), and his life is no less honourable in the eyes of God for that. The military soldier's glory, by contrast, is evidently more conspicuous, and the idea of spiritual warfare with which it is associated in Hopkins's poem on the soldier more obviously exceptional; the effect of Hopkins's stress marks, in particular, is to add specificity to the case, diverting emphasis away from the imprecision of 'some': 'séeing somewhére some mán || do all that man can do'. Yet the idea of both poems is to see wars of the spirit as fought in the world rather than with the world, in ordinary experience rather than in removal from it. Few would claim that 'The Soldier' is among Hopkins's successful poems. It is little discussed by his critics. The poem also sits badly with dominant approaches to his writing, considered either as a project of intellectual distillation or as a drama of inward self. But 'The Soldier' does at least reveal shades to Hopkins's religious understanding, admiring male valour in a way that is neither truly ascetic nor comfortably worldly. There is here the variability in the sense of God and of human experience that Hopkins in his critical reception has too often been denied.

Vulnerable Valour: 'What shall I do for the land that bred me' and 'The Bugler's First Communion'

At the time at which he wrote 'The Soldier', Hopkins had begun to doubt the valour of the army he held dear. To a patriot for whom, as David Alderson remarks, 'the empire was both a Christian obligation and a providential reward', perceived failures of British military courage were profoundly shocking.[35] They led Hopkins, always the arch-Tory, to an ever more bellicose hatred of Gladstone, the Grand Old Man whom he nicknamed 'the Grand Old Mischief-maker'.[36] Such failures also swelled revulsion for the physical deficiencies of the urban masses. He wrote to Bridges of the 1881 Mayday procession in Liverpool that

> While I admired the handsome horses I remarked for the thousandth time with sorrow and loathing the base and bessotted figures and features of the Liverpool crowd. When I see the fine and manly Norwegians that flock hither to embark for America walk our streets and look about them it fills me with shame and wretchedness. I am told Sheffield is worse though. We have been shamefully beaten by the Boers (at Majuba it was simply that our troops funked and ran), but this is not the worse that is to be.[37]

This is a famous passage in Hopkins's letters, notable not least for its emphasis on the Norwegians as 'manly'. Whatever one thinks of the excess of punning on 'Manley' and 'manly' on the part of Hopkins's critics, there can be little doubt about the importance the word held for him. Along with 'sturdy', 'handsome', and 'hardy' (or even 'hardy-handsome', as appears in 'Felix Randal'), 'manly' is part of Hopkins's vocabulary for male brawn, vocabulary in which physical strength is an index to moral integrity. The word's appearance in this letter is typical. Less doubtingly than in 'The Soldier', the impulse of the letter is to associate manly looks with manly callings. Hopkins worried about their fate amid urban squalor ('our whole civilisation is dirty, yea filthy, and especially in the north', he told Robert Bridges).[38] What is striking in the letter is that such worries are seen without pause or explanation to extend from Liverpool and Sheffield to the far reaches of the Empire. The imperial context may be why the vitriol of the letter on the Mayday procession is not simply condescending. Hopkins twice feels shame, an emotion, according to Gabriele Taylor, that 'introduces the notion of an audience, for feeling shame is connected with the thought that eyes are upon one'.[39] Hopkins is here more obviously looking than looked at, but so personally did he take national failings that his imagined audience here might be something like the rest of the world, eyeing Britain's urban and imperial disgraces, the correlation between which is so evident to him that it does not need explanation.

Events at Majuba Hill stayed with Hopkins. A letter of 1888 also engages the British defeat to the Boers as a means of comprehending his disgust at urban poverty:

> What I most dislike in towns and in London in particular is the misery of the poor; the dirt, squalor, and the illshapen degraded physical (putting aside moral) type of so many of the people, with the deeply dejecting unbearable thought that by degrees almost all our population will become a town population and a puny unhealthy and cowardly one. Yes, cowardly. Do you know and realise what happened at Majuba Hill? 500 British troops after 8 hours' firing, on the Dutch reaching the top, ran without offering hand to hand resistance before, it is said, 80 men. Such a thing was never heard in history. The disgrace in itself is unspeakable. Still it might have been slurred over by pushing on the campaign. But Gladstone was equal to himself and the occasion. He professed that the Queen's honour was by this dishonour vindicated, made the convention, and stamped the memory of Majuba in the minds of all African colonists for ever. What one man could do to throw away a continent and weaken the bonds of a world wide empire he did.[40]

Hopkins's fit of rage swings abruptly from debasement at home to humiliation abroad, again without pausing to make clear why these should be seen as equivalent. He was not unusual in his vehemence over Majuba Hill: so stamped in British minds was the disgrace of defeat that 'Remember Majuba' became a battle cry for British troops in the Second Boer War, begun more than a decade after this letter had been penned.[41] Perhaps Hopkins would have been equally angry about what he perceived to be the fundamental causes of defeat had he only known the worst of urban conditions from a distance. As it was, the particular awkwardness of Hopkins's situation was that his work as a priest brought him face-to-face with dire slum poverty. Although he was capable of sympathy and concern for the poor, the experience also served to entrench his reactionary politics.

The letter of 1888 was written not from darkest England, but from an Ireland agitating for Home Rule, a prospect to which Hopkins was sullenly resigned ('Home Rule of itself is a blow for England and will do no good to Ireland', he wrote, 'But it is better than worse things').[42] The especial difficulty of Hopkins's position in Ireland was to be an English patriot serving under the jurisdiction of Irish bishops who supported the nationalist cause. If, in Geoffrey Hill's much-cited phrase, Hopkins upon his conversion suffered, in a large sense, 'an abruption of ... familiar rhythm', a break with habitual patterns of life and thought, he had not before his move to Ireland struggled to reconcile his dual commitments to adopted Church and beloved nation.[43] In particular, the religious basis for his jingoistic fervour remained stable. A letter to Coventry Patmore of 1886 shows him applying only a light varnish to what has been called the 'Anglican imperial meta-narrative', in which empire provides indigenous peoples with 'the best of all Christian worlds'.[44] 'It shd. have been Catholic truth', Hopkins says of the 'civilisation' needing to be spread by British expansion, 'That is the great end of Empires before God, to be Catholic and draw nations into their Catholicism'; yet the question of confessional allegiance is quickly subordinated to the need to spread Christianity of any stripe among the heathens: 'But our Empire is less and less Christian as it grows. There remains that part of civilisation which is outside Christianity or which is not essentially Christian.'[45]

Hopkins's encounter with Irish nationalism was more prone to reveal the strain in his combination of patriotic and religious feeling. He took the measure of nationalist agitation at first hand, going as far as to attend a 'monster meeting' in Phoenix Park in 1885 addressed by William O'Brien MP, after which he remarked in a letter to his mother that 'the grief of mind I go through over politics, over what I read and hear and see, in Ireland about Ireland and about England, is such that I can neither express it nor bear to speak of it.'[46] One means remaining to Hopkins to channel his distress over politics was to spend time in Ireland writing about England, and about England's soldiers. The untitled war-song beginning 'What shall I do for the land that bred me', and written to a melody of Hopkins's own creation, was conceived during an afternoon spent in Phoenix Park in September 1888. This was the site of the notorious murder of British officials two years before Hopkins's arrival in Dublin, a coincidence David Alderson names as 'somewhat ironic', but which Hopkins himself may have found otherwise (he had noted the day of the anniversary of the murders in a letter of earlier that year).[47] 'What shall I do for the land that bred me' is evidently a counterpart to Hopkins's disquiet at military cowardice seen at the far reaches of the Empire. It may also have been an attempt to secure himself against the strangeness of his position closer to home:

> What shall I do for the land that bred me,
> Her homes and fields that folded and fed me?
> Be under her banner and live for her honour:
> Under her banner I'll live for her honour.
>   *Chorus.* Under her banner we live for her honour.
>
> Not the pleasure, the pay, the plunder,
> But country and flag, the flag I am under –
> *There* is the shilling that finds me willing
> To follow a banner and fight for honour.
>   *Chorus.* We follow her banner, we fight for her honour.
>
> Call me England's fame's fond lover,
> Her fame to keep, her fame to recover.
> Spend me or end me what God shall send me,
> But under her banner I live for her honour.
>   *Chorus.* Under her banner we march for her honour.
>
> Where is the field I must play the man on?
> O welcome there their steel or cannon.
> Immortal beauty is death with duty,
> If under her banner I fall for her honour.
>   *Chorus.* Under her banner we fall for her honour.

Sending 'What shall I do for the land that bred me' to Robert Bridges, Hopkins noted how it was 'a task of great delicacy and hazard to write a patriotic song that shall breathe true feeling without spoon or brag'.[48] Sentimentality is the distinguishing mark of popular military song in the period, so this was to desire to remove spooniness where it was actually wanted – a desire shared by other would-be regularisers of martial song in the period, such as Nugent Taillefer in his *Rondeaus of the British Volunteers* (1871) and Charles Williams in his *Soldiers' Songs, for the March, the Camp, and the Barracks* (1898).[49] The ambition was to lay unfulfilled in Hopkins's case, for his song is suffused with exactly the type of feeling he wished to do without.

'What shall I do for the land that bred me' is in no sense a dense work. But if the clunking internal rhymes – '*There* is the shilling that finds me willing', and 'Immortal beauty is death with duty' – perhaps answer to the requirements of the form, 'Her homes and fields that folded and fed me' is a piece of alliteration which engages a favourite Hopkins conceit, playing on 'fold' as both enclosure of land and maternal embrace. The same conceit appears elsewhere in Hopkins's poetry: 'Wound with thee, in thee isled, | Fold home, fast fold thy child', ends the Marian poem 'The Blessed Virgin compared to the Air we Breathe', offering a prayer to be held and protected by the Virgin Mother as are sheep in a pen. 'Her homes and fields that folded and fed me' in 'What shall I do for the land that bred me' may be less conspicuously double in its reference than is the word's appearance in the Marian poem, but it still constitutes a departure from the heartiness Hopkins wanted for his marching song. Even here, it seems, Hopkins could not entirely restrain his ingenuity.

The inspiration for 'What shall I do for the land that bred me' arrived on a significant personal anniversary, coming twenty years to the day since Hopkins had, in the resonant phrase of a few months earlier, 'enlisted ... in the Society of Jesus'.[50] The letter to Bridges which describes the poem's writing makes reference to this anniversary.[51] In these circumstances, and with this poet, an association between soldiers of Christ and soldiers of England might be expected from the poem. This is especially the case given that Hopkins evidently cherished warfare as a figure for the action of spiritual life. There is a risk of overstating the importance of military imagery to the Jesuits at large,[52] but not to this Jesuit in particular. The same retreat notes in which Hopkins talks of having 'enlisted' in the Jesuits, after noting that 'I do not waver in my allegiance, I never have since my conversion to the Church', state that the question of his faithfulness is rather 'how I advance the side I serve on'.[53] A similar idea occurs in a sermon preached a decade earlier, in 1879. Discussing St Paul's appeal to the Ephesians to put on 'the armour of God' (Ephesians 6.11; see also more generally 6.10–17), Hopkins declared, 'The warfare the Apostle speaks of always goes on',

and his notes for the sermon mention 'Choirs of angels, regiments with
officers, ranks, disciplines, subordination'.[54] Earlier that year, he had also
encouraged his congregation to 'learn a precious lesson': that Christ 'is the
king to whom we are to be loyal and he is the general we are to obey', so
that 'The man that says to himself: Christ is my king, Christ is my hero, I
am at Christ's orders, I am to his command, that man is a child of light.'[55]

All this provides a likely religious context for 'What shall I do for the
land that bred me', but one that the poem itself does not really bear out.
In its sole mention of God – 'Spend me or end me what God shall send
me' – 'God' could to all intents and purposes just as well be fate. How
different in this respect is 'The Soldier', in which military service is held
up as a spiritual paradigm. There is a reminder in their divergence that
although Hopkins's strongest poems were religious, he was not uniquely a
religious poet.

Much closer in emphasis to 'The Soldier' is 'The Bugler's First
Communion' (1879), Hopkins's other soldier poem to make of military
service a religious theme. 'The Bugler's First Communion' was written
a few months into Hopkins's curacy at St Aloysius's Church, Oxford, a
mostly unhappy return to a city he continued to love ('I saw little of the
University', he later told a friend known from his undergraduate years,
'But I could not but feel how alien it was, how chilling, and deeply to
be distrusted. I could have wished, and yet I could not, that there had
been no one that had known me there').[56] The place Hopkins knew as
a student he described rapturously in a letter of that period as 'the head
and fount of Catholicism in England and the heart of our Church'.[57]
Oxford had no such thrillingly essential status in Roman Catholicism,
and Hopkins's work there upon his return as a priest proved wearying, in
part because the people he served were felt to be unreceptive: 'I believe
they criticised what went on in our church a great deal too freely, which
is d – d impertinence of the sheep towards the shepherd', Hopkins complained to Robert Bridges: 'if it had come markedly before me I shd. have
given them my mind'.[58]

One of Hopkins's duties in Oxford was to minister to the soldiers stationed at the recently built Cowley Barracks. Inspired by this experience,
'The Bugler's First Communion' takes a soldier for its hero:

> A bugler boy from barrack (it is over the hill
> There) – bóy búgler, born, he tells me, of Irish
>   Mother to an English sire (he
> Shares their best gifts surely, fall how things will),

This very very day came down to us after a boon he on
My late being there begged of mé, overflowing
    Boon in my bestowing,
Came, I say, this day to it – to a First Communion.

Hére he knelt then ín regimental red.
Forth Christ from cupboard fetched, how fain I of feet
    To his youngster take his treat!
Low-latched in leaf-light housel his too huge godhead.

There! and your sweetest sendings, ah divine,
By it, heavens, befall him! as a heart Christ's darling, dauntless;
    Tongue true, vaunt- and tauntless;
Breathing bloom of a chastity in mansex fine.

Frówning and forefending angel-warder
Squander the hell-rook ránks sálly to molest him;
    March, kind comrade, abreast him;
Dress his days to a dexterous and starlight order.

How it dóes my heart good, visiting at that bleak hill,
When limber liquid youth, that to all I teach
    Yields ténder as a púshed péach,
Hies headstrong to its wellbeing of a self-wise self-will!

Then though I should tréad túfts of consolation
Dáys áfter, só I in a sort deserve to
    And do serve God to serve to
Just such slips of soldiery Christ's royal ration.

Nothing élse is like it, no, not all so strains
Us – freshyouth fretted in a bloomfall all portending
    That sweet's sweeter ending;
Realm both Christ is heir to and thére réigns.

O now well work that sealing sacred ointment!
O for now charms, arms, what bans off bad
    And locks love ever in a lad!
Let mé though sée no more of him, and not disappointment

Those sweet hopes quell whose least me quickenings lift,
In scarlet or somewhere of some day seeing
    That brow and bead of being,
An our day's God's own Galahad. Though this child's drift

Séems bý a divíne doom channelled, nor do I cry
Disaster there; but may he not rankle and roam
    In backwheels, though bound home? –
That left to the Lord of the Eucharist, I here lie by;

Recorded only, I have put my lips on pleas
Would brandle adamantine heaven with ride and jar, did
    Prayer go disregarded:
Forward-like, but however, and like favourable heaven heard these.

W. H. Auden wondered of 'The Bugler's First Communion' 'how a poet of Hopkins's sensibility has such a dreadful lapse' (he thought it related 'to a conflict in Hopkins between homosexual feelings and a moral sense of guilt').[59] But an eccentric poem attracts idiosyncratic readers. The modernist poet David Jones, like Hopkins a convert to Roman Catholicism, titled the night march section of his First World War epic *In Parenthesis* (1937) 'The Starlight Order' in an allusion to lines from the fifth stanza of 'The Bugler's First Communion': 'March, kind comrade, abreast him, | Dress his days to a dexterous and starlight order.'[60] Jones would have appreciated the pairing of 'dexterous and starlight' in Hopkins's poem, a pairing of the material and the transcendent which in *In Parenthesis* is still more essential and complete (at the beginning of the night march in Jones's poem, as soldiers assemble, 'the liturgy of their going-up assumed a primitive creativeness, an apostolic actuality').[61] This pairing does not stand for all of Hopkins's poem, however, which has an inconsistent sense of how the world relates to divine reality. Hopkins's language for the ritual on which the poem is focussed swerves unsteadily between the breezy and the archaic, with the tabernacle become a 'cupboard', and Christ himself 'Low-latched in leaf-light housel'. The rhymes are notoriously strained, with that between 'boon he on' and 'Communion' given special notice by Bridges in the preface to the 1918 edition of his friend's poems: 'The rhyme to *communion* in "The Bugler" is hideous, and the suspicion that the poet thought it ingenious appalling.'[62]

For Eric Griffiths, a lack of balance is actually a condition of the poem's faith: 'The Catholic belief in the Real Presence makes the daily species of bread become the substance of divinity; the peculiarities of Hopkins's style here, in its fantastic veering from the supernatural to the mundane, answer to the peculiarities of that doctrine, as Hopkins faces us with it in the workings of language.'[63] It is a hard argument to make about the poem, as Peter McDonald observes: 'There is a difficulty, critically speaking, in crossing the line between perceptively explaining Hopkins's purpose and means in these lines, and holding that the purpose, once perceived, is seen to be aesthetically realized.'[64] Another difficulty is that the poem's language appears less mixed than Griffiths suggests. Thus the turn to prayer in stanza four is also largely a turn away from the mundane, even if the later appeal 'O for now charms, arms, what bans off bad | And locks love ever in a lad!' sustains a kind of homespun lustiness. Christ appears here not as the honest worker-Christ of 'The Soldier' but as a soldier-king, conferring a 'royal ration', meaning that divinity is seen to be exercised regally, an idea of God's action to which Hopkins was frequently drawn.[65] What is more, if the realm in which God reigns is occasionally known in Hopkins by its earthly tokens, whether at large in the 'sweet gift' of mortal beauty ('To what serves Mortal Beauty?', l. 13) or more specially present in the 'Storm flákes' of 'The Wreck of the Deutschland' (l. 168), here it is by contrast 'adamantine', elevatedly unyielding.

Grace and nature might easily fall out of step in 'The Bugler's First Communion', which is one reason why the bugler is imagined as both strapping and vulnerable, seen to maintain an admirable discipline within the world and yet also hoped to remain innocent of it. Hopkins sometimes held that such was Christ's own example in what he named the 'Great Sacrifice'. A letter to Bridges in 1883 gives a remarkable exegesis of part of St Paul's Letter to the Philippians in illustration of the nature of this sacrifice:

> Christ's life and character are such as appeal to all the world's admiration, but there is one insight St. Paul gives us of it which is very secret and seems to me more touching and constraining than everything else is: This mind he says, was in Christ Jesus – he means as man: being in the form of God – that is, finding, as in the first instant of his incarnation he did, his human nature informed by the godhead – he thought it nevertheless no snatch-ing-matter for him to be equal with God, but annihilated himself; taking the form of servant; that is, he could not but see what he was, God, but he would see it as if he did not see it and be it as if he were not and instead of snatching at once at what was all the time was his, or was himself, he emptied or exhausted himself, so far as that was possible, of godhead and behaved only as God's slave, as his creature, as man, which also he was, and then being in the guise of man humbled himself to death, the death of the cross. It is this holding of himself back, and not snatching at the truest and highest good, the good that was his right, nay his possession from a past eternity in his other nature, his own being and self, which seems to me the root of all his holiness and the imitation of this the root of all moral good in other men.[66]

Christ, in the Douay-Rheims translation of St Paul's Letter to the Philippians, 'being in the form of God, thought it not robbery to be equal with God: But *emptied himself*, taking the form of a servant, being made in the likeness of men, and in habit found as a man. He humbled himself, becoming obedient unto death, even to the death of the cross' (2.6–7). Perhaps thinking of the Greek text of the Letter to the Philippians, in

which the ambiguous word 'ἁρπαγμόυ' ('*harpagmon*') is sometimes taken
to mean 'a thing to be snatched at', Hopkins construes Christ as presum-
ing even less than this, not snatching at equality with God as opposed to
not thinking it false to do so. The *kenosis* of Hopkins's version is addition-
ally violent – Christ's self is annihilated and exhausted as well as emptied
in taking on human form – and, crucially, secret, for the particular wonder
of this unworldliness is that it is so much held in reserve and hidden from
view. This maintenance of perfect holiness under the look of the ordinary
provided Hopkins with a model for how the world should be encountered.
'The man who in the world is as dead to the world as if he were buried in
the cloister is already a saint', he once wrote, describing the Jesuit ideal, as
if the active life were a mortification to be lived as though it were a sham.[67]

At the same time, Hopkins could with equal ardour declare in a sermon
Christ 'all the world's hero, the desire of nature', 'a warrior and a con-
queror', 'statesman', 'thinker', 'orator and poet', 'the greatest genius that
ever lived':

> You must not say, Christ needed no such thing as genius; his wisdom
> came from heaven, for he was God. To say so is to speak like the heretic
> Apollinaris, who said that Christ had indeed a human body but no soul, he
> needed no mind and soul, for his godhead, the Word of God, that stood
> for mind and soul in him. No, but Christ was perfect man and must have
> mind as well as body and that mind was, no question, of the rarest excel-
> lence and beauty; it was genius. As Christ lived and breathed and moved in
> a true and not a phantom human body and in that laboured, suffered, was
> crucified, died, and was buried; as he merited by acts of his human will; so
> he reasoned and planned and invented by acts of his own human genius,
> genius made perfect by wisdom of its own, not the divine wisdom only.[68]

The clash between this passage and that previously quoted is not of doctrine but of emphasis. Each in its own way is perfectly orthodox, and each
witnesses to Hopkins's profound reflection on the being of Christ. Yet
each also conveys polarised impressions of human activity, regarded alternatively as bondage and as accomplishment. That Christ incarnate might
be at once self-abasing and self-realising is a possibility opened by his dual
nature, both divine and human, but Hopkins's respective senses of this
are in neither case even-handed. The 'world's admiration' is in one passage
found marginal, whereas in the other it is discovered to be essential. In the
first, Christ practices a secret detachment from the things of the world; in
the second, the worldliness of the world is a thing to be loved.

'The Bugler's First Communion' carries similarly disparate impressions
of worldly activity. The soldier on whom Hopkins based 'The Bugler's First

Communion' was soon to depart on a troopship to India, as the poet noted below his autograph fair copy of the poem: 'ordered to Mooltan [Multan] in the Punjab; was to sail Sept. 30'.[69] The British campaign in Afghanistan was then about to enter a new phase following the massacre of its mission at Kabul in the same month, September, a fact which, notoriously, seems for Hopkins to have lent his poem additional poignancy. 'I am half inclined to hope the Hero of it may be killed in Afghanistan', Hopkins commented upon sending it to Bridges in October, 'presumably', as his biographer Robert Bernard Martin says, 'so that [the bugler's] innocence might be preserved'.[70]

That Hopkins's phrasing is so tentative (his is not a half hope, but only half an inclination to hope) is presumably some recognition of the obstinacy of this thought.[71] The poem itself is more conflicted about the preservation of the bugler's innocence. It sees that the bugler's passage to maturity has begun and glimpses at its desired end. 'Breathing bloom of a chastity in mansex fine' is the image of a boy budding into manhood, and the qualities listed in previous lines – 'dauntless; | Tongue true, vaunt- and tauntless' – seem welcome signs of manhood's flowering, a flowering Hopkins's reversal of the usual positions of noun and adjective ('mansex fine'; 'Tongue true') make individually distinctive. Hopkins's denial of the wish to see the boy in maturity is, moreover, curiously torn:

> Let mé though sée no more of him, and not disappointment
>
> Those sweet hopes quell whose least me quickenings lift,
> In scarlet or somewhere of some day seeing
>   That brow and bead of being,
> An our day's God's own Galahad.

The boy has developed a 'brow', and the proximity of 'bead' to 'brow' encourages the thought of the sweat that might run from it, even if the main emphasis is metaphysical, having to do with 'being'. Of course, the hope to see the boy become man is in several ways curiously imponderable, and the haziness of 'somewhere of some day seeing' catches the possibility of the boy's drifting from the ideal Hopkins creates for him. Yet the fact remains that these notes of anxiety are prefaced with a positive conjecture of the boy's maturity.

The poem's spiritual feeling is highly conflicted. Its regard for the man powerful in human activity is coupled with a profound worry that maturity may prove tainting for the bugler. Hopkins sees that evil needs actively to be warded off. Bernadette Waterman Ward's suggestion, previously quoted, that war for Hopkins stands in imitation of the divine justice 'wrested from a world under occupation by a spirit of lovelessness', is clearly relevant here. The bugler faces a coming siege, with his budding virility intensely liable to corruption: as Peter Swaab observes, Hopkins's point here is to 'assail masculine strength in order to show its vulnerability'.[72] That the poem's hero is not seen as a dominating figure is evidently a consequence of his youth, but it also aligns with a sense that innocence of the world may be preferable to its successful command. Something of the same can be said of 'An our day's God's own Galahad'. This vision of the bugler's future calls upon the kind of Arthurianism to which Hopkins elsewhere objected, lending material achievement paradoxically unworldly form. 'An our day's God's own Galahad' may not imply the 'fantastic charade-playing trumpery Galahad' Hopkins so scorned in Tennyson (it is, after all, 'our day', not that of a lost medieval past), but the decision to cast the bugler as knight nevertheless lends admiration for a secular profession the aspect of legend, lifting it from the ordinary sphere.[73]

Switching between the admiration of earthly exploit and a preference for the safety of unworldly purity, 'The Bugler's First Communion' thus shares the variability of 'The Soldier' in its sense of how God relates to human experience. Both poems at once discover the transcendent in the ordinary and are also anxious about the potentially corrupting influence of material activity. Such ideas about God and faith as are conveyed by the poems are far from complete or consistent; indeed, incompleteness or inconsistency is often what is crucial, as a sign of what in them is spiritually and theologically difficult or conflicted. The difficulty and conflict are not unique to these poems only. Indeed, we might in their light look afresh at what Hopkins, and many others with him, have considered his best poem: 'The Windhover'.

'The Windhover'

In contrast to the poise and steadiness of most of Hopkins's other nature sonnets, 'The Windhover' begins breathlessly:

> The Windhover:
> to Christ our Lord
> I caught this mórning morning's mínion, king-
>   dom of daylight's dauphin, dapple-dáwn-drawn Falcon, in his
>   riding
>   Of the rólling level úndernéath him steady aír, and stríding
> Hígh there, how he rung upon the rein of a wimpling wing
> In his écstasy! then off, off forth on swing,

As a skate's heel sweeps smooth on a bow-bend: the hurl and
    gliding
Rebuffed the bíg wínd. My heart in hiding
Stírred for a bird, – the achieve of, the mástery of the thing!

Brute beauty and valour and act, oh, áir, pride, plúme, here
    Buckle! AND the fire that breaks from thee then, a billion
Tímes told lovelíer, more dangerous, O my chevalier!

    No wónder of it: shéer plód makes plóugh down síllion
Shine, and blue-bleak embers, ah my dear,
    Fall, gáll themsélves, and gásh góld-vermílion.

From the opening line and its mid-word enjambment, the measure of
the poem's excitement at recalling the sight of the bird is that it appears
hard to contain, spilling over the line-ending to create with 'mínion' and
'king- | dom' the first of the regal motifs around which 'The Windhover'
is organised. Hopkins worked and reworked the sonnet, cramming additional words into the octave, with the effect of strengthening this quality
of excitement. He also made distinctive use of patterns of sound to achieve
the same effect. Thinking of the first line especially, Geoffrey H. Hartman
observes that 'the poem's very continuity seems to derive from an on-the-
wing multiplication of the sound of one word into the next, like a series
of accelerating explosions'.[74] Such patterns of sound do not stand above or
outside lexical and grammatical sense in the manner apparently suggested
by the poet's earlier proposal that 'Poetry is speech framed for contemplation of the mind by the way of hearing or speech framed to be heard for
its own sake and interest even over and above its interest of meaning'.[75]
Rather, what we encounter in the opening to 'The Windhover' is an intense
coming together of the sounds of language with its lexical and grammatical referents, in a fusion that makes it difficult to detach or abstract the
poem's propositional statement from its particular arrangement of words.[76]
It would for this reason be very difficult to attach a prose argument to the
poem as Hopkins would later do to his sonnet 'Henry Purcell' (1879) –
even if the quantity of critical ink spilt in debates over the poem's meaning
might on occasion make us wish for this type of clarification.

    All this seems very far from 'The Bugler's First Communion', but
that 'The Windhover' also wavers between the embrace of the world
and its denial makes a common thread between these two poems. 'The
Windhover' shows the hidden life – the life which finds paradoxical freedom in self-limitation – to be vulnerable to the promptings of unexpected
feeling. One way to understand the phrase 'My heart in hiding' is to see
that it traces a version of the self-denying obscurity Hopkins believed to be

the Jesuit ideal. All of Hopkins's nature sonnets actively discover God in the splendour of natural forms; 'The Windhover' has their expansiveness encounter the hidden life of the cloistered. There is here the same tension between ascetical and material impulses also to be found in Hopkins's soldier poems. 'The Windhover' tussles across its *volta* with how admiration for nature's vigour can be reconciled with the seclusion demanded by religious vocation. 'Buckle!' holds the issue in tension, its grammatical ambiguity making it uncertain whether self-surrender – of Hopkins or of the kestrel, depending on one's interpretation of this astonishingly dense poem – is an inclination to be admitted or, alternatively, impelled. Here the fuss made about William Empson's analogy with a collapsing bicycle wheel in *Seven Types of Ambiguity* (1930) has obscured his more essential insight concerning 'Buckle!' – that it might be either indicative or imperative: "'they do buckle here," or "come, and buckle yourself here"'.[77] It is hard to know whether we are encountering a report or a request. However interpreted, 'Buckle!' carries the same sense of a volatile experience of selfhood, fluid and unstable, which animates Hopkins's earlier conception in philosophical notes of 'instress' as 'the flush and foredrawn'.[78] It also has affinities with the reference in his spiritual notes to the 'cleave of being' capable of being raised to Christ: 'points at which God recognizes particular possibilities within the potential of individual selfhood', as Daniel Brown explains, in which the stress of self 'can either fall apart or draw together more completely and elevate itself, according to how it responds to the pressure of divine grace'.[79] Empson's analogies for the word may be improbable – '*buckle* like a military belt, for the discipline of heroic action, and *buckle* like a bicycle wheel, "make useless, distorted, and incapable of its natural motion"' – but in this sense they capture accurately the extreme doubleness of its reference, for 'Buckle!' expresses the instability as well as the dynamism Hopkins understood to characterise the experience of individual being.[80]

It is significant that the pivotal moment of selfhood represented in the poem has a martial aspect, albeit one more elevated than Empson's reference to a 'military belt' perhaps implies. A consistent though surprising element in the poem is the way it identifies the kestrel's flight with knighthood and chivalry. This identification is achieved by the structuring of 'The Windhover' around figures of speech, such as occurs in the dense chain of alliteration and assonance that frames the poem's extraordinary first lines. These figures enable the pairing of likely words of description (such as 'morning' or 'daylight') with unlikely regal language (such as 'minion' or 'dauphin'). The technique is hardly unusual in Hopkins's poetry, forming one of the ways his poetry draws on the inspiration of Anglo-Saxon verse, in which Hopkins discovered a crucial precedent for the thick use of alliteration to bring out stress (he once enlisted *Piers Plowman* as an example of a poem where 'beat is measured by stress or strength, not number', observing of this and other examples that 'It almost seems as if the rhythm were disappearing and repetition of figure given only by the alliteration').[81] Yet there is an extravagance to the language of 'The Windhover' that is unfamiliar in his nature sonnets, within which grouping it appears in all senses the most high-flown of poems. Of the nature sonnets, 'Hurrahing in Harvest' has the closest affinity with 'The Windhover', but even here Hopkins's lavish figurations are foregrounded as if to suggest their specialness: finding Christ in nature, the sestet of 'Hurrahing in Harvest' opens by declaring 'And the azúrous hung hills are his wórld-wíelding shoulder | Majestic – as a stallion stalwart, very-violet-sweet! – ' (ll. 9–10). In these lines, the uncomplicated syntax attunes to the boldness of the initial claim, and the succeeding simile ('as a stallion stalwart') is highlighted to be surprising by the way it is interposed parenthetically. 'The Windhover', by contrast, allows no pause or preparation for the flamboyant use of the language of chivalry; we are not braced for any sudden elevation in its manner, because all of its manner is elevated, from the poem's remarkable opening to its equally remarkable close.

This matters when we consider the way in which the poem presents experience, whether that experience is considered finally to be religious or otherwise (an issue of much debate). 'The Windhover' is close to Hopkins's bugler poem in providing a form of admiration for the world's activity that, in being grandly archaic, manages to transcend ordinary reality. A poem about a moment of sudden openness to the material world, made from within the hidden life, is throughout imbued with a lofty ethic. The princely hero of this poem may or may not be a figure for Christ (Hopkins only added the dedication in 1884, having earlier decided that 'The Windhover' was 'the best thing I ever wrote'), but the self-abnegation described at the end of the poem is certainly in the pattern of Christ's sacrifice – and not the deftly practical Christ lauded in 'The Soldier', but rather the Christ who denies his true nature so that strength might be made vulnerable.[82] The pattern of stress Hopkins marked for 'Fall, gáll themsélves', as Clive Scott has recognised, 'drives enunciation into configurations which are unnatural to it'.[83] It would be more reasonable to speak of burnt-out embers unconsciously giving new colour when in motion, and an emphasis on 'Fall' might just about have given the latitude to interpret the line as though someone or something were poking at the remains of the fire. Hopkins's stress marks make the reality of his meaning impossible to evade, requiring more unusual sense to be made of the action described. We are led more clearly to see the insentient as sentient and the submission of self to be a disciplined action of individual will.

'The Windhover' is more consistent in tenor than Hopkins's soldier poems, with the renunciation embraced at the end of the poem appearing as a true counterpart of the exalted description of the kestrel's flight with which it begins. What 'The Windhover' does share with the soldier poems is a sense of the likely dichotomy between world and spirit upon which its idea of transcendence relies. More clearly than in other nature sonnets Hopkins wrote at around the same time, 'The Windhover' keeps in view the template of a spiritual withdrawal from the world seen in his early, Anglo-Catholic poetry, and also anticipates its later, partial resurfacing in poems including 'The Bugler's First Communion'.

The first reader of 'The Windhover', Robert Bridges, was out of sympathy with Hopkins's high ideal of sanctity. His long poem *The Testament of Beauty* (1929) rails against those who hold that pleasure, 'instead of being an in-itself absolute good | as nature would have had it' is rather 'the pollution of virtue'.[84] The poem recalls in particular a visit made to Hopkins at Roehampton, during which Hopkins objected to Bridges buying some peaches from the gardener:

> And so,
> when the young poet my companion in study
> and friend of my heart refused a peach at my hands,
> he being then a housecarl in Loyola's menie,
> 'twas that he fear'd the savour of it, and when he waived
> his scruple to my banter, 'twas to avoid offence.[85]

A 'housecarl' is a historical term for 'A retainer or member of the household troops', usually of a king or noble (*OED*). Such spiritual soldiery in Bridges's eyes involved an unnatural battle against normal enjoyments. In 'The Windhover', another historical term, 'chevalier', indicates not servitude but courtly dignity, and yet, strange to say, it performs a not dissimilar function, as a marker of exceptional as against ordinary experience. The brilliancy of the event recalled by this poem is in one way immediate – occurring 'this morning' – but it is also outstanding, seen within the world yet by the end of the poem also raised beyond the world. In this 'The Windhover' aligns with 'The Bugler's First Communion'. In both poems the world of natural exploit stands awkwardly to the world of grace. In 'The Windhover' especially, natural desire needs to be denied, even annihilated, in preference to its being fulfilled. It asks to be bruised like a 'púshed péach' that is not to be eaten.

CHAPTER 4

The Martyr

A letter Hopkins wrote to his mother in April 1875 ends by describing 'A heartrending persecution' then taking place in Poland, 'worse than anything that wd. have been thought possible in this century':

> The United Greeks, who are Catholics, are being forced to return to the Russian Church. Cossacks are sent into the village, the peasantry are driven by the knout to the Church, when they refuse they are scourged to blood, then put into the hospital till their wounds are healed sufficiently for them to be flogged again. Some have died under the lash. Women and children are flogged too. In one village the people being brought to the altar and refusing to communicate, their mouths were forced open with the sword and the Precious Blood poured down. Others are starved into submission by having Cossacks quartered on them. They fall into despair and one hears of women dashing their children's brains out when told to give them up.
> Believe me your loving son Gerard M. Hopkins S.J.[1]

The awkwardness of this ending is multiple. It is not only that the letter follows an account of stunning parental violence with a conventional declaration of filial affection, but also that the persecution of the Polish Uniates is itself a curious topic of correspondence for Hopkins and his mother given the confessional divide that existed between them. A much earlier letter drafted by Kate Hopkins to her son, written shortly after she heard of his decision to become a Roman Catholic, breaks off with a cry of anguish that resounds with the seriousness of this difference between them: 'O Gerard my darling boy are you indeed gone from me?'[2] Although in time Kate Hopkins came to accept her son's conversion, it seems that she did not lose her suspicion of his new faith: the inscription inside her copy of the book suggests that she was reading R. F. Littledale's *Plain Reasons against joining the Church of Rome* (1880) more than a decade after Gerard's reception as a Roman Catholic.[3] It is unlikely that she would have shared his ardour in respect of events in Poland.

The way in which Hopkins closes his letter may not be simply thoughtless, however. Rather, his lack of inhibition is likely to have proved authenticating. Something of Hopkins's intention can be known from the fact that the letter conflates a number of separate incidents reported in his source – an article in the Roman Catholic weekly *The Tablet* – and amplifies others: Hopkins's phrasing ('one hears of women') leans towards the identification of one woman's killing of her child as a representative act, whereas it had been singled out as an extraordinary and extreme response by *The Tablet*.[4] The embellishments the letter makes to *The Tablet*'s account suggest that Hopkins admired the woman's defiance as much as he was horrified by its result. According to his description, the woman's response is not isolated, as it had appeared in *The Tablet*'s report, but instead forms part of a powerful demonstration of fidelity to the faith, bringing to light the potency of Roman Catholic belief. Hopkins's own tactlessness towards his mother takes on a similar quality of intransigence in more trivial form.

The poet, as Geoffrey Grigson long ago observed, 'was interested in pain': 'He was interested in the gash, the bloody flow, the bloody hour of the martyrs', Grigson writes, 'Self-humiliation, and pain in others, did not obsess him, but they were always important to him.'[5] Evidence of this interest in pain is not far to seek in Hopkins's letters and journals. To the account given to his mother of the Polish Uniates can be added the report Hopkins offered in an 1888 letter to Bridges, of 'a young man well known to some of our community' in Dublin who had 'put his eyes out': 'He was a medical student and probably understood how to proceed, which was nevertheless barbarously done with a stick and some wire.' 'The eyes', Hopkins felt it necessary to add, 'were found among nettles in a field'.[6]

Grigson believed that a main source of Hopkins's interest in pain was sexual, a view also taken by several later interpreters.[7] This interest could also be ascetical, as when physical suffering was seen to be borne in the cause of faith, as it was in Hopkins's account of the Polish Uniates.[8] Hopkins's several poems on martyrs, in particular, have this ascetical motivation. These poems have tended to be understood by means of the most famous, 'The Wreck of the Deutschland'. Hopkins's earliest editor, Robert Bridges, famously described 'The Wreck' as standing at the opening to Hopkins's poetic maturity 'like a great dragon folded in the gate to forbid all entrance and confident in his strength from past success'.[9] The poem is now more usually taken to herald the arrival in Hopkins's poetry of a system of thought to which his writing is thereafter devoted. Its dominance in views of Hopkins's martyr poems is such that they are often cast squarely in its light and held to exemplify how his poetry constituted a project of intellectual distillation, in which the sacrifice made by the martyr is seen to align with the poet's notion of the 'theological economy of participatory salvation': the notion that sharing in the agony of Christ crucified 'martyrs

gain glory through their wounds; it is Christ's glory, but their whole existence is Christ's and no less their own for being his.'[10]

I wish to bring Hopkins's other poems on martyrdom out from under
the shadow of 'The Wreck' and reveal a different side to their religious
thought. All of Hopkins's poems on the subject have the perception that
martyrdom's most fundamental significance is that it occurs in the image
of Christ's own sacrifice. Impressing the image of Christ's sacrifice upon
the events that his poem describes, Hopkins in 'The Wreck' arrives at a
view of divine providence whose comprehensiveness is exceptional in his
poetry on martyrdom. The poems on the early Christian martyrs Dorothea
and Thecla also lay claim to general significance, holding paradigms of
the religious life, but, contrary to the way in which these poems are often
perceived, they do so differently than would texts of systemised theology.
Instead, communal significance is discovered in the particular local contexts in which these martyrs lived and died, and in the response of others
to their actions. Hopkins's later poem on the recusant martyr Margaret
Clitherow is closer to 'The Wreck' in the formalised nature of its theology,
yet it is able to couple elements of his metaphysical scheme with a profound concern with details of individual history. Rather than take 'The
Wreck' to be exemplary of Hopkins's writing on martyrdom generally,
then, we need rather to comprehend the reasons for its singularity.

Experiments in Hagiography: Hopkins's Early Martyr Poems

Hopkins's earliest surviving poem turns to a gruesome instance of religious suffering in its opening stanzas. 'The Escorial' (1860), which won
his school's poetry prize, briefly recounts the story of the martyrdom of
St Laurence, roasted to death on a gridiron, as part of its description of
the part-monastery, part-royal palace built by Philip II of Spain in the sixteenth century, and dedicated to the saint for the fact that he 'still prais'd his
Master's name | While his crack'd flesh lay hissing on the grate' (ll. 19–20).
At the time when he wrote 'The Escorial', Hopkins had not yet begun to
depart from the moderate High Anglicanism of his parents. It is unsurpris-
ing, then, that King Philip's admiration for the saint earns the poem's scorn.
In one of the young Hopkins's several jibes at Roman Catholic excesses,
that the plan of the Escorial is shaped to resemble a gridiron reveals the
king to have 'grown fantastic in his piety' (l. 23).

Hopkins's own piety would move in a Catholic direction in the years
subsequent to his writing of 'The Escorial', and he would as a consequence
grow less dismissive of the kind of devotion this early poem scorns, going

as far as to declare the 'array of saints and martyrs' celebrated in Roman Catholic devotion to be one of the causes of his decision to convert.[11] His poetry quickly begins to partake of this new enthusiasm. If we include the fragment 'A basket broad', four versions survive of a poem Hopkins wrote on the early Christian martyr St Dorothea; these cross the period of his conversion and the beginning of his Jesuit life, with the earliest version entered in his journal around December 1864, and the last a fair copy made for a fellow Jesuit at Stonyhurst, probably between 1870 and 1871. Hopkins's poem on St Dorothea has received much notice because two among its versions represent Hopkins's first experiment with sprung rhythm. Unlike in the case of sprung rhythm's fuller realisation in 'The Wreck', where only Bridges's transcriptions of the poem survive, the existence of multiple versions of the Dorothea poem enables something of the genesis of his new measure to be traced. As Meredith Martin has noted, these versions are also important for revealing 'an early struggle over how to represent stress graphically'.[12]

Less has been said about the idea of martyrdom the poem embraces. In his invention of sprung rhythm, Hopkins desired to couple 'naturalness of expression' with 'markedness of rhythm'.[13] His treatment of the Dorothea legend is similarly paradoxical in ambition: it attempts to join her youthful ease and poise to a determined pattern of sacrifice. Hopkins's poetic contemporaries shared his attraction to the saint's legend. As well as poems by Christina Rossetti ('"Rivals": A Shadow of Saint Dorothea', 1858), Swinburne ('St. Dorothy', which appeared in *Poems and Ballads* in 1866), and William Morris ('The Story of Dorothea', a tale written for *The Earthly Paradise* between 1861 and 1865, but finally not included), there exists a watercolour by Edward Burne-Jones, entitled *Theophilus and the Angel*, completed between 1863 and 1867.[14] Continuing a family habit of composing poems inspired by paintings, Hopkins intended his lines on Dorothea to accompany a picture; it is not known for certain whose picture, although one possibility is that it was to be Hopkins's own.[15]

According to tradition, Dorothea, a young virgin famed for her beauty and virtue, suffered under the persecution of Christians by the Roman Emperor Diocletian. Said to have been martyred in Cappadocia sometime in the years between AD 287 and 313, she was ridiculed by the lawyer Theophilus on the way to her execution, who asked her mockingly to send him fruits and flowers from the garden of paradise. An angel in the form of a young child subsequently visited Theophilus bearing his demand, an apparition which seemed to him in several ways miraculous, not least because it occurred in the midst of the Cappadocian winter. At this sight

Theophilus was immediately converted, making a declaration of faith that, in leading to his own torture and death, allowed him directly to follow Dorothea's example.

The later versions of Hopkins's poem render distinctive the grace of this apparition by virtue of what Hopkins named his 'peculiar beat', which makes the verse 'stressy', packing emphasis, and so renders insistent what in earlier versions of the poem was only sensuous.[16] Just as importantly, the apparition in later versions is no longer a child emissary, but Dorothea herself, a change which turns the miracle yet more miraculous. The poem also lengthens to include Theophilus's conversion and subsequent arrest, so that instead of ending with his amazement after the departure of an angelic emissary – 'We see | Nor fruit, nor flowers, nor Dorothy' (1864 version, l. 23–24) – it closes with a summons to martyrdom, before giving the final word to Theophilus's persecutors, agents of the governor Sapricius:

> Ah dip in blood the palmtree pen
> And wordy warrants are flawed through.
> More will wear this wand and then
> The warpèd world we shall undo.
> Proconsul! – Is Sapricius near? –
> I find another Christian here.
>
> (Stonyhurst fair copy, ll. 37–42)

The addition of these stanzas brings the story to its culmination, straightening out Hopkins's meaning. As a result, comments Elsie Elizabeth Phare, author of the earliest book-length study of the poet, 'the rather precious naïf grace of the earlier poem is gone: but the poem has, so to speak, been tidied up, the scene has been worked out to a logical instead of to an arbitrary conclusion; all its implications have been exposed.'[17] Theophilus's surprise at the miracle is now but a prelude to his decision to convert.

As Phare recognised, the result of Hopkins's revisions is to widen the poem's reach, framing the individual incident in which Dorothea appears to Theophilus within a larger pattern of suffering and witness so that her death can more clearly be assigned its reason and cause. Yet this remains a poem occupied with the individual history it describes rather than with the formal expression of a theological position. What appears crucial in all the various versions of the Dorothea poem is the saint's unworldly purity. This is also the case in Hopkins's poem on the near-martyr Thecla. The sole surviving autograph copy of 'St. Thecla' dates from around 1876 and appears to have been intended to serve as a presentation piece for display in a Jesuit house, where it would have appeared accompanied by its Latin translation, which also survives. The poem is likely to have been written much earlier, between 1864 and 1865, at a time when Hopkins's Catholic fervour was increasing under the influence of Liddon and Pusey at Oxford. It is thus possible the interest in the early martyrs manifest here and in the Dorothea poem is owed partly to Tractarian influence, given that 'concern for the "tradition" of the ancient and undivided Church is the foundation of Tractarian thought' (a concern which forms part of the interest of Victorian religion generally in what has been called the 'origin of Churches').[18]

This interest in ecclesiastical origins likewise inspired a series of Roman Catholic novels that took the early martyrs for their subject, including Nicholas Wiseman's *Fabiola* (1854) and Newman's *Callista* (1855). Such novels sought to intervene in debates over the historical foundations of Church tradition. The thrust of both 'Lines for a Picture of St. Dorothea' and 'St. Thecla' is by contrast hagiographical, relating incidents from the lives of saints in reverential manner so that their memory may be preserved as an inspiring example of faith in action. Thecla, like Dorothea, was a virgin of the early Church (indeed, 'the virgin *par excellence*' of the Church in late antiquity, hence Hopkins's observation, in ll. 3–4, that 'her name was known, | Time was, next whitest after Mary's own').[19] According to her legend, Thecla was converted to Christianity by the preaching of St Paul, after which she was twice miraculously delivered from martyrdom. Hopkins, in his poem, had not yet arrived at the moment of Thecla's conversion, and perhaps did not intend to relate the conclusion to her story,[20] but his extolling of the saint's grace and beauty at the same time as she is seen to be 'grave past girlhood earnest in her eyes' (l. 20) is already enough to draw the poem close to that on Dorothea. In her adherence to 'the lovely lot of continence' (l. 28), Thecla, as Dorothea, exhibits the virtue of otherworldliness.

'The Wreck of the Deutschland' and the Politics of Martyrdom

In contrast to Hopkins's early poems on Dorothea and Thecla, 'The Wreck of the Deutschland' honours martyrs who were contemporary rather than ancient. They were Franciscan nuns, forced to depart from Germany following Bismarck's repression of the Roman Catholic religious orders, and subsequently drowned in a shipwreck off the Kent coast. This is a fate which for Hopkins displays the integrity of their creed. His poem deals in specific martyrological conventions, just as do the poems on Thecla and Dorothea. Unlike these other poems, however, the brilliance of martyrdom in 'The Wreck' has a direct political relevance, for Hopkins sees the martyr's sacrifice in the context of the secular–Roman Catholic 'culture wars' of the latter half of the nineteenth century. Indeed, this political relevance is increased by the way 'The Wreck' places the individual history of the nuns at a distance in bringing their martyrdom close to type. A poem whose first part records the 'lightning and love' (l. 70) by which God has been known internally becomes greatly more detached from the individual life of belief in its second part, where the response its heroine makes in the moment of her death is known wholly by its affinity with Christ's own suffering at the crucifixion. The poem's consequent determination towards the exposition and proclamation of articles of Roman Catholic belief is exceptional in Hopkins's poems on martyrdom. Yet the turn to general truths of his faith is not at the expense of contemporary politics. My suggestion is that it indicates how 'The Wreck' is motivated as much by current events as by theological ideas.

Underpinning 'The Wreck' is the belief that steadfastness in the face of persecution affords a powerful demonstration of religious truth. One among the Franciscan sisters to drown in the tragedy, the tall nun, is as unyielding in her torment as the Polish Uniates admired in Hopkins's letter to his mother. The tall nun is heralded in the poem as 'A próphetess' who 'tówered in the túmult' (l. 136), her cries sounding God's mercy to her fellow passengers, so that even the 'Comfortless unconfessed of them' (l. 244) among them are

> No not uncomforted: lovely-felicitous Providence,
> Fínger of a ténder of, O of a féathery délicacy, the bréast of thé
>   Maiden could obey so, be a bell to, ring óf it, and
> Stártle the poor shéep back! is the shípwreck then a hárvest, does témpest carry
>   the gráin for thee?   (ll. 245–48)

Robert Lowell comments that 'Hopkins' rhythms even when he is not writing sprung-rhythm have the effect of a hyperthyroid injection.'[21] Even in sprung rhythm, however, Hopkins can be tender, as when the hastening tread of 'Fínger of a ténder of, O of a' slows into the assonantal long vowels of 'féathery délicacy'. The softening is seen in this line's rhythm, which Hopkins cited as an example of how sprung rhythm could accommodate variation in the strength of stress: 'the first two beats are very strong and the more the voice dwells on them the more it fetches out the strength of the syllables they rest upon, the next two beats are very light and escaping, and the last one as well.'[22] Other elements in the stanza are more coercing: Hopkins does not allow the nun's shout simply to reverberate but with the jolt given by 'ring óf it' demands an explicit recognition. '[R]ing óf it' goes against intonational instinct, so that, while the rhythm sustains a broadly falling course, it loses enough fluency for the enjambment to carry a charge of surprise. With 'Stártle the poor shéep back!' any impression that we might be hearing a peal of 'féathery délicacy' is overturned by the visiting of a desperate alarm. Putting scansion at odds with the expected spoken weight of the words so that the voice halts slightly over 'ring óf it' lends the nun's 'calling' of her 'master' (ll. 145–46) its compelling abruptness in the following line. Hers is an evangelism of shock and awe.

Conditions aboard the *Deutschland* as it lay stranded on a sandbank were awful. As the report in *The Times* from which Hopkins drew much of his information stated, the major concern was that 'with the rising tide the ship would be waterlogged', and for 'the intense cold'. For most of those who lost their lives in the tragedy, the actual moment of death was brutally quick: 'Women and children and men were one by one swept away from their shelters on deck.'[23] 'The Wreck' follows such reports in describing how 'lives at last were washing away' (l. 119), and in observing the bitter cold, yet it also intensifies the physical punishment endured by the *Deutschland*'s passengers. The anguish described in the poem sounds as if it might have been inflicted by a sentient persecutor rather than an inanimate sea-storm. The *Deutschland* is battling with natural elements but, having faced the 'béat of endrágonèd séas' (l. 216), that its passengers are 'Crushed' and 'rolled' (l. 131) allows the nuns to share the bodily 'Mark' familiar to the martyr. Hope itself is 'Trénched with téars, cárved with cáres' (l. 115).

The nuns from the convent at Salzkotten faced an indirect martyrdom that took place not at the physical hands of an aggressor, but by shipwreck, following their exile from Germany. Something of this fact may lie behind Hopkins's emphasis on the violence of their deaths, for by such means the nature of their martyrdom is made to seem less unusual. In the passage discussed earlier, 'shípwrack' (l. 248), which departs from the more usual form used elsewhere in 'The Wreck' and is a spelling obsolete by the close of the seventeenth century (*OED*), not only suggests the 'wrack' of marine vegetation but also places an emphasis on 'rack', perhaps of the same variety as the 'rack in Tower' which a sixteenth-century elegy on the Jesuit martyr Edmund Campion, reprinted in 1872 in the Jesuit journal to which Hopkins would later submit his own poem, had seen transformed into 'joys and heavenly bliss'.[24]

To find the note of earlier religious conflict echoed in Hopkins's poem would not be a surprise, for he was steeped in knowledge of the lives and deaths of the English Roman Catholic martyrs of the Reformation. The English religious persecutions of the sixteenth century were a 'favourite Victorian subject'.[25] It was a subject in which Hopkins had particular cause to be interested. Histories of martyrdom provided refectory reading in the Jesuit houses in which Hopkins lived during his training. Research into the Elizabethan recusancy also formed the main part of the intellectual labours of the British Jesuits during Hopkins's lifetime, helping bring about the beatification of fifty-four martyrs of the Reformation in 1886.[26]

Alison Shell finds that the recusant literature of exile and exclusion 'stimulated a mental impregnability' among Roman Catholics, helping instil in them a 'martyrological ideal'.[27] This stress on persecution and victimhood is only part of the story of traditional religion in the Reformation and afterwards and might be challenged in several ways, but it was certainly the inheritance recognised by Victorian Jesuits such as Hopkins's mentor Peter Gallwey. It was Gallwey's belief that

> It is to the courage and fidelity and the blood of the Martyrs, that we ourselves owe it that we too are not sitting in the darkness and the shadow of death. They are the brave soldiers who fought and conquered for us, and by dying saved the inheritance of the true faith for us; and now, if they could make their voices heard, they would speak in words of fire to us, to waken us and rouse us to zeal for all those who are perishing around us.[28]

Hopkins regularly encountered the kind of missionary zeal which saw Roman Catholic endurance of religious persecution as reparation for the nation's guilt and as presaging the return of England to true religion. This was the same impulse that led Newman, in his celebrated 'Second Spring' sermon of 1852, to wonder if the 'suffering of the Martyrs' in England were 'yet exhausted': 'Something, for what we know, remains to be undergone, to complete the necessary sacrifice.'[29]

Sixteenth-century accounts of recusant martyrdoms 'deployed familiar and traditional motifs of hagiography to identify their martyrs, but rather than attributing any personal power to the martyr himself, they portrayed the martyr as having been specially selected as a channel through which God had access to his creation'.[30] Part of the reluctance to lay too much emphasis on personal merit in recusant writings of this period arose from martyrdom itself being a contested category that provided inspiration at once devotional and political: 'The closer the similarity between the details of the death of Christ and the details of the death of the martyr, the more difficult it was to dismiss the martyr as a criminal or a heretic.'[31]

'The Wreck', too, is written with political as well as devotional intent. The nuns are observed by the dedication to be 'exiles by the Falck Laws', and there are hints of political symbolism throughout the poem, of which the exclamation 'O Deutschland, double a desperate name!' (l. 155), signalling that the dire situation of the ship is shared by its nation, is the clearest example. Another clue to the poem's political intent exists in the way in which Hopkins attributes blame for the shipwreck. Exiled from the land of her birth, the tall nun had been forced to embark upon the fateful voyage aboard the *Deutschland* by German anti-Catholic decrees. The poem's logic, however, requires that more than one nation is identified as a guilty party in her death. It is hoped that she will be a conduit for the redemption of Hopkins's own nation by virtue of having perished in English waters; for this to occur, her suffering must be seen to have English as well as German cause. The symmetry of 'Rhíne refúsed them, Thámes would rúin them' (l. 163) thus joins synecdoche and literal meaning in a false equation necessary to Hopkins's purpose, culminating in the poem's final stanza, already discussed in the context of prayer in Chapter 2, in which the sacrifice of the martyr is hoped to be a means of disturbing English religious lassitude and to bear fresh hope to all Britain:

> Dáme, at óur dóor
> Drówned, and among óur shóals,
> Remémber us in the róads, the heaven-háven of the
>   rewárd:
> Our kíng back, Oh, upon Énglish sóuls!
> Let him éaster in us, be a dáyspring to the dímness of us,
>   be a crímson-cresseted east,
> More bríghtening her, ráre-dear Brítain, as his réign rólls,
> Príde, rose, prínce, hero of us, hígh-príest,
> Oür héart's charity's héarth's fíre, oür thóughts' chivalry's
>   thróng's Lórd.

(ll. 273–80)

Strenuous emphasis in this stanza works to achieve communal feeling as the run of collective pronouns ('óur dóor', 'oúr shóals', 'Our kíng', 'the dímness of us', 'hero of us') culminates in a line labouring under the pressure of an ardent desire to see 'ráre-dear Brítain' return to the Roman Catholic fold: 'Oür héart's charity's héarth's fíre, oür thóughts' chivalry's thróng's Lórd.' The stanza shades from prayer into proclamation. At its close, the astonishing sequence of possessives savours the triumphant proving of a religious vision, anticipating how the sacrifice of the nuns might act as a vein for the awakening of the 'unconfessed', in the sense indicated by the *Edinburgh Review* when it commented of Bismarck's *Kulturkampf* that 'the church that has the most martyrs, real or imaginary, is as sure to have the strongest hold on the passions, if not on the beliefs, of a nation'.[32] The only difference is that the martyrs of Hopkins's poem are adopted rather than native.

The double purpose of 'The Wreck', political as well as devotional, may be why a poem whose first part is given over to the turbulence of individual spiritual history turns notably impersonal when faced with the deaths of those in whose honour and memory it is written. The tall nun is known initially by figure and category: she is 'a líoness' (l. 135), 'a próphetess', in whose call to Christ 'a vírginal tóngue tóld' (l. 136). Aside from the fact of her height, the other main distinction of the tall nun from her companions recognised by the poem is that she is said to have been their superior: 'She was first of a five and came | Of a coifèd sisterhood' (ll. 153–54). The convent records actually show that she did not hold this status,[33] but that Hopkins, following *The Times*'s report, got his facts wrong in this respect matters little to the poem's scheme, in which the collective of 'five' has a far larger importance than any individual characteristic or personal history.

Michael Wheeler comments:

> To come upon the names of the five nuns in *The Times* ... – 'viz. Barbara Hultenschmitt, Henrica Fassbaender, Norbeta Reinkober, Aurea Badzinra, and Brigitta Damhorst' – is something of a revelation, so firmly has the poem established in one's mind the sense of a group who are unnamed, and whose identity lies somewhere between [Hopkins's] categories of 'self' and 'human nature', and between individuation and common humanity.[34]

Stanza 22 surrounds their deaths with elaborate symbolism, developed from the significance of the number five as recalling the five wounds suffered by Christ at the crucifixion, 'the finding and sake | And cipher of suffering Christ' (ll. 169–70). Five is described in this stanza as 'Stigma, signal, cinquefoil token | For léttering of the lámb's fléece, rúddying of the róse-fláke' (l. 176), holding a significance that becomes ever more extended: 'Stigma, signal, cinquefoil token' are precise coordinates in a martyrological topography ('cinquefoil' is architectural, as in the five divisions of a pointed arch), yet what they finally correspond to is not strictly mappable; what begins as clear inscription (the 'léttering of the lámb's fléece') ends up as a cast of colour ('rúddying of the róse-fláke'). The associations become larger and more complete. Rose petals are traditionally identified with the wounds of Christ, and with the blood of martyrs, but this 'róse-fláke' is a snowflake, turned from white, the colour of roses associated with Virgin Mary, to become an amalgam of different symbols.

Here and elsewhere, 'The Wreck' has extraordinary scope. Its ambition is very different from Hopkins's other poems on martyrs. Even if the martyrdoms (or near-martyrdoms) recalled in Hopkins's Dorothea poem and 'St. Thecla' occur according to a template, being made in the image of Christ's sacrifice, both these early poems are able to make much of the personal integrity of their subjects: 'Withal her mien is modest, ways are wise, | And grave past girlhood earnest in her eyes', Hopkins writes in 'St. Thecla' (ll. 19–20), preparing us for her remaining so; in the later versions of the Dorothea poem, it is the saint herself who announces her brilliant apparition, exclaiming 'I´ am so´ light and fair´´' (Stonyhurst fair copy, l. 2). The personal details included in these other poems may be martyrological commonplaces, but they are commonplaces that Hopkins in 'The Wreck' avoids, in a detachment from individual history that contrasts markedly with the response of others who had cause to mourn the drowning of the nuns. In his funeral oration for the nuns, Cardinal Henry Manning, having first acknowledged his ignorance of their history ('What can we say, what do we know, of their past?'), nevertheless attempted to imagine the life in Germany that they left behind: 'They had a home peaceful and happy, fruitful in good works, in that great Fatherland in which the Catholic faith strikes root so deeply that no storms can shake it. They were labouring in peace; they were ministering consolation to the sick and the dying; they were training little children in holy fear and love of God and of His blessed mother.'[35]

Hopkins engages scant detail of this kind in 'The Wreck'. Wheeler explains this lack of specificity in terms of the theological ambition of 'Part the second', commenting that 'although the second part embodies a considerable amount of material gleaned from newspaper reports, the Wreck is essentially a religious poem into which documentary data are interpolated'.[36] The massive compass of the poem's final few stanzas – which are discussed further in the next chapter – certainly lend themselves to this conclusion. However, it is also possible that the sacrifice of the nuns exists apart from their individual history so that the poem can more freely engage in contemporary controversy. That the sisters had 'devoted their lives of poverty and contentment to the service of the sick and the fostering of little children' (as Cardinal Manning observed in his funeral oration) is immaterial to Hopkins's poem, I suggest, because saying so introduces a means of comprehending their response that 'The Wreck' seeks to escape.[37]

The tall nun is at one point described as 'The Símon-Péter of a sóul! to the blást | Tárpĕïan-fást, but a blówn béacon of líght' (l. 231). It is a description that ties her recognition of Christ to that of the apostle Peter, but which also hints at her fidelity to his successor as Bishop of Rome, since 'Tárpéïan-fást' refers to the rock on which stands Rome's Capitol, thus 'The nun is like a rock … sharing the immobility of the rock which is the papacy.'[38] It would not be the only moment in Hopkins's poetry to be inspired by Christ's declaration to Simon Peter that 'thou art Peter; and upon this rock I will build my church, and the gates of hell shall not prevail against it' (Matthew 16.18; Douay-Rheims). In 'Andromeda', from 1879, the princess of Greek myth, who appears in Hopkins's poem as an allegorical representation of the Roman Catholic Church, is chained to a 'rock rude' (l. 1), from whence 'Time past she has been attempted and pursued | By many blows and banes' (ll. 5–6), though the poem makes clear that it is a fate from which Perseus – who represents Christ – will in time rescue her. Hopkins in 'The Wreck' prefers symbolism to allegory, but it is not hard to see how, in a poem which ends desiring the reconversion of England to Roman Catholicism, Christ's delivery of a nun who holds fast to the rock of Peter might be taken to foreshadow his delivery of a suffering Church, in like manner to Perseus's anticipated rescue of Andromeda.

Other aspects of 'The Wreck' equally suggest that Hopkins's effort to frame the nun's sacrifice without reference to her individual history has a political as well as a theological motivation. After the lament 'O Deutschland, double a desperate name!' (l. 155) comes a second exclamation, 'O wórld wíde of its góod!' (l. 156), a succession which relies for its logic on the fact that the nuns were far from alone at the time in suffering the anti–Roman Catholic feeling concentrated by the new European democratic nation-states. Pius IX was at this time the self-proclaimed 'prisoner of the Vatican' following the loss of the Papal States, busily expanding his spiritual domain as his temporal powers dwindled; his obdurate resistance to the forces of change sweeping Europe made him both the inspiration and emblem of the persecuted Church. Hopkins took appreciative note of an article in the *Academy* of this period which proposed 'that the policy of Pius IX has been to meet aggression by defiance, almost by provocation; things have been going against him, but he has chosen to play a bold game instead of a cautious one; he has played it with great spirit'.[39]

The advantages of maintaining a bold attitude in the face of persecution are everywhere to be seen in 'The Wreck'. In a poem which draws great significance from dates and numbers, there is a special importance in the fact that the shipwreck it describes occurred on the eve of the Feast of the Immaculate Conception, the 'Féast of the óne wóman withóut stáin' (l. 237). The doctrine that gave rise to this feast had only recently been defined, in circumstances of some controversy; Hopkins in one of his sermons reminds his congregation that at the time of its definition 'there were some who denied it and a small number were left even in 1854 still disputing against it. But when the Pope [Pius IX] spoke they obediently bowed their heads, gave in their submission, and made an act of belief like other Catholics.'⁴⁰ In 'The Wreck', the purity of Mary's conception is seen to parallel the Virgin Birth of Christ ('For so conceivèd, so to conceive thee is done'), which in turn provides the pattern for the tall nun's actions: 'But here was heart-throe, birth of a brain, | Wórd, that héard and képt thee and úttered thee óutríght' (ll. 238–40). According to an editor's gloss, these are lines which propose that 'By thinking of Christ, recognizing his presence, and calling his name out so that others could hear it, the nun has made Christ's presence felt again in the world, "brought it to birth" as Mary did the Incarnated Christ.'⁴¹

It is an immense and extraordinary claim to make of events which Hopkins himself did not witness, and for which the majority of his information came from newspaper reports. The claim has a political edge as well as a devotional significance. A few months before he began to compose 'The Wreck', a report in *The Times*, having observed that the pope had called one of the deposed German bishops 'a martyr of the Church', noted that 'the German Liberal Press resounds with sarcastic articles upon the modern martyr sitting down at the *table d'hôte* of a fashionable resort and discussing the sympathetic brief over a fragrant bottle of hock'.⁴² The enormous scope of the meaning drawn from an unconventional martyrdom in 'The Wreck' comes against what Hopkins clearly knew to be a background of conflicting testimonies about the suffering of German Catholics (his letters and journals of this period are preoccupied with anti-Catholic murmurings in the British and foreign press).⁴³

Offering his own testimony about one instance of German Catholic suffering, Hopkins in 'The Wreck' pores over the meaning of the tall nun's call to Christ while saying little of her unique circumstances and background. Hopkins takes five stanzas to sift the significance of the call, 'O Chríst, Chríst, come quíckly' (l. 191), conjecturing for it a number of possible motives. Was it a desire for death that led her to call on Christ? Or was it rather a wish to suffer in the manner of Christ and achieve the glory of heaven, 'The tréasure never éyesight gót, nor was éver guessed whát for the héaring' (l. 208)? Stanza 27 determines that neither of these explanations will finally serve:

Nó, but it was nót thése.
The jáding and the jár of the cárt,
Time's tásking, it is fáthers that ásking for éase
Of the sódden-with-its-sórrowing héart,
Not danger, electrical-horror; then, further, it finds
The appéaling of the Pássion is ténderer in práyer apárt:
Other, I gather, in measure her mind's
Búrden, in wínd's búrly and béat of endrágonèd séas.

(ll. 209–16)

The subdued conclusion offered here is partly a piece of good staging, rendering more dramatic the appearance of the stanza which comes after. This is the much-discussed *Ipse* stanza, which departs radically from the discursive mode employed just previously, as Hopkins is startled into convulsive excitement at the nun's vision of Christ: 'But how shall I … Make me room there; | Reach me a … Fancy, come faster – | Strike you the sight of it? look at it loom there, | Thing that she … There then! the Master, | *Ípse*, the ónly one, Chríst, Kíng, Héad' (ll. 217–21).

That stanza 27 provides a moment of calm before the succeeding rapture makes it easy to overlook (it is attended by little of the energetic critical debate over the nature of the nun's vision of Christ described in the *Ipse* stanza). But the stanza is important in the sense that it betokens a similar consideration for the truth of the martyr's motivation to that seen in recusant narratives. The desire for death, Hopkins writes, is the preserve of the world-weary, 'the sódden-with-its-sórrowing héart', and the wish to suffer as did Christ is more likely to occur 'in práyer apárt'. By contrast, the tall nun's response is deliberate, but not primed; it appears in the two succeeding stanzas as a pure demonstration of trust in Christ: the tall nun 'Réad the unshápeable shóck níght | And knew the who and the why; | Wording it how but by him that present and past, | Heaven and earth are word of, worded by?' (ll. 227–30).

A few years before he commenced writing 'The Wreck', Hopkins heard read in the Jesuit novitiate a report of the 'Corean martyrs' persecuted in Japan in the 1860s, who 'went to sacrifice their lives in the service of souls': 'They knew what they were doing, and they did it gladly.'[44] More surprised by her fate, the tall nun in 'The Wreck' is still able to 'read' its situation right. The response she makes to the disaster is markedly of its moment, neither closely meditated nor the product of long suffering. This interpretation of events leaves Hopkins free of the complications of personal history in his pursuit of symbolic meaning, constituting another way in which he is 'engaged on a theodicy' rather than a chronicle of events.[45] It equally partakes of Hopkins's determination to secure the political implications of this martyrdom. In recusant narratives it was crucial that martyrs accepted but did not seek martyrdom;[46] 'The Wreck' tries to show something similar about the German nuns, with the effort made across five stanzas to weigh the meaning of the tall nun's cry a way of establishing her right motivation.

In their fusion of immediate and enduring spiritual concerns, these stanzas are instructive for how we read 'The Wreck' generally. If the major effort of Hopkins criticism over the past half-century has been historical in emphasis, countering the trend of early Hopkins criticism by situating the poet more fully in his Victorian contexts, this has often involved attending to religious belief as essentially a cultural matter, resulting in readings of 'The Wreck' that emphasise its controversial and divisive aspects. From this perspective, the *Deutschland* appears 'the symbol of a Protestant nation ... both literal ship and ship of state'; as a consequence, 'The fate of the German ship ... is clearly intended to serve as a warning to anti-Catholic nations'.[47] The extraordinary breadth of Hopkins's spiritual reference makes it tempting to think that large parts of the poem are actually less involved with current historical events. In reality, however, it is impossible to prise apart the religious significance of what Hopkins writes from its political charge, and the politics of Hopkins's poem is as important as its theology in placing 'The Wreck' at a distance from the individual history of its martyrs.

Experiential and Systematic: 'Margaret Clitheroe'

Suffering for one's faith appeared to Hopkins a powerful means of religious witness. Of the Jesuits expelled from Spain after the 1868 revolution there, he wrote: 'To be persecuted in a tolerant age is a high distinction'.[48] It was a distinction Hopkins would not know personally. Born fifteen years after Roman Catholic emancipation, Hopkins lived his Jesuit life in the shadow of recusancy, in which refusal to conform to the Church of England, he believed, had potently attested to one's commitment to Roman Catholic belief. Mary Douglas suggests that 'the greatest source of strength for entrenching a particular cultural bias is the mutual hostility between cultures'.[49] The inspiring precedents found in the recusancy made a number of Victorian Roman Catholics feel the burden of security. Coventry Patmore, for instance, 'maintained that Catholic emancipation had been a mistake; meaning, no doubt, that the Roman Catholic Church in England had been more select and better for having to pay a temporal penalty for its spiritual privileges'.[50]

Patmore was not alone in this feeling. To judge from the succession of controversial pamphlets he produced during the late 1860s and 1870s, it seems the Jesuit Peter Gallwey 'was not altogether unhappy at the prospect of a mild dose of English persecution'.[51] Hopkins's actual and likely encounters with religious prejudice have long occupied his critics, yet to find him fending off entreaties to publication by means of a comparison with the 'counterpoise' of Robert Southwell's career in poetry, the fact that Southwell 'wrote amidst a terrible persecution and died a martyr, with circumstances of horrible barbarity', is to realise that he too was conscious of a disparity.[52] Gladstone, in his best-selling pamphlet on the Vatican decrees, published in 1874, had denounced the recent declaration of papal infallibility as fostering Roman Catholic disloyalty to the nation-state, offering this as a justification for Bismarck's anti-Catholic legislation, and warning that 'it is not Prussia alone that is touched; elsewhere, too, the bone lies ready'.[53] Hopkins's letters of the time indicate that he was absorbed by the short burst of controversy Gladstone succeeded in creating, but he surely also knew that it had never yet been safer to be a Jesuit in England. Manning's estimation that while the German Catholic Church had 'witnessed bishops and their flocks driven to choose between beggary and their duty to their faith … here in England we happily enjoyed all civil and religious liberty', makes this point strikingly.[54]

Unable to share in the 'counterpoise' of Robert Southwell's career, Hopkins was repeatedly drawn to write of the fate which had ended Southwell's life. The deep attraction he felt to the example of the recusant martyrs had issue in the untitled and unfinished poem known as 'Margaret Clitheroe', probably written soon after 'The Wreck', in around late 1876 to early 1877.[55] This poem, on a York recusant crushed to death in 1586 for her refusal to plead when facing a charge of treason, is heavily indebted to the historical work on the recusancy undertaken by Hopkins's Jesuit contemporaries. He seems to have drawn largely on the account given by Clitherow's confessor John Mush, and included in the third volume of John Morris's *Troubles of Our Catholic Forefathers* (1877); Morris was a fellow Jesuit, who worked as professor of ecclesiastical history and canon law throughout Hopkins's period of study at St Beuno's.[56] That Hopkins's poem is likely to have been written in advance of Morris's publication of Mush's account suggests the extent of his familiarity with Victorian Jesuit scholarship on the recusant martyrs.

'Margaret Clitheroe' has much in common with 'The Wreck'. In the earlier poem, the tall nun appears as a pure channel for Christ, her resoluteness displaying his constancy: 'Let him ride, her pride, in his triumph, despatch and have done with his doom there' (l. 224). The same patterning is given to martyrdom in 'Margaret Clitheroe': 'Christ lived in Margaret Clitheroe' (l. 35), Hopkins asserts, with her fixed resolve in the face of extreme suffering said to reflect 'The Christ-ed beauty of her mind' (l. 15). Hopkins's account of the recusant martyr's suffering is also traced with the personal metaphysic that so forcefully appears in 'The Wreck'. Margaret is said to have 'caught the crying of those Three, | The Immortals of the eternal ring, | The Utterer, Utterèd, Uttering' (ll. 24–25): she perceives that the divine spoken word is an actualisation of divine being, in the sense that (as Hopkins would later write) 'God's utterance of himself in himself is God the Word'.[57] According to Daniel Brown, this conception of the act of utterance means that the poem 'presents what are effectively fragments of a manifesto for his mature practice of poetry', in which 'the act and materiality of speech make it analogous to the Word made flesh'.[58]

These distinctive marks of Hopkins's theories of self and being distinguish 'Margaret Clitheroe' as a mature work from the early verses on Dorothea and Thecla. Unlike 'The Wreck', however, it is not entirely a poem of 'discourse' (Hopkins's word to describe the main thrust of 'The Wreck').[59] In 'Part the second' of 'The Wreck', local and particular detail is subordinated to a general paradigm in the interests of what has been called 'narrative stringency', in which the effort is 'to situate phenomena in an order of meaning perpendicular to that of secular continuity'.[60] In 'Margaret Clitheroe', by contrast, the general paradigm is discovered within the unique contours of individual history. Bringing this poem out from under the shadow of its much more famous counterpart reveals new shades to his poetry's thought. It is a crucial poem in Hopkins's oeuvre for its combination of experiential and systematic perspectives.

The combination is not obvious from the way in which 'Margaret Clitheroe' opens, in a manner at once forbidding and foreboding:

> God's counsel cólumnar-severe
> But chaptered in the chief of bliss
> Had always doomed her down to this –
> *Pressed to death*. He plants the year;
> The weighty weeks without hands grow,
> Heaved drum on drum; but hands alsó
> Must deal with Margaret Clitheroe.   (ll. 1–7)

This is a stern view of events, given austere delivery ('cólumnar-severe' is itself a severe variety of compound). As at the opening to 'Part the second' of 'The Wreck', where the account of the shipwreck is ushered in by Death,

beating a drum, this first stanza of 'Margaret Clitheroe' offers a moral-
isation of the poem's action in advance of its commencement. Shaping
the moral, Hopkins strains a metaphor to partner unlike things, requiring
'weeks' to 'grow' so as to align divine sanction with murderous human
agency. Here and over the succeeding stanza – into which enters the question of Margaret's own agency in what occurs – there is an intricate division of responsibility made between the poem's main actors. Margaret is
the 'victim' (l. 8) of persecution and destined to die by God, but for her
suffering to have purpose requires that she foresee its course; her prepara-
tion for death is thus said to recall the way 'water soon to be sucked in |
Will crisp itself or settle and spin' (ll. 9–10), an analogy from laws of
motion that has her alert to the meaning of her fate but at the same time
not inciting of it.[61]

This very precise image is followed by a more casual approximation: 'one
sees that here and there | She mends the way she means to go' (ll. 11–12).
It is a revealing shift in the poem's manner of description. The balance of
compulsion and freedom in the martyr's situation continues to matter to
the story as Hopkins tells it, and similar touches of theological sophis-
tication to that seen early on continue to appear, but in much of what
follows 'Margaret Clitheroe' is a poem less comprehensive in scope than
might be expected from the look of its opening stanzas. This is not only a
consequence of the fact that 'Margaret Clitheroe' is unfinished and exists
only in fragments; nor is it just that, in places, as Eric Griffiths observes,
'the language of the poem takes on and suffers under the savage coarseness
it recounts'.[62] There is also, I want to suggest, an immediacy to parts of
the narration that reveals Hopkins's perspective to be experiential as well
as synoptic.

Such immediacy is especially prominent in the account of Margaret's
death given in the poem's final three stanzas:

> Great Thecla, the plumed passionflower,
> Next Mary mother of maid and nun,
>
> . . . .
>
> And every saint of bloody hour
> And breath immortal thronged that show;
> Heaven turned its starlight eyes below
> To the murder of Margaret Clitheroe.
>
> She held her hands to, like in prayer;
> They had them out and laid them wide
> (Just like Jesus crucified);
> They brought their hundredweights to bear.

> Jews killed Jesus long ago
> God's son; these, (they did not know)
> God's daughter Margaret Clitheroe.
>
> When she felt the kill-weights crush
> She told His name times-over three;
> *I suffer this* she said *for Thee.*
> After that in perfect hush
> For a quarter of an hour or so
> She was with the choke of woe. –
> It is over, Margaret Clitheroe.   (ll. 42–62)

Facing death, Margaret takes her place in tradition. Her last acts are watched by heavenly spectators in whose example she is destined to follow, including Thecla, of whom, of course, the poet had already written. Indeed, the ornate appellation given to this particular spectator – Thecla is 'the plumed passionflower' – savours of the earlier poem, whose devotion is garlanded more elaborately than is that of 'Margaret Clitheroe', in which Hopkins's writing has a different, cruder flavour.

'"Thronged that show"', Griffiths remarks, 'for a moment imagines the company of the blessed as a crowd gawping at a side-show'.[63] The indelicacy of this moment shades easily into the candid piety of what follows. Margaret's suffering is joined to that of Christ with so bare a directness that it is hard to perceive that this is the work of the same poet who, in the poem he completed six months earlier, had in 'The Wreck' developed out of the tall nun's sacrifice such a variety of lush symmetries. The parenthesis enclosing '(Just like Jesus crucified)' is of the kind used to indicate something felt to be nearly obvious, while 'Just like' is phrasing that takes the shortest possible path to the drawing of equivalence. Expanding on such equivalence, the poem's reasoning continues unrefined, with the parallel made between the culpability assumed of the Jews in Christ's death and the guilt of those who perpetrate Margaret's killing rendered in brutally plain statement, absent of the kind of distinction Hopkins would later urge on Patmore when he told the latter that to be of the Jewish race 'is no reproach but a glory, for Christ was a Jew'.[64]

Mush's account of Margaret Clitherow's death is 'a political as well as a theological document'.[65] In his transcription of Mush's account, Hopkins's fellow Jesuit John Morris wished to avoid controversy and so 'removed the more virulent anti-protestant passages of the original'.[66] The sobriety of Morris's treatment won him the respectful hearing he sought from outside the Roman Catholic community, with the *Athenaeum* praising his volume for the fact that 'The theological and polemic element is absolutely eliminated, – the historical is not only in the ascendant, it is paramount.'[67] We do not know if Hopkins had access to Mush's account independent of Morris, but what is clear is that his treatment of the story is quite different in temper from that of his fellow Jesuit, for Hopkins assimilates details from Mush's account in a way that heightens its contentiousness. This is true not only of the prominence 'Margaret Clitheroe' accords to certain aspects of the martyr's suffering, such as the appalling likelihood that 'Within her womb the child was quick' (l. 39), but also in what the poem leaves out: to say of the martyr simply 'She was admired' (l. 17) cuts short the difficult story of her personal reputation yet more finally than it appears even in Mush's report.[68]

'Margaret Clitheroe' is written with a share of caprice, not least in telling of the 'Fawning fawning crocodiles' who visited Margaret in prison, and in describing how 'Days and days came round about | With tears to put her candle out' (ll. 29–31); these were lines which Phare lamented as manifesting Hopkins's 'fondness for a succession of shallow metaphors'.[69] Yet in other respects the poem rests remarkably candid. In 'The Bugler's First Communion', as discussed in the previous chapter, the farfetchedness of Hopkins's rhyming is partly an attempt to have his poem take on something of the youthful pluck of its hero; in 'Margaret Clitheroe', bluntness in rhyme stands in reproach to the deceitful speech of the martyr's accusers. The run of three end rhymes which close each stanza, finishing always with 'Clitheroe', seems to invite the kind of ingenuity in rhyme in which Hopkins specialised, but that he mostly restrains in this poem. The perfect end rhymes of each stanza's final lines are instead emphatically plain, arriving at 'Clitheroe' by way of 'go', 'no', and 'so'; the earlier couplet of Hopkins's *abbaccc* stanza form, too, is often signally unelaborate, as in the lines which follow the praise for Margaret as 'upright, outright': 'Her will was bent at God. For that | Word went she should be crushed out flat' (ll. 37–38).

The risk of such artless rhyming is that it will lapse into bathos, a risk that the poem's closing lines render conspicuous: 'For a quarter of an hour or so | She was with the choke of woe. – | It is over, Margaret Clitheroe.' It is curious to find casual approximation ('quarter of an hour *or so*') given such prominence, appearing here with the kind of incongruity normally reserved to comic verse.[70] Yet this may actually be another effort to remain near to the martyr's experience. Mush's account of Margaret Clitherow exists in two versions. The transcription produced by Hopkins's fellow Jesuit John Morris, drawn from the earlier version, reports of the martyr's death that 'She was dying in one quarter of an hour.'[71] But there had also been another publication, transcribed from the later version of Mush's account, produced in 1849. This has slightly different phrasing: 'She was in dying *about one quarter of an hour*.'[72] We cannot be certain that Hopkins knew this version, but what his poem shares with its phrasing is the sense that Margaret Clitherow's death is being confronted up close, accompanied by the kind of rough estimate (Mush's 'about', Hopkins's 'or so') that might belong to an eyewitness account or verbal report.

In this the poem's ending contrasts with the severe manner in which 'Margaret Clitheroe' opens, where the martyr's fate had been surveyed as if from above, viewed in the largeness of the divine plan. In the final lines, her martyrdom is encountered close to its moment. If the sketchiness of 'quarter of an hour or so' is allowed to represent more than an excuse for a comically bad rhyme, part of its function might be to prepare for the turn made in Hopkins's final line. 'She was with the choke of woe. – | It is over, Margaret Clitheroe': here the shift from past to present tense is a reaching across time, collapsing historical distance, as Hopkins addresses the martyr as if at the moment of her death, and in personal confidence, not – as in the closing speech of 'The Wreck' to the tall nun – after the event of her elevation to the ranks of the martyrs, and by way of petition. Although surprising, the change of tense is not altogether a departure from the poem's method, for it continues the immediacy and directness with which Hopkins imagines the circumstances of her martyrdom; the familiarity assumed here is actually that implied throughout the poem. In the poem's final line, Hopkins offers a word of release to the martyr, calling time on her suffering. The nature of this ending means that, at its close, 'Margaret Clitheroe' is able to encompass particular as well as grand martyrological significance. Hopkins is led to narrate specific and local details of the martyr's story as a means of comprehending the importance of her actions.

The immediacy of this narration has theological implications. Hopkins's frame of reference in 'Margaret Clitheroe' is at once compendious and intimate, able to carry the distinctive mark of his interpretation of Trinitarian belief (God as 'The Utterer, Utterèd, Uttering') as well as the familiarity of personal address ('It is over, Margaret Clitheroe'). Although 'Margaret Clitheroe' could hardly be written from a position of individual subjectivity, as are, for instance, 'The Bugler's First Communion' and the 'terrible sonnets', the poem anticipates in its proximity to the circumstances of the martyr's death the concern of later poems with human experience as inhabited integrally by God's grace. Her martyrdom is brought close to type, as is that of the tall nun in 'The Wreck'; but unlike in the case of the tall nun, it is also framed by individual history, having a share of contingency ('quarter of an hour or so'). The German nuns in 'The Wreck', it has been claimed, 'have been transformed into religious symbols'; the same cannot be argued of 'Margaret Clitheroe'.[73] Hopkins is instead able to move between personal confidences, experiential circumstance, and large martyrological significance with rare and surprising freedom.

Christopher Ricks, reviewing a biography of Hopkins, observes that 'something must be acknowledged as happening to masochism once it is institutionalized as mortification':

> I for myself wish that Hopkins had not wished for his hair-shirt, for his sore chain, for his scourge, and for his 'custody of the eyes' (the penance of looking nowhere but at the ground); but all of these self-inflictions were not self-inflictions to him, and they are his business – or are his understanding of what it was for him to be about his Father's business. The stakes being what they were for him, he would have gone singing to the stake.[74]

That in 1881 Hopkins still expected 'some, I cannot guess what, great conversion or other blessing to the Church in England' from the 300th anniversary of the martyrdom of Edmund Campion suggests how he continued to be attuned to the idea that bloody witness could yield spectacular return. Nothing survives of Hopkins's 'great ode' on Campion, which the same letter mentions that he had begun, but his declared intention that it should be 'in sprung rhythm of irregular metre' gives a tantalising hint of the way his attunement to the fruits of martyrdom might have had prosodic implications.[75] The loss of the Campion ode to modern English poetry is, as Geoffrey Hill observes, 'grievous'.[76] Given the range of Hopkins's writing on martyrdom, part of our regret should be that we cannot know whether a poem which sounds likely to have been of grand vision would also, like 'Margaret Clitheroe', have remained close to the martyr's experience.

PART III

Last Things

CHAPTER 5

Death and Judgement

Death to Hopkins appeared fearful, and thus all the more necessary to con-template. 'We have the fate of others before our eyes for our warning', he declared in a meditation on hell, 'our sins are like their sins but not our fate – not hitherto: let us while we can make ourselves safe, *make our election sure.*'[1] This warning, provided by the fate of those already departed, would to Hopkins have stood largely impersonal, for, saints apart, it was to him a tenet of faith that the individual destiny of the dead cannot be known for certain by those whom they leave behind. Such uncertainty sometimes lent Hopkins's attitude to the last things a deep vulnerability. In 1877 he told his mother upon hearing of her father's death that he was glad it had coincided with the feast of the Holy Rosary, a feast which that year also overlapped with the anniversary of the event which had inspired its proclamation, the battle of Lepanto in 1571. This coincidence promised to Hopkins a double boon:

> I receive it without questioning as a mark that my prayers have been heard and that the queen of heaven has saved a Christian soul from enemies more terrible than a fleet of infidels. Do not make light of this, for it is perhaps the seventh time that I think I have had some token from heaven in con-nection with the death of people in whom I am interested.[2]

Hopkins alone in his family is likely to have been convinced of the efficacy of such prayers in aiding the souls of the departed. As a moderate High Anglican, Kate Hopkins would have viewed warily the belief that the peti-tions of the living could benefit the dead, which is the likely reason why her son's confidence is given touchy report: Hopkins wants to share his feeling, but he is also aware that across the confessional divide, not least in invoking the intercession of the Virgin Mary, it cannot be mutual.

Written a decade earlier, Hopkins's answer to parental pleas to reconsider his decision to convert to Roman Catholicism is similarly torn in feeling:

> You ask me if I have had no thought of the estrangement. I have had months to think of everything. Our Lord's last care on the cross was to commend

His mother to His Church and His Church to His mother in the person of St. John. If even now you wd. put yourselves into that position wh. Christ so unmistakeably gives us and ask the Mother of sorrows to remember her three hours' compassion at the cross, the piercing of the sword prophecied by Simeon, and her seven dolours, and her spouse Joseph, the lily of chastity, to remember the flight into Egypt, the search for his Foster-Son at twelve years old, and his last ecstasy with Christ at his death-bed, the prayers of this Holy Family wd. in a few days put an end to estrangements for ever.[3]

A devotion to the *Mater Dolorosa*, the Mother of Sorrows, was also a badge of Anglican ritualist piety at the time, but here it signals the zeal of the soon-to-be convert to Rome, announced in a manner more likely to provoke than to reassure Hopkins's parents.[4] The letter's stagey parade of new devotional clothes appears cruel, but it is likely to be an insensitivity born of anxiety, in the sense Hopkins later suggested was true of a number of replies to his parents at a time when 'every new letter I get breaks me down afresh': 'Your letters, wh. shew the utmost fondness, suppose none on my part and the more you think me hard and cold and that I repel and throw you off the more I am helpless not to write as if were true.'[5] Hopkins's reply to his mother on hearing of his grandfather's death was composed long after relations between them had been repaired. It too, however, is at once hard and helpless in the manner of its affection, following a prickly spiritual logic which seems unlikely to have consoled his mother.

The letter speaks of an intercessory relationship that is not dissolved by death, yet its brittle reasoning suggests the difficulty death posed to Hopkins's trust in divine solidarity with humanity. The difficulty is clearly seen in his poetry, which senses that the rupture of death serves to reveal the disharmony which exists between humankind and God. This sense of disharmony may be thought unlikely in a poet whose work is most obviously absorbed with the indwelling of the natural and the human by God's grace. Surprising as it may seem, however, Hopkins's expansive sense of the divine energy current in the world and alive in human selves only falteringly persists into his notion of their end. Of course, the celebration of creation and Incarnation in Hopkins is necessarily predicated upon the final purpose towards which he understood that these move, namely, the redemption of the world and its peoples. But as others have noticed, the 'apocalyptic angst' seen in Hopkins's response to energy physics is actually a general feature of his writing: one recent essay states that the belief in judgement after death 'challenged [Hopkins's] enquiring mind with its enigmatic inevitability'.[6] Indeed, his poetry's commitment to the created order can be seen to reach its limit in an eschatology absorbed by the new cosmic order as cataclysmic event, and by the punitive character of the judgement which precedes the world's end.

We see here a tension between Hopkins's perception that the natural order represents sacramentally the supernatural reality of God and his contrasting awareness of a deep rift between temporal and eternal realities.

John Morris, a Jesuit who taught Hopkins in the course of the latter's priestly training, once wrote of death 'as the completion of what God has done and is to do for me by the works of grace'.[7] In his student's poetry, by contrast, this world and the next appear more discontinuous. Death for Hopkins frequently marks the smallness and brevity of human life, with the latter seen forlornly in a late sonnet as inhabiting a mere 'scaffold of score brittle bones' ('The shepherd's brow', l. 5). Hopes and fears for the departed are for Hopkins neither vague nor shadowy, but often crudely graphic. An exception is provided by the closing stanzas of 'The Wreck of the Deutschland', in which, attached to a boldly panoramic vision of the history of salvation, death makes manifest the fundamental stability of God's presence and action. As this chapter will suggest, the assurance of 'The Wreck' in respect of the last things is afforded partly by its distance from the contingency of individual circumstance. Elsewhere, Hopkins's deep sense of the proximity of grace to personal history barely survives the drama of life's culmination in death and judgement. Only in 'That Nature is a Heraclitean Fire and of the comfort of the Resurrection' (1888) does Hopkins manage to alleviate his bleak sense of what awaits at life's end with confidence in God's final transformation of individual experience.

The Fate of the 'Unconfessed'

What did Hopkins believe happened at the moment of death to those, like his grandfather, who died outside the Roman Church? The hope in 'The Wreck' is that the 'unconfessed' who died aboard the *Deutschland* were granted God's mercy at the last, in what Hopkins knew as the grace of final perseverance, 'the timely coming of death while the soul is at peace with God'.[8] This is what allows Hopkins to conceive that the 'shipwráck' his poem describes might to God constitute a 'hárvest' (l. 248). Although the grace of final perseverance cannot be merited, it must be demanded; St Alphonsus Liguori, whose affective spirituality exerted a large influence on nineteenth-century Roman Catholicism, and on its eschatology in particular, puts the matter directly: 'Whoever prays will obtain it; whoever does not pray will not obtain it, and will be lost.'[9]

Behind the desire of 'The Wreck' that the *Deutschland*'s passengers achieve this penitence lies a delicate theological question. Attentive to pronouncements from Rome on the status of non-Catholics,[10] Hopkins is unlikely to have missed the clarification of the doctrine of *extra ecclesiam nulla salus* ('outside the Church there is no salvation') attempted by Pope

Pius IX in the mid-1860s, just ahead of Hopkins's conversion to Rome. Those 'who labor in invincible ignorance', the pope had declared, but 'who, zealously keeping the natural law and its precepts engraved in the hearts of all by God, and being ready to obey God, live an honest and upright life, can, by the operating power of divine light and grace, attain eternal life'.[11] As the *Syllabus of Errors* Pope Pius issued a year later insists, however, this should not be taken to mean that 'Good hope at least is to be entertained of the eternal salvation of all those who are not at all in the true Church of Christ'; the fate of those outside the Roman Church remains perilous, and confidence in their rescue by God would be misplaced.[12]

As a convert, Hopkins well understood the awkwardness of the issue. Earlier Tractarian converts to Rome had broken with the Anglican Church partly to relieve anxiety for their salvation. The unease Hopkins felt for his own soul prior to becoming a Roman Catholic had been calmed by Newman's words of fellow feeling at their initial meeting: 'Amongst other things [Newman] said that he always answered those who thought the learned had no excuse in invincible ignorance, that on the contrary they had that excuse the most of all people.'[13] Later, however, when Hopkins's own need for excuse had been removed, he was unwilling to extend the same margin to a friend wavering between the Churches of England and Rome: 'if God says that without faith it is impossible to please Him and will not excuse the best of heathens with the best of excuses for want of it what is to be said of people who knowing it live in avowed doubt whether they are in His church or not?'[14]

In Hopkins's poems, appeals for mercy for those dying outside the Roman Church are so convoluted as to mark only narrow hope for salvation. In 'The Loss of the Eurydice' (1878), the suddenness of the shipwreck exposes the danger of unpreparedness for death. A particular source of distress in the poem is the wilful destruction of Roman Catholic shrines and holy places at the time of the Reformation: 'Deeply surely I need to deplore it, | Wondering why my master bore it' (ll. 97–98). Such violence is seen to have opened a distance between what Hopkins calls 'My people and born own nation' (l. 87) and Roman Catholic faith which the fate of those in the shipwreck brings troublingly into focus. The poem closes with a call to the bereaved to pray for those drowned in the disaster:

> O well wept, mother have lost son;
> Wept, wife; wept, sweetheart would be one:
>   Though grief yield them no good
> Yet shed what tears sad truelove should.
>
> But to Christ lord of thunder
> Crouch; lay knee by earth low under:

'Holiest, loveliest, bravest,
Save my hero, O Hero savest.

And the prayer thou hearst me making
Have, at the awful overtaking,
    Heard; have heard and granted
Grace that day grace was wanted.'

Not that hell knows redeeming,
But for souls sunk in seeming
    Fresh, till doomfire burn all,
Prayer shall fetch pity eternal.   (ll. 105–20)

The confidence shown here in the possibility of divine relief is painstaking. The idea motivating the third of these stanzas is that if God lives in the eternal present we are able to petition him for a change in the past.[15] It is a perfectly orthodox thought, and one that to Hopkins seems to have been a great solace, yet it remains, as Dennis Sobolev observes, 'an expression of the deepest anxiety to propose such a prayer, with its theologically sophisticated argument, to the wives of the drowned sailors as a last resort'.[16] The imperative the stanzas deliver is severally convoluted by grammatical anomalies, as in the omission of the relative pronoun in 'Save my hero, O Hero savest', or when Hopkins commends the weeping of 'mother have lost son', in which the preference for 'have' over 'who has' appears, curiously, like something more than a compression. There is also a strange version of a conventional archaism ('hearst' for 'hearest'). Some of these intricacies can be understood as strenuous efforts at precision: the absence of the relative pronoun from 'O Hero savest', for instance, has been proposed to mean that the connection between 'Hero' and 'savest' can 'stand no break whatever'; 'the Hero is invoked in this line precisely in so far as He saves men.'[17] The intricacies are also partly offset by the simplicity of the verse form, composed of quatrains in rhyming couplets. Yet even this last aspect of the poem returns us in a different way to the anxiety about a lack of preparation for death, for the strained rhymes of earlier in the poem – that between 'portholes' and 'mortals' (ll. 39-40) is perhaps the most obvious example – become with the rhyme of 'burn all' with 'eternal' also blunt, staked between stark alternatives.

We feel here the polarity of creature and Creator in a way common to several of Hopkins's poems on death and judgement but which stands contrary to attempts to order all of his writing by a systematic theory based on the sacramental awareness of the natural order. The insights of these poems are in fact more mixed. The plea entered at the opening of 'Henry

Purcell' (1879) actually enlists the method recommended by 'The Loss of the Eurydice', that of retroactive prayer. It does so in very condensed form, requiring grammatical somersaults to be turned in the process:

> Have fáir fállen, O fáir, fáir have fállen, so déar
> To me, so arch-especial a spirit as heaves in Henry Purcell,
> An age is now since passed, since parted; with the reversal
> Of the outward sentence low lays him, listed to a heresy, here.

(ll. 1–4)

'Henry Purcell' shows an effort to harbour generous feelings towards the dead within the confines of a strict conscience about their fate. Purcell's music was to Hopkins 'something necessary and eternal'.[18] He was less sure of the eternal destiny of its composer. That the outward fact of dying a Protestant might not tell against Purcell is the poem's hope, and it finds in the opening lines what is – even for Hopkins – remarkably dense expression. For all that the lines have the appearance of a question ('Have the fair fallen?'), they are actually, as Hopkins explained to a confused Robert Bridges, in the perfect imperative:

> Have is not a plural at all, far from it. It is the singular imperative (or optative if you like) of the past, a thing possible and actual both in logic and grammar, but naturally a rare one. As in the second person we say 'Have done' or in making appointments 'Have had your dinner beforehand', so one can say in the third person not only 'Fair fall' of what is present or future but also 'Have fair fallen' of what is past.[19]

The tone of this is typical of Hopkins's exchanges with Bridges over matters of poetry, which manage (as Michael Hurley observes) simultaneously to 'affirm Hopkins's faith in Bridges's critical acumen and also his belief that any faults of incomprehension lie with Bridges the reader rather than Hopkins the writer'.[20] In this case, Bridges's difficulty with the lines from 'Henry Purcell' may not have been much relieved by Hopkins's gloss, for it is an odd kind of explanation, with a strangeness that is itself revealing of the poem described. The analogy Hopkins provides to Bridges relates only to tense, of course, and yet the incongruous banality of his example – 'Have had your dinner beforehand' – indicates the lengths of explanation to which he was forced by such difficult lines. The strain of this explanation demonstrates something of the challenge Hopkins's eschatological severity posed to his admiration for worldly achievement.

'Henry Purcell' holds seemingly anomalous beliefs in parallel, vaunting what Hopkins's prose gloss describes as Purcell's ability to utter in music 'the very make and species of man' even as it subjects the composer's eternal fate to the juridical categories of 'outward sentence' and 'listed to a heresy'. Such categories are also prominent in Hopkins's spiritual prose. The Roman Catechism distinguishes a particular judgement in advance of the general judgement, with the former said to occur at the moment of death, at which point each individual is 'instantly placed before the judgement seat of God, where all that he had ever done, or spoken, or thought, during life, shall be subjected to the most rigid scrutiny'.[21] According to this scheme, the Day of Judgement can be expected to enact a sentence that has already been decided. Frederick William Faber, also a Roman Catholic convert, commented, 'The soul knows its fate beforehand, and so has no hope: thus it is an execution rather than a judgment.'[22] Hopkins's own reflections on the necessity of judgement at death are intricate:

> Why at death? Not by a physical necessity, as I think, but because life, being, by God's decree, one moral whole, namely a state of probation, it is befitting that some judgement on it should take place as soon as it is over. And yet this judgement is, as I suppose, in some manner unofficial, unformal, and its issue is rather the prisoner's plea allowed, not gainsaid, than the judge's own sentence. Or it is even formal but not a vindictive or punitive sentence formally, but of formal excommunication, non-communion, breaking off of intercourse, and detention till judgement.[23]

The thought here is not only tangled but also cramped, pressed between thinly discriminated punishments. Behind its legal categories can be sensed a large awareness of the human tendency to err and transgress. Of course this is in the nature of the subject, given that Hopkins is writing of sin and lost souls, but it still says much that it is hard to conceive from his account how the particular judgement might work otherwise and initiate a process of reformation. There is the same eschatological narrowness here also seen in 'Henry Purcell'. This narrowness would have its most important appearance in the poetry in what Hopkins teasingly described as 'the longest sonnet ever made and no doubt the longest making': 'Spelt from Sibyl's Leaves'.[24]

The Difference of Death: 'Spelt from Sibyl's Leaves'

'Spelt from Sibyl's Leaves' does not fit into any neat conceptual scheme. Even its subject is difficult to classify, in part because the poem is of such varied inspiration, owing as much to Virgil as to the Book of Revelation. When taken as a vision of the end-times, however, it suggests that Hopkins's notion of final judgement was just as narrow as his idea of particular judgement. Here is the poem in full:

Earnest, earthless, equal, attuneable, || vaulty, voluminous, … stupendous
Evening strains to be tíme's vást, || womb-of-all, home-of-all, hearse-of-all
    night.
Her fond yellow hornlight wound to the west, || her wild hollow hoarlight
    hung to the height
Waste; her earliest stars, earlstars, || stárs principal, overbend us,
Fíre-féaturing héaven. For éarth || her béing has unbóund; her dápple is at
    énd, as-
Tray or aswarm, all throughther, in throngs; || self ín self stéepèd and
    páshed – qúite
Disremembering, dísmémbering || áll now. Heart, you round me right
With: Óur évening is óver us; óur night || whélms, whélms, ánd will énd us.
Only the beakleaved boughs dragonish || damask the tool-smooth bleak
    light; black,
Ever so black on it. Óur tale, O óur oracle! || Lét life, wáned, ah lét life wínd
Off hér once skéined stained véined varíety || upon, áll on twó spools; párt,
    pen, páck
Now her áll in twó flocks, twó folds – bláck, white; || ríght, wrong; réckon
    but, réck but, mínd
But thése two; wáre of a wórld where bút these || twó tell, eách off the óther; of a
    ráck
Where, selfwrung, selfstrung, sheathe- and shelterless, || thoúghts agaínst
    thoughts ín groans grínd.

'Day of wrath, that day when the world is consumed to ash as David and the Sibyl testify' opens the *Dies Irae*, the Latin hymn used in the Roman Catholic liturgy as the sequence for the Requiem Mass. At the end of 'Spelt from Sibyl's Leaves', which likely echoes the hymn, God's judgement yields a narrow dichotomy between the lost and the saved. It is fitting that the penultimate lines of the poem are formed largely of bare monosyllables, for in their allusion to Matthew's Gospel these lines imagine the division of the sheep from the goats yet more starkly than does the biblical original: here there are only 'twó flocks, twó folds' rather than two species, as if even the mark of difference found in the Gospel story allowed for too much gradation. Moreover, although these 'twó flocks, twó folds' are parted, there is no departure, no dispersal; they are instead held in terrible friction, each telling 'off the óther', in what Helen Vendler calls a 'strange tautological synonymy'.[25] This hellish vision becomes in the final line a vision of hell, in which physical and mental pains appear to coalesce, with Hopkins's language no longer spare but instead circular, turned in upon itself.

We see here the discrepancy between Hopkins's perception of the dignity of created life and his notion of the potential hideousness of its end. This can be sensed even at the level of the individual word. He began writing

'Spelt from Sibyl's Leaves' in October 1884, a few months after he had moved to Dublin. It took him almost two years to complete the poem. There is some debate about the derivation of 'throughther', but that at least 'Disremembering' is agreed to be an Irish dialect word confirms that 'Spelt from Sibyl's Leaves', for all its concern with the end-times, is also steeped in a particular time and place.[26] Writing of another poet fascinated by local words, Hopkins commented that the Dorset dialect poems of William Barnes held a 'Westcountry "instress"', elsewhere praising Barnes's 'natural-ness', and proposing him to be 'like an embodiment or incarnation or man-muse of the country, of Dorset, of rustic life and humanity'; this admiration for Barnes partakes of Hopkins's own conviction that the language of poetry should 'arise from, or be the elevation of, ordinary modern speech' and ren-der, by special emphasis of patterns of sound, the deep particularity of indi-vidual words.[27] 'Disremembering', which Hopkins may have encountered in Richard Chenevix Trench's *English Past and Present* (1855), has, however, a philological interest that differentiates it from the ordinariness of 'Jack' or 'patch' in 'That Nature is a Heraclitean Fire' or the demotic 'Áh well, God rést him áll road éver he offénded!' of 'Felix Randal'; its vernacularity is more obscure, strange in a way that, like the rest of the poem, relies on the excavation of what Hopkins believed were true etymological correspond-ences between pairs of words, thereby hinting at the possible unity of lan-guage which had long preoccupied him (these pairings include 'vaulty' and 'voluminous', 'bend' and 'unbound', and 'wrong' and 'wrung'; they frame in particular the extraordinary opening line, which builds towards 'stupen-dous' both in its dramatic one-stress rest – 'voluminous, … stupendous' – and through intricate sound patterning between and across pairs of words).

'Disremembering', then, is a word whose inclusion here is inspired by theories of language which relate closely to Hopkins's belief in Christ as Word made flesh. Yet the manner in which 'Disremembering' is paired, in this case to indicate the terror of final judgement, suggests how Hopkins's intricate verbal patterning has not always the shapeliness we might antic-ipate from a poem framed according to such theories. It is coupled with 'dísmémbering', comprising what Valentine Cunningham calls 'a broken rhyme': 'The second item of the pair returns, claiming rhyming partner-ship, but returns with a loss, with a bit broken off, amputated, *dismembered* in fact.'[28] The 'broken rhyme' of 'Disremembering' and 'dísmémbering' is one of a number of ways in which a poem fashioned with an ear to grandly emphatic performance – Hopkins, by now increasingly drawn to terms of musical duration to describe prosodic effects, recommended 'long rests, long dwells on the rhyme and other marked syllables', so that it 'shd. be

almost sung' – is prone to upset or disturb its elaborate correspondences
of sound and word origin.[29] Many of Hopkins's stress marks move against
'natural' speech rhythms, as in the disconcerting emphasis given to 'ín' in
'thoúghts agáinst thoughts ín groans grínd'. More generally, the intense
patternedness Hopkins sought to achieve in poetic language is here felt
slightly to come apart. The line 'Her fond yellow hornlight wound to the
west, || her wild hollow hoarlight hung to the height', for instance, shares
in its symmetry a concern with the exact description of sunsets evident in
Hopkins's remarkable letter to the journal *Nature* in the aftermath of the
Krakatoa eruptions of 1883, in which he observed that the intensity of the
sun's after-glow meant that 'the fields facing west glowed as if overlaid with
yellow wax'.[30] But, unlike in the *Nature* letter, sunset in 'Spelt from Sibyl's
Leaves' is part of the immense drift characterising the world's dusk, in
which the apocalyptic collapse is shown to involve a vast unravelling. The
main verb towards which 'Her fond yellow hornlight wound to the west, ||
her wild hollow hoarlight hung to the height' is directed ('Waste') is only
engaged belatedly, once the enjambment has been crossed. The extraordinary vowel patterning of these lines is also faintly out of shape. To its echo
of the previous line's 'west', 'Waste' adds the vowel sounds which thereafter
come to prominence in 'her earliest stars, earlstars, || stárs principal', but it
also tilts out of balance the previous line's anaphoric poise, pressing us over
the line-ending. In what follows, for a moment 'earliest stars, earlstars, ||
stárs principal' traces a pattern of sound which by contrast appears com-
pacted ('earliest stars' condensed into 'earlstars'), but this too then disperses
('stárs principal' continues the verbal echo, but more diffusely). Such res-
tiveness is the signal feature of this imagining of the world's end.

Recent conceptual approaches to Hopkins tend to expect all of his
work to adhere neatly to the poetic theory and personal metaphysic which
frame the early phase of his creative maturity. 'Spelt from Sibyl's Leaves'
is more fluctuating and agitated. The agitation makes it no surprise that
it should be this poem of Hopkins, above all others, which appears most
to have captured the attention of one of the most profound readers of his
work, Geoffrey Hill, who sees the language of 'Spelt from Sibyl's Leaves'
as emblematic of Hopkins's method ('HOPKINS LANGUAGE IS, IN A
SENSE "THROUGHTHER"', Hill declares in unpublished lecture notes,
for it 'goes down into the domain of throughther, where the recondite +
the idiomatic cohabit').[31] Hill's Hopkins is not the fluent and assured poet
of 'God's Grandeur' or 'Pied Beauty' (neither poem appears in all of Hill's
extensive critical commentary on Hopkins); he is rather one whose fascination for Hill lies in the way, as a poem from Hill's collection *The Orchards*

of Syon (2002) puts it, 'Hopkins, who was self- | belaboured, crushed, cried out being uplifted'.[32] Indeed, the quality Peter McDonald discerns in Hill's own poetry might serve to describe what draws Hill to Hopkins, and to 'Spelt from Sibyl's Leaves' in particular: 'Hill's style never rests: no phrase is allowed to settle back on itself without being upset by what succeeds it; no isolated effect, however brilliant, is allowed to remain unshadowed.'[33]

Hill holds to no assumption that the work produced at the outset of Hopkins's poetic maturity provides an exact template by which to judge all of his later writings. There is not here the inflexible view of the poetry which, expecting that Hopkins's writing should form a continuous project, places 'Spelt from Sibyl's Leaves' simply as 'a stunning rejection of the staunchly held Scotism that had structured all the great poems of his Welsh years'.[34] As discussed in the next chapter, the way 'Spelt from Sibyl's Leaves' envisions hell certainly involves a startling application of Hopkins's theories of self and being. But rather than rigidly appraising all of his poetry by identical theoretical criteria, we should notice the diversity in its perspectives and insights. This requires us to return once again to the poem which above all others has been used to define the character of Hopkins's writing. The contrast between this poem, 'The Wreck of the Deutschland', and 'Spelt from Sibyl's Leaves', cannot in fact be reduced to whether they espouse or invert the same grand system; rather, it is also in being quite different poems that these arrive at alternative notions of final ends.

A Grand Vision: 'The Wreck of the Deutschland'

An 'end', St Augustine observes in *The City of God*, can mean either 'finished so that it does not exist' or 'perfected and fulfilled'.[35] The end imagined in 'Spelt from Sibyl's Leaves' is more rupture than completion, not least because the day of reckoning the poem imagines is left isolated from the Christian narrative of which it might otherwise have formed part: until its final lines, 'Spelt from Sibyl's Leaves' is more substantially a poem of apocalypse than of eschatology. In the final stanzas of 'The Wreck of the Deutschland', by contrast, Hopkins's idea of the coming of the future age stands fully and deliberately within the pattern of human fall and redemption, in which the world is 'perfected and fulfilled' rather than ended. Writing of these final stanzas, Michael Wheeler remarks that in widening his focus from the suffering of the tall nun, Hopkins 'effects a transition at the end of the poem from the sharply focused drama of her agony and death to the broader expression of its significance in relation to the corporate life of the Roman Church'.[36] This puts matters carefully for the massive scope of this closing sequence, a sequence that, in distinction to 'Spelt from Sibyl's Leaves', blends eschatology with soteriology in declaring Christ's victory over sin and evil and in lauding the atonement by which salvation is made possible. To describe the poem using these terms of systematic theology is appropriate, for never again is Hopkins's poetry so grandly synthesising. As Wheeler observes, 'The Wreck' does nothing less than articulate 'a theology of death which is grounded in Christ's own death and passion'.[37]

The amplitude of the salvation sounded in the final stanzas of 'The Wreck' is not an entirely new theme within the poem. Midway through 'Part the second' we encounter Christ's astonishing perspective on the shipwreck tragedy: 'Storm flákes were scróll-leaved flówers, lily shówers – sweet héaven was astréw in them' (l. 168). Here a Hopkins coinage, the verb 'astréw', beautifully carries the sense that God's mercy is 'strewn', liberally scattered rather than narrowly concentrated. But it is only really at the close of 'The Wreck', in the declamatory final stanzas, that Hopkins's vision of God's triumph over death becomes truly expansive. The sweep and ambition of these stanzas is remarkable for a poet, who, as Francis O'Gorman argues, had an 'imaginative habit of declining to contemplate vastness, literal or conceptual, in almost any form'.[38] They are unique in Hopkins for the fullness of the sense that final judgement is not an overturning of human history and experience, but instead the fulfilment of divine action already manifest in the world.

Beginning from stanza 32, 'The Wreck' opens out from the drama of the shipwreck to contemplate the majesty of God's saving action. The urgency of earlier sections is moderated by a sense of the stability of divine presence:

> I admíre thee, máster of the tídes,
> Of the Yóre-flood, of the yéar's fáll;
> The recúrb and the recóvery of the gúlf's sídes,
> The gírth of it and the whárf of it and the wáll;
> Stánching, quénching ócean of a mótionable mínd;
> Gróund of béing and gránite of it: pást áll
> Grásp Gód, thróned behínd
> Déath, with a sóvereignty that héeds but hídes, bódes but abídes;
>
> (ll. 249–56)

The identification of 'béing' with God, familiar from the Platonic tradition of Augustine and Anselm, is here made emphatically material ('Gróund' and 'gránite'). Yet the lines themselves make space for delicate verbal shades amid the heavy scorings. Michael Hurley suggests that it is 'the very springiness of sprung rhythm that allows Hopkins such range, which he realises through the juxtaposition of stress with looser, smoother, more delicate sound patterns'.[39] The particular quality of the stanza employed in 'The Wreck' is its capacity for such variability, at one moment bunching its stresses and in another dispersing them again, as happens here when the insistent beat of 'Grásp Gód, thróned behínd' gives way to the swiftly falling tread of 'Déath, with a sóvereignty that héeds but hídes, bódes but abídes', a recovery of supple movement reciprocated in the fluid exchange of vowels among similarly placed consonants across 'héeds but hídes, bódes but abídes', this last a technique Hopkins named '*vowelling off*', which he likely derived from the alliterative tradition of Anglo-Saxon verse.[40]

'Death is certain and uncertain', Hopkins once observed, 'certain to come, uncertain when and where'.[41] God's command over death in stanza 32 of 'The Wreck' is also imagined as at once assured and hidden from view, but with the difference that obscurity is here a cause for trust rather than fear. '[B]ódes' is often taken to be a borrowing from Anglo-Saxon, meaning 'order' or 'decree',[42] but – among other possibilities – it may also be a derivation of 'bide' (*OED*: 'To remain in a place, or with a person, as opposed to going away; to stay'), thus making 'bódes but abídes' into something less than a contrast, with the hiddenness of God's action appearing as a token of his patience.

Fear of sovereign death does not dominate these stanzas, which distinguishes their last things from those presented in other Hopkins poems. It also differentiates the close of 'The Wreck' from the opening to the poem's second part, where Death, personified, had appeared as recruiting sergeant, 'on drum', ominously ever-present but still unrecalled by his charges, who 'forget that there must | The sóur scýthe crínge, and the bléar sháre cóme' (ll. 83; 87–88), a line whose thick sound relations require that its short words make a slow procession of their dire foretelling. This is death seen terrifyingly in its moment. At the close of 'The Wreck', by contrast, death appears cast as part of the larger drama of salvation in Christ, drama which occurs at a remove from the terms of individual experience. The eschatology that earlier in the poem was 'internalized', as Wheeler describes, is here 'externalized', driven outwards.[43]

That this section of 'The Wreck' does not begin from experience, but rather surveys it, is part of the poem's uniqueness. Hopkins's conviction of the basic goodness of the natural order here aligns not only with his poetry's perception of the origin of the created world but also with that world's destiny. In stanza 33, the poem pictures the harrowing of hell, Christ's triumph over the powers that hold humankind in bondage. Attention is fixed on the recovery of the relationship with God enabled by Christ's action, as opposed to humanity's fault:

                    With a mércy that oútrídes
                    The all of water, an ark
            For the lístener; for the língerer with a lóve glídes
                    Lówer than déath and the dárk;
        A véin for the vísiting of the pást-prayer, pént in príson,
        The-last-breath penitent spirits – the uttermost mark
                    Our passion-plungèd giant risen,
        The Christ of the Father compassionate, fetched in the storm
            of his strides.

                                                        (ll. 257–64)

The sense in which the 'pént in' become 'penitent' here (in the near-anagram
of earlier in the stanza) is obscure, partly because of the difficulty of ascer-
taining precisely what kind of break is announced by the dash before 'the
uttermost mark'. Is 'mark' here the furthest point of distance from God, or
does it instead designate the extent of Christ's saving action? A third possibility has also been suggested: that those on the fringes of salvation 'mark', as
in recognise or behold, Christ.[44]

Perhaps we do not need to decide between these possibilities. In any case, the
dense syntax of the stanza makes it hard to distinguish what 'was' from what 'is'.
Compare the account given in one of Hopkins's sermons of the same moment,
in which Christ rises from the dead to vanquish his enemies: 'they did not
know that their seeming triumph was total defeat, that his seeming defeat was
glorious victory. For it was not the world Christ had come to fight but the ruler
of this world the Devil.'[45] What is gained by Christ's victory is the promise of
salvation, and Hopkins's choice of tense in the sermon implies the distinction
between the renewal of life in the present (and its perfection in the future) and
the past action on which it depends. The more fluid relation between past and
present seen in stanza 33 of 'The Wreck' is the product of compressed language.
It suggests a different aspect of the belief Hopkins declared in the sermon: that
salvation is both process and event, for its meaning is always being created
anew in human responses to the atonement, responses that are neither antici-
pated nor presumed (Christ saves; he has not, in advance, saved).[46]

After stanza 33, the poem goes backwards in order to move forward,
returning to the event of the Incarnation, and then shifting again to declare
the goodness of God's judgement. In the movement between Incarnation
and divine judgement, Hopkins captures the perception that God's kingdom is inaugurated in the present rather than reserved to the future. The
progress of this drama of salvation is not shattering, and only a little apocalyptic. Stanza 34 may be different from other stanzas at the close of 'The
Wreck' in having an eye to the judgement expected at the end of time, but
even here the criss-cross of events from Christian history works to lessen
the extremity of the world's final destiny:

> Now burn, new born to the world,
> Double-naturèd name,
> The heaven-flúng, heart-fléshed, máiden-fúrled
> Míracle-in-Máry-of-fláme,
> Mid-numberèd he in three of the thunder-throne!
> Not a dóomsday dázzle in his cóming nor dárk as he
> cáme;
> Kínd, but róyally recláiming his ówn;
> A released shówer, let flásh to the shíre, not a líghtning of fíre
> hard húrled.

(ll. 265–72)

A 'thunder-throne' is a seat of judgement (see Revelation 6.1; 8.5) to which, in this scenario, the Incarnation stands in large contrast, being an exercise of divine majesty close to the 'língering-óut swéet skíll' described in 'Part the first' (l. 78). Christ is 'heaven-flúng, heart-fléshed, máiden-fúrled', a description which has been taken to exemplify sprung rhythm's tendency to heavy and deliberate emphasis, but which might actually be said to illustrate exactly the opposite: a complex latticework of sound.[47] There is, to be sure, an obvious harshness to the gathering of alliterative fricatives, which the stress pattern accentuates, but also a certain delicacy in the mellowing of 'flúng' into 'fléshed' and, especially, 'fúrled', this last a break on the verbal propulsion provided by the *fl-* openings.

Such delicacy is important, for the enveloping protection afforded by the Virgin Mother aligns here with the pattern of Christ's saving action. Christ's action, too, has its lightness, which is seen even amidst the poem's vehement closing appeal. I have already discussed this closing appeal in previous chapters, but it is worth further consideration in this context. We see here the particular felicity of the stanza form Hopkins uses in 'The Wreck', which remains open to diverse rhythmic currents and variegated sound patterns:

> Dáme, at óur dóor
> Drówned, and among óur shóals,
> Remémber us in the róads, the heaven-háven of the
> rewárd:
> Our kíng back, Oh, upon Énglish sóuls!
> Let him éaster in us, be a dáyspring to the dímness of us,
> be a crímson-cresseted east,
> More bríghtening her, ráre-dear Brítain, as his réign rólls,
> Príde, rose, prínce, hero of us, hígh-príest,
> Oür héart's charity's héarth's fíre, oür thóughts' chivalry's
> thróng's Lórd.

(ll. 273–80)

As much as the final stanza is thick with spondaic accents, pressing home the advantage gained to England by the martyrdom achieved on its shores, fluidity can still be glimpsed in the line 'Let him éaster in us, be a dáyspring to the dímness of us, be a crímson-cresseted east,' an appeal that stays for a moment with the rising sun before finding its object in the following line. Having a series of close alliterative returns (between 'dáyspring' and 'dímness', and also 'crímson' and 'cresseted') bracketed within the more distant recurrence across the line between 'éaster' and 'east' also allows these to be encompassed by Christ's rising at the Resurrection even as the poem lingers unforcingly with the dawning sun across the enjambment.

The density of these closing stanzas is extreme and is matched only by their breadth, as 'The Wreck' turns soaringly synoptic in order for the individual narrative of martyrdom it has earlier recounted to be understood as paradigmatic of God's action generally. What occurs in the particular instance of the tall nun's death is used to reveal the universal rule of divine life. Hopkins insisted his poem was not a narrative but an 'ode',[48] a designation that begins to make sense if we see that 'The Wreck' fulfils what Paul H. Fry has classified as the ode's hymnic functions: 'theurgy, celebration, genealogy'.[49] As previous chapters have shown, much of the rest of Hopkins's poetry is not so consolidative, with the fastening of individual experience to the cosmic and to the communal having the effect of emboldening that experience rather than making it ideal. The greater compendiousness of 'The Wreck' allows it to surmount what the more specifically apocalyptic of Hopkins's poems contend with: a sense that 'the hour of death', as one of the spiritual manuals Hopkins knew puts it, 'is the hour of *undeceiving*, in which I shall judge of all things differently from what I do now', a break with rather than the consummation of an individual's previous history.[50] At the close of 'The Wreck' by contrast, the last things are given a genealogy that enables their invocation also to be a celebration.

The Change of 'That Nature is a Heraclitean Fire'

'The Wreck' was written whilst Hopkins was still a seminarian, and it has a seminarian's ardour to bring Christ's truth to a world he is eager to confront. The later poetry Hopkins wrote out of priestly event and incident faces the last things more anxiously, attempting to find reassurance amid the waywardness of personally encountered lives, as occurs in the nervy enquiry made of the hero of 'The Bugler's First Communion': 'may he not rankle and roam | In backwheels, though bound home?' (ll. 42–43). Such lives, it is hoped, will be transformed by a reality that is universal, but the drama of death and judgement in these poems still occurs on an individual scale that only awkwardly becomes monumental. The final lines of 'Felix Randal' provide one example: 'How far from then forethought of, all thy more boisterous years, | When thou at the random grím fórge, pówerful amídst péers, | Didst fettle for the great grey drayhorse his bright and battering sandal!' (ll. 12–14). Here the inclusion of 'sandal' to make the rhyme with 'Randal' is not less heavy-handed for 'sandal' possibly being technical, the name for a type of horseshoe. Rather, the crossing of the workaday and the classical hauls the man into myth.[51] Like 'The Bugler's First Communion', 'Felix Randal' is a poem as much about the act of ministry as about the person being ministered to, and it stays close to the matter of pastoral encounter, imagining a good death, but only glancing at what a good death makes possible. The poem's opening line ('Félix Rándal the fárrier, O is he déad then? my dúty all énded') is typical in that its equivocality is all priestly, with what seems, as Seamus Perry remarks, 'an unthinking response to an unexceptional death', nevertheless complicated by the spurning of the commonplace 'Oh' for what might conceivably be an exclamation of lament ('O').[52]

The poetry Hopkins later wrote in Ireland provides a new opening into the immensity of the last things. 'Spelt from Sibyl's Leaves' presents the end of everything, 'tíme's vást, || womb-of-all, home-of-all, hearse-of-all night'. 'That Nature is a Heraclitean Fire and of the comfort of the Resurrection', a poem with which 'Spelt from Sibyl's Leaves' is often paired, contrasts man's end with nature's endless, shape-shifting renewal. I have discussed the final lines of 'That Nature is a Heraclitean Fire' in Chapter 1, but here is the poem in full:

> Cloud-puffball, torn tufts, tossed pillows || flaunt forth, then chevy on an air-
> Built thoroughfare: heaven-roysterers, in gay-gangs || they throng; they
>   glitter in marches.
> Down roughcast, down dazzling whitewash, || wherever an elm arches,
> Shivelights and shadowtackle ín long || lashes lace, lance, and pair.
> Delightfully the bright wind boisterous || ropes, wrestles, beats earth bare
> Of yestertempest's creases; in pool and rutpeel parches
> Squandering ooze to squeezed || dough, crúst, dust; stánches, stárches
> Squadroned masks and manmarks || treadmire toil there
> Fóotfretted in it. Million-fuelèd, || nature's bonfire burns on.
> But quench her bonniest, dearest || to her, her clearest-selvèd spark
> Mán, how fást his fíredint, || his mark on mind, is gone!
> Bóth are in an únfáthomáble, áll ís in an enórmous dárk
> Drowned. O pity and indig || nation! Manshape, that shone
> Sheer off, disseveral, a star, || death blots black out; nor mark
>   Is ány of him at áll so stárk
> But vastness blurs and time || beats level. Enough! the Resurrection,
> A héart's-clarion! Awáy grief's gásping, || joyless days, dejection.
>   Across my foundering deck shone
> A beacon, an eternal beam. || Flesh fade, and mortal trash
> Fáll to the resíduary worm; || world's wildfire, leave but ash:
>   In a flash, at a trumpet crash,

I am all at once what Christ is, || since he was what I am, and
Thís Jack, jóke, poor pótsherd, || patch, matchwood, immortal diamond,
            Is immortal diamond.

'[L]ately I sent you a sonnet, on the Heraclitean Fire, in which a great deal
of early Greek philosophical thought was distilled', Hopkins told Bridges
of this poem.[53] Various Pre-Socratic philosophers have been suggested as
inspirations for the poem, although Heraclitus is evidently the source from
which Hopkins draws most significantly. At the heart of Heraclitus's theory of motion is what one of Hopkins's undergraduate essays describes as
'the certainty of change', which leaves 'no unity but a stream of alteration'.[54]
According to Heraclitus, all of nature comes under this 'certainty of change',
which may to Hopkins have been part of the theory's appeal, for, as Catherine
Phillips observes, Heraclitus allows for 'the integration of various parts of
nature, the binding together of everything', in a perpetual flux that joins
earth and sky.[55] This constant reshaping of nature has violent and unruly vigour in Hopkins's poem, as clouds appear 'torn' and 'tossed', light is splintered
('Shivelights'), and the wind 'ropes, wrestles, beats earth bare'. Prior to any
reflection on the human condition, nature's state of constant motion and
transformation appears a cause for delight. Yet it is hard to escape hints in
the poem's opening description of the coming unhappy comparison with the
fate of man. That the wind 'beats earth bare' prefigures the awful levelling of
time which further on in the poem 'beats level'; and if the imprint on nature
of 'Squadroned masks and manmarks' can happily be done without, much
less so the 'mark on mind' of man whose disappearance will later be a cause
for the exclamation 'O pity and indig || nation!' (an exclamation made all the
more emphatic for bestriding the mid-line caesura). Fear of death is always
on the poem's horizon. Take line 7: 'Squandering ooze to squeezed || dough,
crúst, dust; stánches, stárches'. The alexandrine as Hopkins employs it is a
grand line, but equally a restless one, unwieldy in a manner prone to having
a phrase or effect turn back on itself, as happens with the drying of mud in
'dough, crúst, dust', where the chain of metaphor ('dough, crúst') is replaced
by sound echo ('crúst, dust'), an echo which, we realise, is also a reversal of
metaphor (mud really has become dust). The consequent prominence of
'dust' is ominous given what follows in succeeding lines.

   Here, the poverty of man's end is felt in sharp contrast to nature's buoyant
powers of self-renewal. Finally, of course, this feeling will be overturned, as
the Heraclitean pre-Christian vision is eclipsed in the poem's codas by the
Christian hope of salvation, but the fearfulness of death is first expressed
by its apparent elimination of what Hopkins held most precious: unique
self-being. The description of man as 'her bonniest' is owed to a fateful echo

with 'nature's *bonfire*'. This and the succeeding 'dearest to her' apart, however, the poem's report of what is lost to death highlights individual distinctiveness in terms that are characteristic to Hopkins's theory of the self.
His idea, as it is put in notes of 1882, was that 'Self is the intrinsic oneness
of a thing', and so not accidental, but essentially and indivisibly singular.[56]
Human nature, for Hopkins, was 'more highly pitched, selved, and distinctive than anything in the world'.[57] Thus in 'That Nature is a Heraclitean
Fire', man is nature's 'clearest-selvèd spark', the most intensely individuated
of all created things. The particular awfulness of death is that it removes
difference, flattening distinctive marks of being, and rendering singularity
imperceptible (the dominant metaphor here is of a loss of sight: 'death blots
black out' and 'vastness blurs'). Hopkins's lament is for specialness lost, for
that which has 'shone | Sheer off, disseveral', with 'sheer' as adjective mean-
ing 'bright, shining; existing by itself', as adverb 'completely, absolutely', and
with 'disseveral' indicating an existence too particular to be grouped.[58]

The hope of the Resurrection, when finally called upon in the poem's
codas, promises to liberate and elevate individual distinctiveness. The
poem changes perspective to represent the enormity of this hope. What
had been a poem conducted in the third person, grieving for 'Mán' and
'Manshape' at large, alters to become about 'Thís Jack' specifically (a shift
the stress Hopkins indicated for 'Thís', at the expense of 'Jack', renders
emphatic). In his meditation notes, Hopkins was drawn to think of individual distinctiveness particularly in relation to his own self, for 'nothing
else in nature comes near this unspeakable stress of pitch, distinctiveness,
and selving, this selfbeing of my own ... searching nature I taste *self* but at
one tankard, that of my own being.'[59] Part of the 'comfort' held out by the
Resurrection in 'That Nature is a Heraclitean Fire' resides in its capacity
to be spoken of personally, enabling the proud assertion of individual self
seen in the closing lines, in which the phrase 'I am' appears twice ('I am
all at once what Christ is, || since he was what I am'). The phrase is also
carried over into 'd*iam*ond', in an incorporation that helps makes sense of
what might otherwise appear contrived or fanciful in Hopkins's closing
lines: the rhyme of 'I am, and' with 'diamond'. Thought of in this way, the
rhyme, though unlikely, is actually part of the logic of Hopkins's reflections, for salvation is seen here to ensure that singularity of self is made
permanent and unbreakable, 'I am' become 'diamond'.

This reversal in the poem's idea of the human condition is abrupt partly
because it aligns with no formal division in Hopkins's sonnet. Divisions of
structure instead occur separately to sense in 'That Nature is a Heraclitean
Fire': although the end of the octave can just about be distinguished

(concluding 'nature's bonfire burns on'), the sestet runs over, with the change of direction signalled by the cry of 'Enough!' in line 16 occurring after we have entered the sonnet's codas. The unexpectedness of this change of direction is such that Norman White complains it is arbitrary: 'Dogma has been impersonally introduced without the elaborate and close engagement that there was in the description of nature … The enthusiastic last four lines carry a special charge, but depend on the reader's thoughtless acceptance of the unexplained sudden switch to another way of thought.'[60]

White is wrong to suggest that the switch involves the neglect of the personal, for the particular effort of these lines is to meld dogma with individual experience. Another point in their defence might be the potential for the cry of 'Enough!' to signal not only the interruption of Hopkins's lament but also, as Lesley Higgins has argued, an affirmation of sufficiency, a 'declaration that the Resurrection alone is "Enough!" to transform the perpetual flux of natural matter into a triumphant, theological pattern of redemption'.[61] We might also draw on Geoffrey Hill's claim that what he describes as the 'uncouth anacoluthon' of 'Enough! the Resurrection' constitutes 'one of the greatest grammatical moments in nineteenth-century English poetry': 'It has been criticised for its arbitrariness, but arbitrariness is the making of it. The Resurrection is a kind of eschatological anacoluthon; no amount of standard grammar can anticipate or regularize that moment.'[62] The style of thought here is quite different from the intensely logical and proclamatory poetry written at the outset of Hopkins's creative maturity. What we have at the close of 'That Nature is a Heraclitean Fire' is not an exact formula of faith but rather an arduous testimony of future hope made from within the disorderliness of individual history. The abruptness with which the testimony is offered is integral to Hopkins's meaning.

The ending to 'That Nature is a Heraclitean Fire' appears all the more unique and surprising when seen against Hopkins's reflections on death and judgement in his spiritual prose. Here, God's action in relation to death and judgement could seem to Hopkins troublingly uncertain. Notes for a meditation he made in 1884 on the New Testament parable of the proud Pharisee and repentant tax collector are full of anxiety on this score:

> This one incident, which lasted perhaps but a few minutes, is all we hear. In that short time all was done, one man put in to the way of salvation; the other, as wd. seem, of eternal ruin. There is then a suddenness about the story and the suddenness seems rather to terrify than to comfort, as if the way of God were full of incalculable hurricanes and reverses, in an instant building up and in the same casting down, making it seem better (which God forbid) to live recklessly and trust to a single hearty act of sorrow than

to toil at prayers and mortifications which a breath of pride may in one fatal instant shatter and bring to nothing.[63]

The worry here is of being found on the wrong side of the story, as one who toils at spiritual observances that provide no guarantee of final safety; it is the fear of the unknown in God's action. The same fear recurs in much of Hopkins's later poetry. As the next chapter will discuss, there are likewise parts of Hopkins's later poetry in which heaven cannot be comprehended, whether it figures as impassive obstruction – in 'To seem the stranger lies my lot, my life', the complaint is of 'dark heaven's baffling ban' (l. 12) – or as violent adversary: in 'Not, I'll not, carrion comfort', there is wonderment at 'The héro whose héaven-handling flúng me, fóot tród | Me' (ll. 12–13). 'That Nature is a Heraclitean Fire', by contrast, does not attempt to understand what heaven is like, but only the transformation that it requires. The effort is to realise how the future life stands to human experience. Images of shipwreck and safety (such as that of the 'foundering deck') give the impression of heaven as a haven, a refuge from life's struggle, with eternity seen in opposition to mortality. Yet the sheerness of the contrast subsides at the poem's last, in a fate which is not a delivery from the trouble and effort of ordinary life, but rather its perfection.

Hopkins's own life came to an end on 8 June 1889. His death followed a short illness, resulting from typhoid fever. Having received the final blessing and absolution, his last words, at least as reported in his obituary, were 'I am so happy, I am so happy.'[64] Writing to one of Hopkins's oldest friends a few days afterwards, the happiness his mother imagined for him was to have 'begun that higher life of which this is but a shadow or a symbol'.[65] Her son, when alive, would surely not have disagreed with this notion of the hereafter, but it is equally certain that his poetry stands differently to it, at once more emphatic in the sense of what finite reality reveals of God, and less convinced that life's end in death and judgement will not be its rupture. Of course the comparison is not an equal one, given how far the circumstance of Kate Hopkins's letter requires the more conventional sentiment. But her son's poetry too shares in conventional impressions of the last things, not least, as the next chapter suggests, in being absorbed with the psychological rhetoric of hellfire familiar to Jesuit tradition. 'That Nature is a Heraclitean Fire' is in this sense a prodigious exception. For Hopkins's poetry to see beyond the terror of final ends, ends both individual and general, required that his originality be at its most strenuous.

CHAPTER 6

Heaven and Hell

Hopkins's early reputation was as a writer ahead of his time, belonging more truly among the moderns than the Victorians – an idea of the poet best epitomised by F. R. Leavis's pairing of Hopkins with T. S. Eliot and Ezra Pound in *New Bearings in English Poetry* (1932). He is now more likely to be compared to writers of his own period. As Finn Fordham says, however, the 'historicizing turn' in the study of Hopkins 'can turn Hopkins into an effect and a symptom rather than a cause'.[1] According to Fordham, 'it also underestimates the skill and daring with which the modernist critics energetically promoted Hopkins' importance and it unintentionally dehistoricizes his impact on modernist criticism and on subsequent poetry.'[2] Affinities with modernist writers are still worth contemplating. One such affinity even coincides with a shared biographical context. Among the points of connection that exist between Hopkins and James Joyce, whom Anthony Burgess believed in their innovations of literary style 'pursued the same end out of the same temperament', is that they knew several of the same institutions and personalities: Joyce began his studies at University College Dublin, where Hopkins was Professor of Greek and Latin Literature, less than a decade after the latter's death; in his earlier schooling, Joyce had also been taught by Jesuits well known to Hopkins, including John Conmee, rector of Clongowes Wood College when Joyce was a student there, who makes several appearances in Joyce's fiction, most notably at the start of the 'Wandering Rocks' episode of *Ulysses* (1922), and Joseph Darlington, Hopkins's colleague at University College, upon whom Joyce likely based the dean of studies in *A Portrait of the Artist as a Young Man* (1916).[3]

'You allude to me as a Catholic', Joyce is reported to have once remarked; 'you ought to allude to me as a Jesuit.'[4] There are many suggestive glimpses in Joyce's writing of the Catholic and Jesuit culture Hopkins inhabited, albeit rendered in a manner analogous to the fashion in which Buck Mulligan understands Stephen Dedalus in *Ulysses*: 'you have the cursed jesuit strain in you, only it's injected the wrong way'.[5] One such glimpse is of the vividly material understanding of hell current in Catholic belief of this period. 'Sin, remember, is a twofold enormity', declares the Jesuit preacher Father Arnall in *Portrait of the Artist*: 'It is a base consent to the promptings of our corrupt nature, to the lower instincts, to that which is gross and beastlike; and it is also a turning away from the counsel of our higher nature, from all that is pure and holy, from Holy God Himself.'[6] For this reason, Arnall explains, those damned to hell can expect separate physical and spiritual punishments. First, 'the blood seethes and boils in the veins, the brains are boiling in the skull, the heart in the breast glowing and bursting, the bowels a redhot mass of burning pulp, the tender eyes flaming like molten balls.'[7] What is worse, however, is affliction of mind: 'ever to be shut off from the presence of God ... ever to have the conscience upbraid one, the memory enrage, the mind filled with darkness and despair, never to escape'.[8]

Schooled in the same Ignatian practice of 'composition of place' to which Joyce has Arnall subscribe, Hopkins did not so clearly divide hell's punishments. At the end of 'I wake and feel the fell of dark, not day', the choking self-enclosure described by the poem is likened to the anguish of the damned, anguish that appears at once mental and physical:

$$\text{Selfyeast of spirit} \begin{cases} \text{a dull dough sours} \\ \text{my selfstuff sours. I see} \end{cases}$$

$$\text{The lost are like this, and their} \begin{cases} \text{scourge} \\ \text{loss} \end{cases} \text{to be}$$

$$\begin{cases} \text{As I am mine, their sweating selves;} \\ \text{Their sweating selves as I am mine, but worse.} \end{cases} \quad \text{(ll. 12–14)}$$

These lines – which have several uncancelled variants – do not collapse the standard scholastic distinction between the *pœna damni*, the pain of separation from God felt by lost souls, and the *pœna sensus*, their material torment, but they do render the distinction less entire, disturbing the tidiness of the traditional scheme. Where Joyce's Arnall distinguishes between forms of suffering in hell, Hopkins's 'sweating selves' lends the inner penalty of the damned the fleshly quality of its external twin: the agony of isolated selfhood is given bodily description, as if it too is able to know the heat of hellfire. Rather than delineate varieties of punishment, as does Joyce's Arnall, Hopkins's poem has the suffering of the lost appear appallingly whole.

This vision of hell is especially shocking because offered with a clarity absent from the rest of the poem. Running clear of the clotted syntax of 'Selfyeast of spirit a dull dough sours', the closing sentence of 'I wake and feel' in its later version is newly lucid: 'I see | The lost are like this, and their scourge to be | As I am mine, their sweating selves; but worse.' The earlier version reads 'Their sweating selves as I am mine, but worse'. Hopkins altered his word order in revision and introduced a semicolon in place of a comma ('As I am mine, their sweating selves; but worse'), making it less likely that the affliction the poem describes would be mistaken as 'worse' than hell. What is 'worse' in the revised version is clearly the fate of the lost. If this comparison with the fate of lost souls is evidence of emotional strain, the poem's ultimate emphasis is on the difference between these states, so that as much as the final line is anguished, there is in 'but worse' a last-ditch confidence in the human will and in the likelihood of divine relief, a confidence which is all the more notable because it can sometimes appear out of reach elsewhere in the 'terrible sonnets'.

Hopkins realised that to lend physical form to the abstract pains of hell, as does 'I wake and feel', involved a departure from convention: writing of hell, he complained of the inability of 'our scholastics' to 'see that there is an intellectual imagination', comprising a unity between spirit and matter.[9] It is a remark that suggests Hopkins's frustration with the abstract and syllogistic nature of the scholastic theology he was taught. The manner of 'I wake and feel' in its conception of hell could not be more different, and yet here too doctrinal truth is of primary concern. Geoffrey Hill proposes that the distinction entered by the final line of 'I wake and feel' is in one sense 'a doctrinal formality, a matter of status; there is a touch of forensic dryness in the placing of that semi-colon; a dryness which is as significant as the extremity of suffering.'[10] Such scrupulousness is familiar to Hopkins's imagining of heaven and hell in his poetry, in which startlingly physical depictions of mental suffering in hell exist alongside rectitude about the future lot of those still to face God's judgement; the same combination of reserve and concreteness can also be seen in Hopkins's attempts to conceive of the glory of heaven.

Little has been written about notions of the afterlife in Hopkins's poetry, probably because it is not one of his main subjects. Indeed, the relative infrequency of references to heaven and hell in the poems has itself been proposed to show that '[Hopkins's] mind, for all its absorption with the divine and the highest things, is of the earth.'[11] This is perhaps to be expected from a poet who once expressed how 'my life is determined by the Incarnation down to most of the details of the day', a determination that seems more often to have allowed the things of the earth to be viewed sacramentally, as tokens of divine presence in the ordinary ('the details of the day'), than it led to thoughts of the final salvation Hopkins believed Christ makes possible.[12] What is more surprising is that when impressions of the future life do appear in his poetry, they tend to mark the distance Hopkins saw between created and divine orders, particularly in representing the deep sinfulness and fallenness of humanity in its alienation from God. Hopkins's writing on the future life exists at a remove from the perception of an intimate connection between creation and divine grace on which his nature poetry, in particular, rests; it conceives of divine reality more extrinsically to human existence than is usually believed possible for Hopkins. What this shows is that the poet's adherence to his personal metaphysic does not make the spiritual awareness of his poetry single or unvarying. To consider the poet's view of the future life, I suggest, is to see the asceticism that existed alongside the sacramentalism of his mature vision, and to recognise that this was more than a product of the bleakness of parts of his later work, instead appearing as a constant factor in all of his writing.

Warning of Hell: 'Spelt from Sibyl's Leaves'

The stringency in Hopkins's vision of the future world was not inevitable or automatic. Others who knew similar religious contexts found ways to alleviate their eschatological anxiety. According to Geoffrey Rowell, purgatorial devotion grew increasingly important to nineteenth-century Roman Catholics, providing them with a means by which 'the sharp contrast between heaven and hell could be made less harsh'.[13] Hopkins, however, appears to have had little desire to lessen this disparity, either in his spiritual writing or in his poetry. Indeed, his poetry's insistence on the physical reality of the mental suffering known in hell helps underline the difference between eternal fates. Hopkins's contemporary Henry James Coleridge, great-nephew to the poet, and the editor who rejected 'The Wreck of the Deutschland' from publication in a Jesuit magazine, wrote in a tract on purgatory of how 'the discord and savage tumult of Hell reflect the internal miseries of the souls there, preying upon themselves, and as it were tearing themselves to pieces'.[14] In Hopkins, internal and external pains of hell are brought together yet more nearly. 'I wake and feel', in this respect, is not a one-off; there is also the close of 'Spelt from Sibyl's Leaves', which I began to discuss in the previous chapter:

> Now her áll in twó flocks, twó folds – bláck, white; ‖ ríght, wrong;
>   réckon but, réck but, mínd

But thése two; wáre of a wórld where bút these || twó tell, éach
   off the óther; of a ráck
Where, selfwrung, selfstrung, sheathe- and shelterless, || thoúghts agaínst
   thoughts ín groans grínd.

                                          (ll. 12–14)

It is just possible that 'selfwrung, selfstrung' describes intellectual suffering, and that 'sheathe- and shelterless' names its physical equivalent, even if 'wrung' and 'strung' seem material actions, and 'sheathe- and shelterless' appear to relate more than the literal absence of home or habitat. But if these types of pain remain distinct in the opening to the final line, they fuse in its climax, as 'thoúghts agaínst thoughts ín groans grínd' locates the mind's sensation of hell's pains, in writing that is strenuous not only because weightily alliterative across the expanse of the eight-stress line but also because awkward to voice: 'By putting the emphasis on the *in*', Susan Stewart observes, 'Hopkins makes us push down the emphasis on the second *thoughts* and *groans*, forcing down our voices and foregrounding the carrying over of sound from *in* to *grind*.'[15]

Unlike 'I wake and feel', 'Spelt from Sibyl's Leaves' is a poem whose imparting of material form to mental agony occurs in the attempt to warn and counsel, even if the object of its address (which is perhaps the poet's self, or else perhaps others) is not made explicit. The caution offered in the final lines involves the narrowing of what was already binary: 'Spelt from Sibyl's Leaves' speaks of a reduction to 'twó flocks, twó folds', but it ends more singly, telling only of hell. In offering this warning, Hopkins desires to keep heaven in mind: the final lines can be said to insist on the necessity of choice in our actions as the means to safeguarding our salvation. Yet it is also the case that at its close, the accent of the poem is firmly on lost humanity and makes no mention of an alternative. Hopkins concentrates on the danger to be avoided in the future life rather than on any hope to be embraced.

In this, Hopkins's poem shares ground with the rhetoric that Joyce has Arnall deploy in *Portrait of the Artist*. Much is owed in both cases to the tradition of Roman Catholic preaching on hell that developed out of the Counter-Reformation, in which preachers (as John Casey observes) 'wanted to give people an imaginative sense how the other world was as real as this one, and how the sinner might find himself precipitated with terrifying unexpectedness into it'.[16] What is unique to 'Spelt from Sibyl's Leaves' is that the insistent newness of 'selfwrung' and 'selfstrung' adver-tises that the poem's sense of this other world engages a special conception of selfhood, the same conception of selfhood which earlier, in an untitled poem of 1877, had led to the declaration that

> As kingfishers catch fire, dragonflies draw flame;
>   As tumbled over rim in roundy wells
>   Stones ring; like each tucked string tells, each hung bell's
> Bow swung finds tongue to fling out broad its name;
> Each mortal thing does one thing and the same:
>   Deals out that being indoors each one dwells;
>   Selves – goes its self; *myself* it speaks and spells,
> Crying *What I do is me: for that I came.*   (ll. 1–8)

These lines provide a supreme illustration of what Patricia Ball identifies as the guiding principle of Hopkins's observation of the natural world: 'Everything is to be looked at with the expectancy that it will speak its nature to the receptive eye.'[17] All the elements in creation are seen to be united in proclaiming their own utter distinctiveness, what Hopkins elsewhere named as their 'selfbeing'.[18] The poem's intense patterning in alliteration, assonance, and other kinds of verbal chiming is shaped to the same end, directed to the quality Hopkins held to be essential in art: 'what I call inscape, that is species or individually-distinctive beauty of style'.[19] In effect, the close of 'Spelt from Sibyl's Leaves' turns the process of individuation described in the 1877 sonnet inside out. Here too Hopkins emphasises the stress of self, in verbs that habitually designate the pressure and strain of being in his poetry ('wrung' and 'strung'), but with the difference that selfhood is now stripped of any awareness of others – or, which is yet more awful, of God. The self no longer 'Deals out', sharing in a unity of action, but is instead held captive to itself, existing in cramped isolation.

The final line of 'Spelt from Sibyl's Leaves' condenses what Hopkins had earlier realised in private meditation notes which discuss the nature of the deprivation experienced by those in hell: that in the situation of the lost, 'the understanding open wide like an eye, towards truth in God, towards light, is confronted by that scape, that act of its own, which blotted out God and so put blackness in the place of light … Against these acts of its own the lost spirit dashes itself like a caged bear and is in prison, violently instresses them and burns, stares into them and is the deeper darkened.'[20] He wrote elsewhere that the fall of Lucifer resulted from 'dwelling on his own beauty, an instressing of his own inscape'.[21] The use of a similar language of selfhood at the close of 'Spelt from Sibyl's Leaves' reveals the symmetry that exists between Hopkins's conception of present time and his notion of future time, for the departure from God's presence in this poem does not occur in an entirely unfamiliar pattern but rather follows a distorted and excessive version of principles of being the poet so cherished that he invented for them a technical language all of his own.

The way the picturing of hell in 'Spelt from Sibyl's Leaves' is framed by Hopkins's distinctive theories of self and being may appear to place it at a distance from the coarse image of eternal suffering propounded in the Jesuit preaching of his day and earlier, preaching of the type Joyce has Arnall undertake in *Portrait of the Artist*, which has its roots in the Counter-Reformation, when Roman Catholicism – as Casey remarks – 'developed a rhetoric and psychology that aimed at bringing hell home to the faithful in the most dramatic manner possible'.[22] Yet 'Spelt from Sibyl's Leaves' has more in common with this tradition than we might assume. The modernist theologian George Tyrrell in an essay of 1899 criticised the 'extravagance' of notions of hell then promoted in Roman Catholic writing and preaching, complaining that 'the particular gratification that certain minds get out of the *materiality* of the fire can only be accounted for by a nervous dread of in any way making the doctrine mysterious, or removing it from the jurisdiction of common-sense – of that semi-rationalism, which delights to express and explain things spiritual in terms of matter and motion, of chemistry and mechanics'.[23] Even with the distinctive slant given by Hopkins's concern with the 'intellectual imagination' and with principles of being, the materiality of hell in 'Spelt from Sibyl's Leaves' should be understood within similar terms: as part of a commitment to the physical definition of spiritual realities. Indeed, the final lines of 'Spelt from Sibyl's Leaves' have their own share of 'extravagance', as an elaboration of what was already elaborate, a refinement of the traditional scheme of eternal punishment so that it corresponds with a unique theory of intellectual apprehension.

Handled by Heaven

Perhaps the difference in spiritual awareness seen between Hopkins's nature poetry and his writing on hell is inevitable given their respective subjects. Yet what underlies conceptions of hell in Hopkins's poetry is not reserved to these conceptions alone: the way Hopkins describes heaven's action actually implies a similar sense of the fracture between divine and created orders. Alphonsus Liguori, the eighteenth-century saint whose conservative eschatology is said by Jill Muller to have influenced Hopkins, remarked on the difference of heavenly from earthly life:

We are unable to understand the joys of paradise, because we have no conception but of the joys of this earth. If horses were capable of reasoning, and they knew that their master had prepared a grand banquet, they would imagine that it could consist of nothing else but of good hay, oats, and barley, because horses have no notion of food except such as this. Even thus do we form notions of the joys of paradise.[24]

There is a different emphasis here to the typological expectation had by Kate Hopkins on the occasion of her eldest son's death, cited in the previous chapter: that this life stands to the future life as 'a shadow or a symbol'. What must by definition be the case – that the next world is hidden from this world – hardens into the perception that the future life utterly transcends human understanding. Liguori comprehends that what we take to be the signs of the future life can in truth only be its deception. Behind his reserve about heavenly bliss stands the realisation of the gulf between nature and grace that Hopkins heard so much about in the spiritual texts used as refectory reading in the course of his Jesuit training. For many of these texts, as one baldly states, 'The world is a cheat: it sells its glory, which is nothing, at a high rate.'[25]

This denigration of the worldly lay opposite to the impulse which motivated most nineteenth-century hopes for the future life, which tend to be characterised by the reunion of friends and loved ones, in what Phillipe Ariès terms 'a transference of the emotional demands of earthly life'.[26] The relief provided by heaven was seen to be as much from the vexation of life as from the danger of sin, a view of celestial glory readily apparent in the final stanza of a poem by Manley Hopkins, Gerard's father, entitled simply 'Rest':

> 'Vision of Peace!' we seek thy pearly gate,
> 　　Eternal Rest; profound in God's great love.
> Thirsting, and oft in tears thy children wait,
> 　　Such restless pilgrims here. Lift us above
> Earth's fretful joys and tears. Give us true rest,
> 　　Tranquil, unbroken, on the Saviour's breast![27]

This is an entirely comforting vision of heaven, which is understood by Manley Hopkins in reassuringly human terms. His son's poetry does not imagine heaven directly. Instead, it describes marks of heaven in the world. There are occasions when heaven's action is seen to be gentle, notably in 'Epithalamion' (1888), in which water 'with heavenfallen freshness down from moorland still brims' (l. 39), and also in 'To what serves Mortal Beauty?' (1885), which desires that the admiration of 'heaven's sweet gift' (l. 13) be properly directed. More generally, though, a classical reserve about future bliss is punctuated by a startlingly concrete sense of how heaven's action is felt in this life, as against the life to come. In several poems the tokens of heaven in the world are known with a violence that portends their exceptionality. Hopkins's sense of this violence is the product of a sharp distinction between the gift of grace and the place of its reception; it is rooted in the same profound awareness of human corruption seen in the view of hell's pains given at the close of 'Spelt from Sibyl's Leaves'.

We see the rarity of heaven's action especially vividly in 'Not, I'll not, carrion comfort'. In this poem, cited in full in Chapter 2, there is wonder at 'The héro whose héaven-handling flúng me, fóot tród | Me' (ll. 12–13). Such an assailant cannot be the personified 'Despair' of the poem's octave. His nature is as uncertain as that of the divine adversary seen in the most important of the poem's several biblical inspirations, Genesis 32.24–30, in which Jacob wrestles night-long with a being at Peniel, an Angel of the Lord whose identity here and elsewhere in the Old Testament is mysterious, but who has often been thought (as Hopkins's High Church mentor Henry Parry Liddon observed) to constitute 'not direct appearances of a Person in the Godhead, but Self-manifestations of God through a created being'.[28] The adversary imagined in 'Not, I'll not, carrion comfort', who is described as a 'héro', appears more clearly to be the person of Christ; Christ's heroism was precious to the poet, of course, not least in the military form discussed in Chapter 3. But the revisions Hopkins made to line 12 of the poem, turning it steadily heavenward, from 'hero whose force there flung me' to 'hero whose heavenforce flúng me', before arriving finally at 'héro whose héaven-handling flúng me',[29] increase the strangeness of the encounter in a way that mirrors the paradox of the identity of Jacob's assailant, the man or angel of whom Jacob is able to say 'I have seen God face to face, and my life is preserved.'[30] As with Jacob at Peniel, the realisation that the encounter has been with God occurs only after the event. As is also true of the biblical story, the particular nature and terms of the encounter remain enigmatic, with 'héaven-handling' implying the other-worldliness of God's action. To hold in the hands can be an act of intimacy, or at least of nearness, but 'handling' here also has the sense of a person managed or manipulated as if more remotely, in this case on unequal terms: that the 'handling' is by 'héaven' works to emphasise the verticality of the relation the poem describes.

As Hopkins would have received it from Aquinas, the theocentric conception of heaven emphasises the beatific vision to be an act of intellectual understanding in which 'the face-to-face vision of the divine essence cannot be an act of bodily sight, for it is enjoyed even now by angels, who are pure spirits, and by blessed souls separated from their bodies'.[31] Hopkins in his poetry is less concerned with the future beatific vision than with heaven as a force or energy in the present. When heaven is mentioned, it is usually to make clear a sharp distinction between this world and the next: to speak of deeds of heaven is not to speak of heaven itself but rather a way for Hopkins to refer to God's action as impersonal and unreadable. There is rarely here the celebration of Christ manifest in the created order which elsewhere distinguishes his writing. Where heaven is given agency in Hopkins's poetry, holding the power over this life seen in 'Not, I'll not, carrion comfort', it is most often to emphasise the exceptionality of God's presence and action in a world that requires to be denied.

This is true even of 'The Wreck', which here aligns with the trend of Hopkins's poetry generally. In stanza 34 of the poem, Christ in his first coming is described as 'The heaven-flúng, heart-fléshed, máiden-fúrled | Míracle-in-Máry-of-flále' (ll. 267–68). As discussed in the previous chapter, these are lines which retain their verbal delicacy amid the insistent roll of successive compounds. At the same time, 'heaven-flúng' signals the same violence and suddenness later seen in 'Not, I'll not, carrion comfort', which describes being 'flúng' by a divine adversary. The 'flúng' of 'heaven-flúng' in 'The Wreck' is the odd word out in a section of the poem which seeks to assert the generous constancy of Christ's saving exploit, with his first coming described later in the stanza as 'A released shówer, let flásh to the shíre, not a líghtning of fíre hard húrled' (l. 272).

Hopkins usually ascribed the Incarnation with steady origin. He took from Scotus the idea that for Christ to become man was creation's reason and cause: this is what is meant by the declaration early in 'The Wreck' that the divine stress felt on earth comes not from God's bliss, 'Nor first from heaven', but from Christ's sacrificial assumption of human nature (l. 43). Perceiving creation's inherent orientation to divine life, Hopkins developed his sacramental understanding of the natural order. He saw, as the poem later puts it, that 'Heaven and earth are word of, worded by' Christ (l. 230), able to be paired for the fact of drawing their energy from an identical source.

With 'heaven-flúng', by contrast, we arrive at the sense which drove the dominant mode of Roman Catholic theology in Hopkins's day, of a breach between nature and the supernatural, in which the prominence accorded to miracle and prophecy as instruments of God's revelation indicate the extremity needed to overcome the rupture that exists between this world and the next. Christ's assumption of created nature is lent the aspect of sensational rescue and deliverance. The same can be said of the assigning in 'The Wreck' of heavenly character to the mischances of bad weather.

Midway through 'Part the second' Hopkins writes that in hastening the tragedy, 'Storm flákes were scróll-leaved flówers, lily shówers – sweet héaven was astréw in them' (l. 168). If the coinage 'astréw', as noted in the previous chapter, connotes a liberal scattering of God's mercy, this is a scattering that arrives emphatically from above, in dramatically vertical relation, and which needs to be seen alongside a similar reference in 'The Loss of the Eurydice', a poem about a shipwreck that was for Hopkins a more entirely forlorn occurrence than even the wrecking of the *Deutschland*:

> And you were a liar, O blue March day.
> Bright sun lanced fire in the heavenly bay;
>   But what black Boreas wrecked her? he⌐
> Came equipped, deadly-electric,
>
> A beetling baldbright cloud thorough England
> Riding: there did storms not mingle? and
>   Hailropes hustle and grind their
> Heavengravel? wolfsnow, worlds of it, wind there?   (ll. 21–28)

The coinage 'Heavengravel' primarily describes a shower of hail but also renders ominous what a few lines earlier appeared only deceptive, casting the 'heavenly' of 'Bright sun lanced fire in the heavenly bay' as more than simply a property of the sky (this in the sole appearance of the word 'heavenly' in Hopkins's mature poetry).[32] 'Heavengravel' is far from the 'sweet héaven' seen in 'The Wreck'; rather than signalling God's bliss, it hints that bad weather is the bearer of heavenly wrath. The poem does not see the wrecking of the *Eurydice* as an act of divine vengeance, but Hopkins makes a point of observing that the tragedy occurs to God's anxiety, and that it elicits God's sorrow, in that the drowned are not afforded the protection of what, in Hopkins's mind, was God's true Church. It suits Hopkins to have with 'Heavengravel' at least the implication of God's larger concern for the souls of the drowned sailors, in which a product of the skies, a natural phenomenon, carries a hint of what awaits in divine judgement.

The hint is of a judgement that appears impersonal and unfeeling. 'Boreas', in the stanza cited earlier, refers to the Greek god of the North Wind reputed to have wrecked the Persian fleet; it is he who comes with lightning bolts 'deadly-electric', enacting a form of sudden violence – as this and other poems show – which appears to have fascinated Hopkins.[33] By contrast, 'Heavengravel', being a type of rock rather than a person, stands anonymous. The invented word has the awe of Psalm 147 as its likely inspiration – 'He sendeth his crystal like morsels: who shall stand before the face of his cold?' (Douay-Rheims) – but without the realisation of God's personal agency seen in the psalm. In the regular style of Hopkins's noun compounds, 'Heavengravel' is not hyphenated, making it harder to prise its two terms apart, just as the word that follows immediately after – 'wolfsnow' – has the same tightness of association also seen in the Joycean compound that appears close to it in the *OED*, taken from the 'Circe' episode of *Ulysses*: 'Her wolfeyes shining'. Used adjectivally, as in the 'heaven-flúng' of 'The Wreck', 'heaven' is recognisably an active agent; combined with 'gravel' to form a noun, it is more of a blank for being a substance. Thus if 'Heavengravel' is indeed associated with God's heaven, it gives an impression I have been arguing is familiar to Hopkins's poetry: once more, even in physical proximity, tokens of heaven are made to stand for what in the life of God is unreadable and impersonal.

The Cosmology of 'To seem the stranger lies my lot, my life'

'To seem the stranger lies my lot, my life | Among strangers' begins one of the least consoled of Hopkins's 'terrible sonnets'. The opening of 'To seem the stranger' is so unassuaged as to refuse even the temptation to linger over sorrow. The enjambment instead prises apart the plaintive sonority of 'my lot, my life': if for a moment 'my life' looks like a rhetorical flourish, there is a necessary readjustment to register its orientation in chiasmus towards the second line ('my life | Among strangers'). This is not the only way in which the opening reveals fresh shades to its sadness the closer it is looked at. 'The words "To seem the stranger"', as Jane Wright notices, 'may mean "to appear to be a stranger when not really". But they could also mean "to have the feeling of being a stranger," or "to appear to become all the more strange"'.[34] In this most starkly personal of poems, all three possibilities stand in painful contrast to what was Hopkins's own childhood motto: 'To be rather than seem'.[35]

At the close of the poem, these frustrations are given immense and remarkable magnitude. Here is its sestet:

> I am in Ireland now; now Í am at a thírd
> Remove. Not but in all removes I can
> Kind love both give and get. Only what word
>
> Wisest my heart breeds ⎰ baffling heaven's dark ban
> ⎱ dark heaven's baffling ban
> Bars or hell's spell thwarts. ⎰ This to hoard unheard,
> ⎱ Thoughts hoarded unheard
> Heard unhéeded, ⎰ leaves me a lonely began.
> ⎱ [leave]
>
> (ll. 8–14)

Tracing a private and individual anguish, the poem evokes a cosmic geography. Line 12 has an uncancelled variant ('baffling heaven's dark ban'); earlier drafts of the poem also have a different version of this line, which this time was rejected: 'Wisest my breast holds still to bear some ban'. The reference to heaven, then, was added in revision, and of this amendment Daniel A. Harris remarks that 'when Hopkins changed "some ban" to "dark heaven's baffling ban," and thereby ascribed the failure of colloquy to God, he made the most radically heterodox gesture of his poetry'.[36] In fact, the poem's frustration has less to do with an absence of communication with God than with the failure of life to bear fruit; it is written from the same position as the later poem '*Justus quidem tu es, Domine*', with a feeling that one is unable to 'breed one work that wakes' (l. 13). But Harris is right to highlight the significance of the revision. A 'ban' which had been of uncertain origin is by this change given clear attribution, as the work of powers from above whose action is agonisingly hard to fathom.

What of the difference between Hopkins's two alternatives for this revised line, 'baffling heaven's dark ban' and 'dark heaven's baffling ban'? The second alternative was preferred by Bridges for his edition of Hopkins and is the more hopeful of the two word orders. The idea that 'God's providence is dark' (as Hopkins put it in one of his sermons) indicates that divine ways are obscure to human reasoning; this is the sense of 'dark heaven's baffling ban', where what is 'baffling' is the obstruction presented, whereas heaven itself stands mysterious. '[B]affling heaven's dark ban', by contrast, implies that it is heaven that is bewildering, and its action that is hidden or elusive. The decision in editions of Hopkins that do not include variants to prefer 'dark heaven's baffling ban' offers the potential for the incomprehension of divine action to appear natural. The suggestion becomes that God's ways are inherently strange to human understanding, with the consequent implication that his designs may eventually work themselves out, regardless of whether or not one is able to make sense of them.

Of course, even if this version of the line is preferred, the poem's sense of the unknowability of God's will can hardly be said to be comfortable. The 'ban' felt in 'To seem the stranger' comes from heaven, which must by association indicate God, but it remains important that the prohibition is suggested as coming from a place first of all, and only by correspondence from a divine person. The image of 'dark heaven' plays on the meaning of 'heaven' as physical sky, here clouded, as well as on the idea that the realm of God is itself celestial, beyond the visible horizon. In this 'To seem the stranger' has an idea of heaven close to other poems in which Hopkins wrote of eternity. As with 'Heavengravel' in 'The Loss of the Eurydice', for example, 'dark heaven's baffling ban' appears the more remote for not invoking the person of God, but only the location of his kingdom. There is in the poem a profound sense of isolation, something which the celestial geography it draws upon – invoking the heights of heaven and the depths of hell – serves to intensify, for there is a kind of mismatch between the immense firmament conjured in the poem's final lines and the individual heart 'dark heaven' thwarts, a mismatch which the doubling up of adjectives to describe heaven's opposition serves to intensify ('dark heaven's ban' would make different sense but also, in its lack of excess, be less emotionally true). In so cosmic an expanse, the cause which the poem pursues feels small, as if it might easily get lost amid the vastness.

The extremity of the poem's feeling is spectacularly rendered in the closing lines by the direct adjoining of 'dark heaven's baffling ban' or 'baffling heaven's dark ban' to 'hell's spell'. This pairing of heaven and hell offers the form of a cosmic battle between opposed powers without any of their expected hostility; their only apparent difference in respect of the situation described is that heaven thwarts by its remoteness whilst hell appears an active agent. If the internal rhyme of 'hell' and 'spell' is one to which the poet was drawn, carrying here the sense of a struggle with malign spiritual energies that was a large element in his conception of Christ's redemption, the poem's description of hell involves the same eschatological framework seen in its notion of heaven.[37] 'To seem the stranger' is one of several places in his writing where Hopkins's adherence to the reality of the Devil's personal existence demanded by Roman Catholic doctrine took on, if not quite conventionally, the colour of popular imagination, even as he pored over minute theological particulars. Setting itself in competition to the chorus led by Christ, the song of Lucifer, in the fall of the angels, was, Hopkins reflected, 'an incantation: others were drawn in; it became a concert of voices, a concerting of selfpraise, an enchantment, a magic, by which they were dizzied, dazzled, and bewitched'.[38] 'To seem the stranger' has the image of this same war between polar opposites, albeit only in form, in an antithesis it is a mark of the poem's feeling of torpor not to be able to bear out. Casting a 'spell', hell enchants and deceives in a manner like that of Lucifer's song, as if by strategy, with the semblance of Satan's emissaries as the positive entities Hopkins believed them to be.

These emissaries are not identified concretely, meaning that 'hell's spell' might also attach to a different notion of the diabolic, one associated with scholastic theology, in which, as Jeffrey Burton Russell explains, the standard view was that 'evil was privation, lacking any ontological reality in itself'.[39] Duns Scotus, whom Hopkins followed in thinking of Satan's fall as the result of solipsistic pride, was among those to perceive that 'Deficiency or evil in a (created) being comes about by the absence of a perfection that it could actually have.'[40] The diabolic aggressor of 'To seem the stranger' is not named as an actual spirit, but instead identified as a location in an immense cosmology. The effect is to render the oppression of 'hell's spell' more featureless and abstract than it would be otherwise (just as in the case of 'dark heaven' standing for God's providence). As much as the description of 'hell's spell' hinges on Hopkins's vivid awareness of real diabolic presence, then, hell's power is known here by what it prevents rather than by what it causes. In that respect, 'dark heaven's baffling ban' and 'hell's spell' form a true pair, expressing how the absence of perfection in life is the poem's complaint. Both imply the gulf between the eschatological vision of God and the world of the individual believer. The 'terrible sonnets', as discussed in Chapter 2, have as the framework for their frustration and despair a strong expectation that nature and grace are not opposed and that divine presence should ordinarily be known intimately in personal history. That is true of 'To seem the stranger' also, but here the same framework has to share ground with a quite different perception of the relationship between the life of the world and the life of God, in which the afterlife stands for what is unknown and featureless in divine action.

Hell-rook Ranks and Sweet Endings

'To seem the stranger' was written in Dublin, a place Hopkins found uncongenial personally and politically. Commenting on the prominence of the last things in the poetry he wrote there, Jill Muller proposes that in consequence of his personal unhappiness, and influenced by trends in English Roman Catholic writing of the period, 'Hopkins turned increasingly from the empty prospects of this world to eschatological speculation': 'The dark spirituality of the sonnets of desolation flatly denies the incarnationalist message of the earlier Catholic poems.'[41] The symmetry of this view of Hopkins is familiar, for, even if its terms are different, there is the exact transformation ordained here as in older interpretations of Hopkins's vulnerability to the religious doubts of his age, where (according to the most famous of the older interpretations) the dramatic overturning of 'what is, in Victorian poetry, an almost unique sense of the immanence of God in nature and in the human soul' results in a 'shattering experience of the disappearance of God'.[42] It is familiar in another sense, too, in attributing to his writing the same fixed ambition seen in recent studies that assume the coherence of Hopkins's work as a systematic venture, from which, in this case, the later poetry is seen to fall away.

If we allow that the determination of Hopkins's poetry is less single, however, our sense of its progression need not be so rigid. To set the spiritual awareness of Hopkins's 'terrible sonnets' in blunt opposition to his earlier poetry is to constrain each to a single type of insight, existing at a contrary pole from the other, and free of opposed currents of thought. In reality, the spiritual awareness of his poetry is more mixed. A profound incarnationalism exists in tension with a more ascetical sense of spiritual life. In the nature sonnets of 1877, the joyous celebration of nature's variety may have pressed this ascetical sense to the margins of his writing, but it remained always with Hopkins, leaving its trace even in poems which honour the individual attention given to humankind by God.

One such poem is 'The Bugler's First Communion'. Midway through this poem, which is cited in full in Chapter 3, heavenly protection is entreated for the poem's hero to see off the evil powers seen to threaten his virtue:

> Frówning and forefending angel-warder
> Squander the hell-rook ránks sálly to molest him;
> March, kind comrade, abreast him;
> Dress his days to a dexterous and starlight order.   (ll. 17–20)

It has been said that 'hell-rook ránks' signals the difference between life in barracks and 'army field conditions', but the reference seems rather to be to an infernal presence than to stages in military deployment.[43] In their *Catholic Dictionary* of 1884, Hopkins's Oxford friend William Addis and his Dublin colleague Thomas Arnold affirm of the devil and evil spirits that 'Their personal existence is clearly taught', and that, 'Although condemned to the pains of hell immediately after their fall, still from time to time the devil and his angels wander in the air and over the earth.'[44] 'The Bugler's First Communion' has not the caution of the dictionary definition in characterising demonic activity. Emissaries from hell at once military and bird-like in demeanour harass the boy-soldier. It is a strange combination of qualities, but one which leaves little doubt that the danger he faces is held to be an external, ontological reality. Evil does not manifest itself as absence or deficiency, but is instead witnessed as a greedily active presence.

This conception of evil has an inflexibility that others at the time were prepared to leave behind. Speaking of demons in one of his early Roman Catholic sermons, John Henry Newman suggested that 'the present war with evil spirits would seem to be very different from what it was in former ages', for 'they attack a civilised age in a more subtle way than they attack a rude age'. The attack occurs 'not grossly, in some broad temptation, which everyone can understand, but in some refined way they address themselves

to our pride or self-importance, or love of money, or love of ease, or love
of show, or our depraved reason, and thus have really the dominion over
persons who seem at first to be quite superior to temptation'.[45] The dominion held by evil spirits in 'The Bugler's First Communion' by contrast rests
thoroughly 'rude'. There is here a raw trust in the reality of evil spirits upon
which other Roman Catholic converts of the time were keen to improve.

  Not that the poem is all dark. Instead, there exists alongside the fearful
idea of hell's threat a much happier notion of heaven's bliss. A few lines on
from the description of the 'hell-rook ránks', the boy-soldier is described
as 'freshyouth fretted in a bloomfall all portending | That sweet's sweeter
ending; | Realm both Christ is heir to and thére réigns' (ll. 30–33). The
fragility of this continuity between present and future time is the poem's
worry, but that it exists at all – and is indeed able to be given priestly nur-
ture and protection – is a source of delight. There is in these lines a sense
of gradation in the desired movement from earth to heaven, in which the
youth who is already so 'sweet' that he can be wholly identified with this
quality (hence the conversion of an adjective into a noun: 'That sweet') will
become still yet 'sweeter'.

  'In appointing us guardian angels', Hopkins observed in an 1880 sermon,

> God never meant that they should make us proof against all the ills that
> flesh is heir to … but he meant them, accompanying us through this world
> of evil and mischance, sometimes warding off its blows and buffets, some-
> times leaving them to fall, always to be leading us to a better; which bet-
> ter world, my brethren, when you have reached and with your own eyes
> opened look back on this you will see a work of wonderful wisdom in the
> guidance of your guardian angel.[46]

The declaration becomes more generous and hopeful as it proceeds, and
in the anadiplosis of the 'better world' following from our being led 'to a
better' in this world is conceived a striking reciprocity between the lives
known on earth and in heaven. Equally, though, this reciprocity is prefaced by the same darker conception of a 'world of evil and mischance', to
which, in 'The Bugler's First Communion', God's angels are sent as special
envoys, dispatched to hostile territory. In both sermon and poem, there is
the mixed insight Hopkins has only rarely been allowed in recent criticism
determined to make of his thought a full edifice.

  The same point can be made in respect of 'Felix Randal', another poem
in which disparate impressions of eternal life reveal the shifting nature of
Hopkins's spiritual awareness. In that poem, it is said that the sick man 'cursed
at first, but mended | Being anointed and all; though a heavenlier heart began
some | Mónths éarlier, since Í had our swéet repríeve and ránsom | Téndered

to him' (ll. 5–8). The sacrament offered by the priest is Felix's 'repríeve and ránsom': Christ's sacrifice makes satisfaction for his sin and pays the price of redemption. Sweetening the doctrinal language of salvation, however, is not only the idiomatic casualness of 'Being anointed and all', but also 'heavenlier'. The adjective allows for degrees of heavenliness; it also makes apparent that the final end of the life with which the poem is concerned will involve the perfecting of a process already begun in the present, and not its rupturing.

'I find within my professional experience now a good deal of matter to write on', Hopkins told Bridges of 'The Handsome Heart'.[47] The turn to professional experience made in 'Felix Randal' and 'The Bugler's First Communion' inspired Hopkins to emphasise continuity between this life and the next that is rare for his poetry to imagine. Even here, however, the continuity is only partial. Elsewhere, the tokens of heaven in the world are known even less consolingly, in a departure from what is usually taken to constitute the tenor of Hopkins's writing. James Finn Cotter comments that 'For Hopkins, Christ stands on this side of time, with man in history, one with the world he made and redeemed': 'Christ in glory is not removed from men, but linked now more closely than was ever possible in his earthly existence … In his sermons and poetry, Hopkins insisted on the intimacy of divine life, its saturation of everyday living.'[48] The originality of Hopkins's incarnational awareness dominates our perception of his work. But it would be a mistake to think that Hopkins was wholly relieved of the ascetical disposition adopted by the spiritual writers to which as a Jesuit he was exposed, with their continual refrain that 'True tranquillity of mind cannot be obtained but by a contempt of the world and conquest over ourselves.'[49] His sacramental vision of creation was seldom pure or complete. The ascetical awareness evident in the stark advice given to a friend in 1868 went deep and was never entirely supplanted: 'Until you prefer God to the world and yourself you have not made the first step.'[50]

The fluctuations in Hopkins's spiritual and theological awareness are especially apparent in the later poetry. Seen against the pattern of work produced in the early part of his poetic maturity, the poems Hopkins wrote after he left Wales would seem failures in a project of synoptic understanding. Allowed a different perspective and ambition, they witness to Hopkins's interest in the promise and difficulty of human striving for God in day-to-day life. The unevenness in their thought is less the defeat of a system than a manifestation of the variety in Hopkins that his poetry of religious experience serves to make prominent.

Notes

Introduction

1. Robert Bridges, *Selected Letters of Robert Bridges*, ed. by Donald E. Stanford, 2 vols. (Newark: University of Delaware Press, 1983), I, 186.
2. Elizabeth Bishop, 'Gerard Manley Hopkins: Notes on Timing in His Poetry' (1934), in *Prose*, ed. by Lloyd Schwartz (London: Chatto & Windus, 2011), pp. 468–74 (p. 468).
3. *CW*, II, 813.
4. *LPM*, p. 348.
5. Elizabeth Bishop, 'Efforts of Affection: A Memoir of Marianne Moore' (c. 1969), in *Prose*, pp. 117–40 (p. 140).
6. *CW*, I, 362.
7. *CW*, III, 423.
8. *CW*, I, 317.
9. Elsie Elizabeth Phare, *The Poetry of Gerard Manley Hopkins: A Survey and Commentary* (Cambridge: Cambridge University Press, 1933), p. 129.
10. See Martin Dubois, 'The *Month* as Hopkins Knew It', *Victorian Periodicals Review*, 43 (2010), 296–308.
11. *CW*, I, 252.
12. Jude V. Nixon, '"Goldengrove unleaving": Hopkins' "Spring and Fall," Christina Rossetti's "Mirrors of Life and Death," and the Politics of Inclusion', *Victorian Poetry*, 43 (2005), 473–84 (p. 477).
13. *J&P*, pp. 253–54.
14. *CW*, I, 357.
15. Norman H. MacKenzie, *Hopkins* (Edinburgh: Oliver and Boyd, 1968), p. 10.
16. *CW*, II, 681.
17. *CW*, I, 306.
18. *CW*, II, 813.
19. *CW*, I, 494.

20. Confession numbers are recorded each year in *Letters and Notices*, the in-house Jesuit publication. During Hopkins's first year in Liverpool, 1880, a total of 72,810 confessions were heard. In the year of his departure for Dublin, 1884, this number had risen to 87,053. Issues of *Letters and Notices* are held at the Archives of the British Province of the Society of Jesus at Farm Street, London (*Archivum Britannicum Societatis Iesu*). Other details are taken from John McDermott, 'Hopkins in Liverpool', in *Hopkins' Lancashire: Sesquicentennial Essays*, ed. by John McDermott (Wigan: North West Catholic History Society, 1994), pp. 19–25.

21. *CW*, II, 942. On Hopkins's work in Ireland, see the editorial introduction to *CW*, VII, 23–34.

22. *CW*, I, 273.

23. *CW*, I, 502.

24. A remark quoted by Katharine Tynan, *Memories* (London: Eveleigh Nash & Grayson, 1924), p. 155.

25. Anon., 'Father Gerard Hopkins', *Letters and Notices*, 20 (1890), 173–79 (p. 174).

26. I. A. Richards, 'Gerard Hopkins', *Dial* (1926), repr. in *Gerard Manley Hopkins: The Critical Heritage*, ed. by Gerald Roberts (London: Routledge, 1987), pp. 140–46 (pp. 143–44). See for the opposing view, e.g. John Pick, *Gerard Manley Hopkins: Priest and Poet* (London: Oxford University Press, 1942).

27. R. K. R. Thornton, *Gerard Manley Hopkins: The Poems* (London: Edward Arnold, 1973), p. 10.

28. Isobel Armstrong, in her landmark study *Victorian Poetry: Poetry, Poetics and Politics* (London: Routledge, 1993; repr. 1996), observes in Hopkins's poetry an effort to expound theories of stress and Being first outlined in his 1868 notes on Parmenides. According to Armstrong, Hopkins's attempt to find in language a bulwark against the Paterian philosophy of flux is ill-fated, for a poetic theory based upon 'the authority of the Word made flesh through the incarnation of Christ', which requires the absolute unity of word and thing, unravels when Hopkins attempts to put it into practice: 'the frantic, hysterical attempt to fix meaning is the very cause of its dissolution' (pp. 420, 435).

29. Most significant here is the work of Daniel Brown, whose *Hopkins' Idealism: Philosophy, Physics, Poetry* (Oxford: Clarendon Press, 1997) establishes the significance of Hopkins's undergraduate encounters with philosophical Idealism as well as his awareness of the new energy physics coming into prominence around the mid-century. Brown's compelling revision of our familiar impression of Hopkins's intellectual life also attributes the philosophical vision of his poetry with logical consistency and unifying principles; he has written elsewhere of Hopkins's effort to determine 'a systematic understanding of the world' (*Gerard Manley Hopkins* [Tavistock: Northcote House, 2004],

p. 104). By this account, Hopkins's 1868 notes on Pre-Socratic philosophy constitute 'an imaginative and syncretic metaphysic which provides the master discourse for his later writings in theology and poetry' (*Hopkins' Idealism*, viii). Other recent commentators who also argue for the comprehensiveness of Hopkins's vision include Philip A. Ballinger, *The Poem as Sacrament: The Theological Aesthetic of Gerard Manley Hopkins* (Louvain: Peeters Press, 2000), and Bernadette Waterman Ward, *World as Word: Philosophical Theology in Gerard Manley Hopkins* (Washington, DC: Catholic University of America Press, 2002).

30. Helen Vendler, 'I have not lived up to it', *London Review of Books* (3 April 2014), 13–18 (p. 14).

31. William James, *The Varieties of Religious Experience*, ed. by Matthew Bradley (Oxford: Oxford University Press, 2012), p. 31.

32. Philip Endean, S.J., 'The Spiritual Exercises', in *The Cambridge Companion to the Jesuits*, ed. by Thomas Worcester (Cambridge: Cambridge University Press, 2008), pp. 52–67 (p. 53).

33. Ignatius of Loyola, *Spiritual Exercises*, trans. by Charles Seager (London: Charles Dolman, 1847), p. 14. This is the twentieth of the so-called Annotations placed by Ignatius at the outset of his book. Hopkins in 1869 received a copy of the *Spiritual Exercises* in the Latin translation of the Spanish autograph text which had been published by Johann Philipp Roothaan in 1835. Seager's translation is of the authorised Latin version of the *Spiritual Exercises* which had until then been in wide use, but it also takes account of Roothaan's work on the Spanish autograph text.

34. Geoffrey Hill, 'What you look hard at seems to look hard at you', Oxford Professor of Poetry lecture, 6 May 2014, www.english.ox.ac.uk/news-events/regular-events/professor-poetry [accessed 21 September 2014].

35. Hill, 'What you look hard at seems to look hard at you'.

36. Philip Endean, S.J., 'Christian Spirituality and the Theology of the Human Person', in *The Blackwell Companion to Christian Spirituality*, ed. by Arthur Holder (Oxford: Blackwell, 2005), pp. 223–39 (p. 233).

37. Ballinger, p. 233.

38. Carlo Ginzburg, 'Morelli, Freud and Sherlock Holmes: Clues and Scientific Method', *History Workshop*, 9 (1980), 5–36 (p. 21).

39. Ginzburg, p. 21.

40. Notable studies on the latter include Walter J. Ong, S.J., *Hopkins, the Self, and God* (Toronto: University of Toronto Press, 1986); David Anthony Downes, *The Ignatian Personality of Gerard Manley Hopkins* (Lanham: University Press of America, 1990); and Maria R. Lichtmann, *The Contemplative Poetry of Gerard Manley Hopkins* (Princeton: Princeton University Press, 1989). In Lichtmann's book, contemplation, as opposed to meditation, is proposed as

the dominant mode of Hopkins's writing. One previous study has examined Hopkins and religious experience: Donald Walhout's *Send My Roots Rain: A Study of Religious Experience in the Poetry of Gerard Manley Hopkins* (Athens: Ohio University Press, 1981). Walhout writes as a philosopher, and his interest 'lies wholly with the substance, not the style, of Hopkins's poetry ... The focus is phenomenological, not literary' (p. 4). The effort is to comprehend Hopkins's poetry in relation to the religious believer's 'postcommitment experience of dryness and renewal', in what Walhout calls 'the ENG experience', composed of engagement, nature, and grace (p. 8).

41. *CW*, III, 570–71.

42. *CW*, IV, 311.

43. Dennis Sobolev, *The Split World of Gerard Manley Hopkins: An Essay in Semiotic Phenomenology* (Washington, DC: Catholic University of America Press, 2011), p. 43.

44. See Meredith Martin, *The Rise and Fall of Meter: Poetry and National Culture, 1860–1930* (Princeton: Princeton University Press, 2012), p. 62.

45. *CW*, III, 511.

46. *CW*, IV, 315.

47. James I. Wimsatt, *Hopkins's Poetics of Speech Sound: Sprung Rhythm, Lettering, Inscape* (Toronto: University of Toronto Press, 2006), p. 3; *J&P*, p. 289.

48. *CW*, II, 881.

49. A point made by Harold Bloom in his introduction to *Gerard Manley Hopkins*, ed. by Harold Bloom (New York: Chelsea House, 1986), p. 3. For Hopkins's comment on 'luxuries of poetry', see *CW*, II, 914.

50. *CW*, III, 483.

51. Hilary Fraser, *Beauty and Belief: Aesthetics and Religion in Victorian Literature* (Cambridge: Cambridge University Press, 1986), p. 68.

52. Fraser, p. 99.

53. Ward, *World as Word*, p. 3: 'His philosophy and its outworking in arresting poetry may be sampled in a few lines of "That Nature is a Heraclitean Fire and of the Comfort of the Resurrection"'. The sense that the poetry is primarily occupied with elucidating 'inscape' and 'instress' as concepts is also what causes Hans Urs Von Balthasar to value 'The Wreck of the Deutschland' and 'The Loss of the Eurydice' over other poems in his theological interpretation of Hopkins in *The Glory of the Lord: A Theological Aesthetics*, 7 vols. (Edinburgh: T&T Clark, 1982–91), III (1986), 353–99.

54. Matthew Campbell, *Rhythm and Will in Victorian Poetry* (Cambridge: Cambridge University Press, 1999), p. 189.

55. Peter McDonald, *Sound Intentions: The Workings of Rhyme in Nineteenth-Century Poetry* (Oxford: Oxford University Press, 2012), p. 295.

56. Meredith Martin, 'Hopkins's Prosody', *Hopkins Quarterly*, 38 (2011), 1–30 (p. 3).

57. This notion is what leads J. Hillis Miller to claim that 'Hopkins's linguistic underthought undoes his Christian overthought' in his *The Linguistic Moment: From Wordsworth to Stevens* (Princeton: Princeton University Press, 1985), p. 265.

58. *CW*, IV, 307.

59. *CW*, I, 904.

60. Randall McLeod, 'Gerard Hopkins and the Shapes of His Sonnets', in *Voice, Text, Hypertext: Emerging Practices in Textual Studies*, ed. by Raimonda Modiano, Leroy F. Searle, and Peter Shillingsburg (Seattle: University of Washington Press, 2004), 177–297 (p. 265).

61. McLeod, 'Gerard Hopkins and the Shapes of His Sonnets', p. 265.

62. The comments on 'mastery' are those of Christopher Ricks, speaking in *'How Meet Beauty': An Enquiry into the Current Reputation of Gerard Manley Hopkins*, a radio programme transmitted by the BBC on 23 June 1977; I cite from the transcript given in *Gerard Manley Hopkins: Poetry and Prose*, ed. by Walford Davies (London and Vermont: J. M. Dent, 2002), pp. 218–25 (p. 224).

63. *CW*, II, 914.

64. A. E. Housman, *The Letters of A. E. Housman*, ed. by Archie Burnett, 2 vols. (Oxford: Clarendon Press, 2007), I, 397.

65. T. S. Eliot, *After Strange Gods: A Primer of Modern Heresy* (New York: Harcourt, Brace and Company, 1934), p. 52.

66. T. S. Eliot, 'Religion and Literature' (1935), in *Selected Essays*, 3rd edn (London: Faber and Faber, 1951; repr. 1999), p. 390; *For Lancelot Andrewes: Essays on Style and Order* (London: Faber and Gwyer, 1928), p. 124.

67. Morris Dickstein, 'Is Religious Poetry Possible?' *Literary Imagination*, 2 (2000), 135–51 (p. 137).

68. Dickstein, pp. 136, 143.

69. Michael Symmons Roberts, 'Poetry in a Post-Secular Age', *Poetry Review*, 98 (2008) 69–75 (p. 72).

70. Daniel Karlin, 'Victorian Poetry and the English Poetry Full-Text Database: A Case Study', *Literature Online*, 6 May 2014, http://collections.chadwyck .co.uk/marketing/karlin.jsp [accessed 28 June 2016].

71. Brian Cummings, *The Literary Culture of the Reformation: Grammar and Grace* (Oxford: Oxford University Press, 2002), p. 378.

72. John Henry Newman, *An Essay in Aid of a Grammar of Assent* (London: Burns & Oates, 1870), p. 249.

73. Clark M. Brittain highlights the importance to Hopkins of the Tractarian revival of patristic studies in 'Logos, Creation, and Epiphany in the Poetics of Gerard Manley Hopkins', unpub. PhD thesis, University of Virginia, 1988. I am grateful to Philip Endean for alerting me to Brittain's work.

74. *CW*, I, 204. The fullest description of these studies is provided by Alfred Thomas, S.J., *Hopkins the Jesuit: The Years of Training* (London: Oxford University Press, 1969), pp. 93–97.

75. Tom Muir, 'A May Magnificat? Hopkins and Stonyhurst 1870-84', in *Hopkins' Lancashire*, ed. by McDermott, pp. 27–35 (p. 31).

76. Hopkins was required to argue otherwise in both cases in his defence of theses in natural theology in the Stonyhurst philosophy examination of 1872 (Gonzaga 32:2). Of course, this method of disputation was a test of understanding and skill in argument, not a reflection of actual adherence to one or the other side of the debate.

77. *CW*, IV, 304–5.

78. *CW*, IV, 216.

79. *CW*, II, 619.

80. Newman declined Hopkins's offer to write a commentary: see *CW*, II, 571, 575. The best account of the influence of the *Grammar of Assent* on Hopkins is provided by Ward in *World as Word*, pp. 100–31.

81. Trent Pomplun, 'The Theology of Gerard Manley Hopkins: From John Duns Scotus to the Baroque', *The Journal of Religion*, 95 (2015), 1–34 (p. 33).

82. *CW*, III, 531.

83. The edition of Scotus Hopkins happened upon at Stonyhurst dates from the early sixteenth century and remains in good condition, but it is not easy to interpret. The edition is now held by Heythrop College Library, London. The four volumes are leather bound in two books, with the text in double columns. They were printed by the Venetian printer Gregorio de Gregori in 1514. The other edition of Scotus owned by the English Province in Hopkins's lifetime, which was then kept at St Beuno's, is now also held by Heythrop College Library. It was edited by the Irish Franciscans of St Isidore, Rome, and printed at Lyon in 1639.

84. Christopher Devlin, S.J., 'Scotus and Hopkins', in *S*, pp. 338–51 (p. 338). Most discussions of Hopkins and Scotus take their bearings from Devlin's essay, about which doubts have been raised: see Ballinger's careful chapter on Hopkins and Scotus in *The Poem as Sacrament*, pp. 103–50. Another crucial intervention is Ward, *World as Word*, pp. 158–97. Trent Pomplun suggests that Hopkins 'seems to have been familiar with several arguments found not in the writings of Scotus himself but rather in the baroque disciples of the Subtle Doctor and their Jesuit interlocutors'. He adds: 'Whether Hopkins read such sources directly or knew them by hearsay is difficult to determine' (p. 19).

85. *CW*, III, 531–32.

86. See Joseph J. Feeney, S.J., 'Hopkins' "Failure" in Theology: Some New Archival Data and a New Reevaluation', *Hopkins Quarterly*, 13 (1986–87), 99–114.

87. Pomplun, p. 2.

88. *J&P*, p. 249.

89. The phrase is that of Hopkins's Jesuit contemporary Joseph Rickaby, S.J., in *Scholasticism* (London: Archibald Constable, 1908), p. 43. As Ballinger says, 'The fact may be that the influence was general or simply confirming in nature' (p. 111). Anthony Bischoff, S.J., who was decades at work upon a life of Hopkins, thought that 'The basic attraction to Scotus was that in him Hopkins found a mind akin to his own, a man who delighted, as he did, in bypaths, originality, daring, etc.' (Letter to Christopher Devlin, S.J., 23 July 1948, Gonzaga 55:2; also cited by Ballinger).

90. *S*, p. 129; *CW*, III, 489. On Hopkins's sacramentalism, see especially Jeffrey B. Loomis, *Dayspring in Darkness: Sacrament in Hopkins* (Lewisburg: Bucknell University Press, 1988); Waterman Ward's chapter 'Sacraments and Poetry' in *World as Word*, pp. 131–57; and Ballinger.

91. *CW*, VII, 80.

92. Adrian Grafe, *Gerard Manley Hopkins: la profusion ténébreuse* (Lille: Septentrion, 2003), p. 30. See also more generally on nineteenth-century theological contexts, pp. 29–35.

93. *CW*, I, 84.

94. Philip Endean, S.J., 'The Spirituality of Gerard Manley Hopkins', *Hopkins Quarterly*, 8 (1981), 107–29 (p. 108).

95. *CW*, I, 308.

96. Geoffrey Hill, 'What you look hard at seems to look hard at you'.

97. See Jill Muller, *Gerard Manley Hopkins and Victorian Catholicism: A Heart in Hiding* (New York and London: Routledge, 2003), pp. 37–68; and Maureen Moran, *Catholic Sensationalism and Victorian Literature* (Liverpool: Liverpool University Press, 2007), pp. 231–83. See also Moran's 'The Heart's Censer: Liturgy, Poetry and the Catholic Devotional Revolution', in *Ecstasy and Understanding: Religious Awareness in English Poetry from the Late Victorian to the Modern Period*, ed. by Adrian Grafe (London: Continuum, 2008), pp. 27–45.

98. The spiritual diet at the fashionable Mayfair church at Farm Street, London, where Hopkins spent a few months in 1878, was more ostentatious, but the notice books for the Jesuit church in Oxford, where Hopkins was posted later that year, and at Bedford Leigh, where he was sent the year after, show little more exotic than an occasional procession in honour of the Virgin Mary. The notice books survive in the archives of the British Province of the Society of Jesus at Farm Street, London (*Archivum Britannicum Societatis Iesu*). Pizza's remark appears in 'Hopkins' Counter Stress', *Literature and Theology*, 25 (2011), 47–63 (pp. 51–52).

99. Jonathan Z. Smith, *Imagining Religion: From Babylon to Jonestown* (Chicago and London: University of Chicago Press, 1982), xii.

100. Simon Humphries, 'Hopkins's Silent Men', *ELH*, 77 (2010), 447–76 (p. 448).

1 Bibles

1. *S*, pp. 83; 81. Hopkins's self-deprecation in recounting these difficulties is well conveyed by the revisions to his record of the former incident, made to display the full artlessness of his parishioner's remark: 'After this sermon one of my penitents told me, with great simplicity, that I was not to be named in the same week as Fr. Clare [the Rector and a renowned preacher]. "Well" [I] said "and I will not be named in the same week. But did you hear it all?" He ~~slept during parts of it, he~~ said he did, only that he was sleeping for parts of it' (MS F, fo. 102r, Campion Hall, Oxford).

2. *CW*, II, 522. This comes with reference to the mission Hopkins preached at Maryport in 1882.

3. Anon., 'Father Gerard Hopkins', p. 174.

4. *S*, p. 62.

5. *S*, p. 89.

6. Joseph J. Feeney, S.J., *The Playfulness of Gerard Manley Hopkins* (Aldershot: Ashgate, 2008), p. 169.

7. *CW*, I, 437. The remark about singularity was made by Richard F. Clarke, S.J., in an entry of 1872 in his notes on spiritual meditations (Gonzaga 31:1).

8. The recollection of Hopkins's fellow Jesuit Henry Marchant, a not always reliable source of information on the poet's life, reported in *J&P*, p. 421.

9. *S*, p. 70.

10. *S*, p. 30.

11. *S*, pp. 225–33.

12. *S*, p. 233.

13. *S*, p. 231.

14. *S*, pp. 225–26. This part of the manuscript is full of deletions and revisions, indicating something of the care Hopkins took over his analogy (MS L, fo. 2, Campion Hall, Oxford).

15. Justus George Lawler, *Hopkins Re-Constructed: Life, Poetry, and the Tradition* (New York: Continuum, 1998), p. 227. When the reference is to a translation Hopkins actually encountered, the critical preference tends to be for the Roman Catholic Douay-Rheims Bible, but the contributor of a chapter on Hopkins in the recent *Blackwell Companion to the Bible in English Literature* limits himself to the Anglican King James Version and Coverdale's version of the Psalms in the *Book of Common Prayer* 'as being two of the translations from Scripture with which Gerard Manley Hopkins would have been familiar': see Paul S. Fiddes, 'G. M. Hopkins', in *The Blackwell Companion to the Bible in English Literature*, ed. by Rebecca Lemon, Emma Mason, Jonathan Roberts, and Christopher Rowland (Chichester: Wiley-Blackwell, 2009), pp. 563–76 (p. 575).

16. The first part of Hopkins's Vulgate is held by the Jesuit Archives in Dublin (J11/13). It is signed by him 'Gerardi Manley Hopkins. Octobris xxxi, in vigil, omn. Sanct. MDCCCLXVI'. The Anglican Bible he owned in the period prior to his conversion is kept at the John J. Burns Library at Boston College. See for the latter, James Finn Cotter, 'Hopkins' Notes on the Bible', in *Gerard Manley Hopkins Annual*, 1993, ed. by Michael Sundermeier and Desmond Egan (Omaha: Creighton University Press, 1993), pp. 89–101.

17. *CW*, I, 150. The poem was 'Barnfloor and Winepress'. As one of Hopkins's editors observes, 'Though the epigraph varied a little in Douay … other changes for this reason would have been slight' (*PW*, p. 237).

18. The view of Hopkins's Jesuit contemporary Sydney Fenn Smith, as given in his 'Our English Catholic Bible', *The Month*, 90 (July 1897), 43–62 (p. 47). Smith's view was not unusual. The convert Frederick William Faber's comments on the King James Version, made a few years after he had crossed to Rome, had their fame ensured by being quoted selectively in R. C. Trench's *English, Past and Present* (1855). The King James Version, Faber wrote, 'lives on in the ear like a music that never can be forgotten', yet (and this Trench excluded from his citation) 'who would dream that beauty was better than a blessing?' See *English, Past and Present: Five Lectures* (London: Parker, 1855), p. 30; Trench is citing from the *Dublin Review*, 34 (June 1853), 466, itself citing Faber's *The Life of S. Francis of Assisi* (1853).

19. As noted in the unsigned introduction to the *Sermon Notes of John Henry Cardinal Newman, 1849–1878*, ed. by The Fathers of the Birmingham Oratory (London: Longmans, 1913), vi.

20. Thus on hearing of Newman's plan to undertake a new translation of the Bible, an old Catholic clergyman named Charles Husenbeth wrote to him describing 'a serious apprehension lest an endeavour should be made to assimilate our version to that of the establishment… This fear is the more natural from the preference which you must have from long habit for what is called the "authorised version"': see *The Letters and Diaries of John Henry Newman*, ed. by Charles Stephen Dessain et al., 32 vols. (Oxford: Clarendon Press, 1973–2008), pp. XXXI, 62.

21. *S*, pp. 93, 13, 71, 73. The italics are Hopkins's own (as they are in all subsequent quotations from his sermons).

22. *CW*, I, 364.

23. *CW*, I, 477.

24. Cited and discussed by Ronald Knox, *On Englishing the Bible* (London: Burns and Oates, 1949), pp. 21–22.

25. The King James Version shows the same difference – 'He shall cover thee with his feathers, and under his wings shalt thou trust' (King James) – though the *Book of Common Prayer* version is slightly closer to the poem and a more likely

source. The difference is not consistent, however: Psalm 17 in the *Book of Common Prayer* asks that God 'hide me under the shadow of thy wings' (17.8); the Vulgate also has 'wings' ('*alarum*') in this instance (according to its numbering, 16.8). Compare also *Book of Common Prayer* Psalm 36.7 and Vulgate 35.8.

26. Diane D'Amico, *Christina Rossetti: Faith, Gender, and Time* (Baton Rouge: Louisiana State University Press, 1999), pp. 13–15.

27. Most important in terms of commentary on Hopkins and the Bible is the work of James Finn Cotter. I discuss Cotter's article on Hopkins and Job later; see also his 'Apocalyptic Imagery in Hopkins's '"That Nature is a Heraclitean Fire and of the Comfort of the Resurrection"', *Victorian Poetry*, 24 (1986), 261–73; 'The Song of Songs and "The Wreck of the Deutschland"', in *Gerard Manley Hopkins and Critical Discourse*, ed. by Eugene Hollahan (New York: AMS Press, 1993), pp. 57–64; and *Inscape: The Christology and Poetry of Gerard Manley Hopkins* (Pittsburgh: University of Pittsburgh Press, 1972). Other notable accounts include Maria R. Lichtmann's study of the influence on Hopkins of parallelism in Hebrew poetry, *The Contemplative Poetry of Gerard Manley Hopkins* (Princeton: Princeton University Press, 1989), and George P. Landow, *Victorian Types, Victorian Shadows: Biblical Typology in Victorian Literature, Art, and Thought* (Boston: Routledge and Kegan Paul, 1980), pp. 179–87.

28. '*Ipse*' is sometimes related to Luke 24.15 (see e.g. *PW*, p. 344), but Cotter also gives persuasive evidence for its connection to Colossians 1.15–20 in *Inscape*, pp. 157–60. The new prominence of Church Latin in Hopkins's devotional life after his conversion is also reflected in the occasional verses and translations he produced between joining the Jesuit novitiate in 1868 and writing 'The Wreck of the Deutschland' in 1875–76, many of which are in (or from) Latin.

29. *CW*, II, 903.

30. *CW*, II, 748.

31. *CW*, II, 749.

32. Martin, 'Hopkins's Prosody', p. 8.

33. David Nowell Smith, *On Voice in Poetry: The Work of Animation* (Basingstoke: Palgrave Macmillan, 2015), p. 146.

34. Wimsatt, p. 53; *CW*, I, 282.

35. James Finn Cotter, 'Hopkins and Job', *Victorian Poetry*, 33 (1995), 283–93 (p. 291).

36. James Anthony Froude, 'The Book of Job', in *Short Studies on Great Subjects*, 4 vols. (London: Longmans, 1877–83), I (1877), pp. 283–84.

37. *CW*, I, 365.

38. Eleanor Cook, *Against Coercion: Games Poets Play* (Stanford: Stanford University Press, 1998), p. 117.

39. Brown, *Hopkins' Idealism*, p. 179.
40. See Jack Goody, 'What's in a List?', in *The Domestication of the Savage Mind* (Cambridge: Cambridge University Press, 1977), pp. 74–111; I quote from p. 104.
41. *CW*, II, 516.
42. *CW*, VII, 74–75; 138–41; 156–57.
43. *S*, p. 289.
44. Eric Griffiths, *The Printed Voice of Victorian Poetry* (Oxford: Clarendon Press, 1989), p. 289.
45. MS F, fos. 44v–45r, Campion Hall, Oxford.
46. Griffiths, p. 290.
47. Henry Parry Liddon, *Sermons Preached before the University of Oxford*, 3rd edn (London: Rivingtons, 1869), p. 209.
48. Jude V. Nixon, *Gerard Manley Hopkins and His Contemporaries: Liddon, Newman, Darwin, and Pater* (New York: Garland, 1994), p. 7.
49. *CW*, I, 506–7.
50. *CW*, I, 365.
51. *CW*, II, 906.
52. *CW*, I, 365.
53. James Milroy, *The Language of Gerard Manley Hopkins* (London: André Deutsch, 1977), p. 30.
54. See Alfred Thomas, S.J., 'Hopkins's "Felix Randal": The Man and the Poem', *Times Literary Supplement* (19 March 1971), 331–32.
55. *MW*, p. 365.
56. Thomas makes the connection with this passage in '"Felix Randal"', p. 331.
57. *MW*, p. 365.
58. This is version (b) in *PW*. For the sermon, see *S*, p. 47.
59. John R. Beard, 'Lessons in English', *The Popular Educator*, 2 (1853), 378–80 (p. 379). Cary H. Plotkin rightly cautions that 'fettle' 'is not peculiar to Lancashire' but recognises that its effect in the poem is to convey 'an entire world beyond the precincts of polite society': see *The Tenth Muse: Victorian Philology and the Genesis of the Poetic Language of Gerard Manley Hopkins* (Carbondale: Southern Illinois University Press, 1989), p. 78.
60. Two-and-a-half pages are devoted to 'fettle' in the *English Dialect Dictionary*. Meanings include 'To clean, tidy up, put to rights'; 'To repair, mend; to prepare, make ready, put in working order, set to rights': see *The English Dialect Dictionary*, ed. by Joseph Wright, 6 vols. (London: Henry Froude, 1898–1905).
61. See C. J. T. Talar, 'Innovation and Biblical Interpretation', in *Catholicism Contending with Modernity: Roman Catholic Modernism and Anti-Modernism in Historical Context*, ed. by Darrell Jodock (Cambridge: Cambridge University Press, 2000), pp. 191–212.

62. *Essays and Reviews: The 1860 Text and Its Reading*, ed. by Victor Shea and William Whitla (Charlottesville: University Press of Virginia, 2000), p. 504. Hopkins in 1865 made a note to read *Essays and Reviews*: see *CW* III, p. 277. He would have known about Renan from his attendance at Henry Liddon's Bampton Lectures of 1866: Liddon asserted the divinity of Christ and opposed Feuerbach, Renan, and Higher Criticism more generally.

63. Addis's comments appear in a letter to G. F. Lahey, S.J., cited in the latter's *Gerard Manley Hopkins* (Oxford: Oxford University Press, 1930), p. 19.

64. 'Allowing 25 years only to a generation, & each patriarch to have twenty children and none barren', Manley Hopkins arrived at the figure of 888,888 persons, which he thought plenty, though it had to be acknowledged that 'this is taking an extreme case' and required many possible intervening factors to be ignored (Hopkins Family Papers, Gonzaga, 39:3).

65. For Hopkins and parallelism, see Lichtmann. Hopkins mentions the subject in his 'Notes for Roman Literature and Antiquities', made in Dublin in the 1880s: 'Poetry is the art of utterance in verse, or, to include Hebrew poetry, in which the figure of Parallelism is used, and other possible kinds, of utterance in some figure or pattern of language independent of the matter' (Campion Hall, Oxford, MS G.II, fo. 10r).

66. See Stephen Prickett, *Words and The Word: Language, Poetics and Biblical Interpretation* (Cambridge: Cambridge University Press, 1986).

67. *CW*, II, 565.

68. See especially Frank Kermode, *The Genesis of Secrecy: On the Interpretation of Narrative* (Cambridge, MA: Harvard University Press, 1979); Robert Alter, *The Art of Biblical Narrative* (London: George Allen & Unwin, 1981); and Gabriel Josipovici, *The Book of God: A Response to the Bible* (New Haven: Yale University Press, 1988).

69. Harold Bloom, *The Book of J* (London: Faber and Faber, 1991), p. 44.

70. Josipovici claims that a preoccupation with questions of translation is a symptom of the larger problem of treating the Bible differently from other literary texts: 'Once again it is our anxiety in relation to this particular book that makes us concentrate on whether we are accurately understanding the details while ignoring the challenge of responding to the whole' (p. 34).

71. Prickett, *Words and the Word*, p. 42.

72. The poem is untitled and is identified usually by its first line – 'Thou art indeed just, Lord, if I contend' – or occasionally by the first words of its epigraph. I have chosen the latter option, for reasons that will become apparent.

73. The poem appears in *The Cathedral, or the Catholic and Apostolic Church in England* (Oxford: John Henry Parker, 1838).

74. The earliest version of 'Barnfloor and Winepress' – and the only one in Hopkins's own hand – does not have the epigraph, suggesting that it may have been added later; the sole autograph of 'Nondum' does have its epigraph (*EPM*, pp. 113–14; 220–21). The dense biblical typology of 'Barnfloor and Winepress' has been explored by Landow, pp. 180–84.

75. See Alister E. McGrath, *Iustitia Dei: A History of the Christian Doctrine of Justification*, 2 vols. (Cambridge: Cambridge University Press, 1986), I, 3.

76. Thomas Ward, *Errata of the Protestant Bible* (Dublin: James Duffy, 1841), p. 75. One of the theses required to be defended in the 'Ad Grad' examination at St Beuno's in 1877 – the occasion of Hopkins's 'failure' to do well enough to progress to a fourth year of theology – runs as follows: '*Homo justus per bona opera, en gratia Dei factor, vere meretur gratiae sanctificantis augmentum et vitam aeternam*' ('Man is just by good works, behold in grace made by God, truly meriting the advancement of sanctifying grace and eternal life'). I cite from Gonzaga MS 33:9.

77. This is not the only point in the poem where Roman Catholic modes of translation are important: see Dennis Sobolev's remarks on the preference for 'contend' rather than the King James's 'plead' to stand for '*disputem*' in his 'Semantic Counterpoint and the Poetry of Gerard Manley Hopkins', *Victorian Literature and Culture*, 35 (2007), 103–19 (p. 110).

78. *S*, p. 262. These notes were dated by Hopkins 'Jan. 1 1888', but this was a slip for 1889.

79. *Chapters into Verse: Poetry in English Inspired by The Bible*, ed. by Robert Atwan and Laurance Wieder, 2 vols. (New York: Oxford University Press, 1993), I, 411–12.

80. S. E. Gillingham excludes the epigraph, and makes a comparison with the King James Version of Job, hence translating '*Justus*' as 'righteous' rather than 'just'. See her *The Poems and Psalms of the Hebrew Bible* (Oxford: Oxford University Press, 1994), pp. 8–9.

81. *The Psalms in English*, ed. by Donald Davie (London: Penguin, 1996), p. 290. Davie also leaves out the epigraph from the Vulgate.

82. Jonathan Z. Smith, *Map Is Not Territory: Studies in the History of Religions* (Leiden: E. J. Brill, 1978), p. 301.

83. Ong, p. 126.

84. *CW*, II, 654.

85. *CW*, I, 505.

86. Endean, 'The Spirituality of Gerard Manley Hopkins', p. 126.

87. The recollection of one of two of Hopkins's Liverpool parishioners, Edward McCloughlin and 'old Mrs Campbell', interviewed by Anthony Bischoff, S.J., in 1949 (Gonzaga 41:12).

2 Prentice

1. *LPM*, pp. 340–43.
2. Walter Brueggemann, *The Psalms and the Life of Faith*, ed. by Patrick D. Miller (Minneapolis: Fortress Press, 1995), p. 104.
3. The name given to this group of poems is not Hopkins's own. It originates with Robert Bridges, who, in the edition of Hopkins he published in 1918, wrote of his 'high admiration and respect' for the 'terrible posthumous sonnets' ('Preface to Notes', in *Poems of Gerard Manley Hopkins*, ed. by Robert Bridges [London: Humphrey Milford, 1918], p. 101). Some commentators prefer to call them 'Sonnets of Desolation'. There is no agreement over which poems should be covered by the designation, but most critics would include the untitled poems which begin respectively: 'To seem the stranger lies my lot, my life', 'I wake and feel the fell of dark, not day', 'No worst, there is none. Pitched past pitch of grief', 'Not, I'll not, carrion comfort, Despair, not feast on thee', 'Patience, hard thing! the hard thing but to pray', and 'My own heart let me more have pity on'.
4. Graham Storey, *A Preface to Hopkins* (Harlow: Longman, 1981), p. 35.
5. *S*, p. 132.
6. David Anthony Downes, *The Ignatian Personality of Gerard Manley Hopkins* (Lanham: University Press of America, 1990), p. 96. Downes is the most dedicated of a cluster of critics to have adapted for Hopkins the celebrated thesis offered in Louis L. Martz's *The Poetry of Meditation: A Study in English Religious Literature of the Seventeenth Century* (New Haven: Yale University Press, 1954) about the influence of Counter-Reformation meditative techniques on seventeenth-century English poets.
7. I am indebted here to Philip Endean S.J.'s remarks in 'How Should Hopkins Critics Use Ignatian Texts?' in *Gerard Manley Hopkins: Tradition and Innovation*, ed. by P. Bottalla, G. Marra, and F. Marucci (Ravenna: Longo Editore, 1991), pp. 161–76.
8. Philip Sheldrake, *A Brief History of Spirituality* (Oxford: Blackwell, 2007), p. 6.
9. Philip Sheldrake, *Spirituality and History: Questions of Interpretation and Method*, rev. edn (London: SPCK, 1995), p. 85.
10. James Clare, S.J., *The Science of Spiritual Life, According to the Spiritual Exercises* (London and Leamington: Art and Book Company, 1896).
11. Daniel A. Harris, *Inspirations Unbidden: The 'Terrible Sonnets' of Gerard Manley Hopkins* (Berkeley: University of California Press, 1982), xv; p. 75.
12. Paul L. Mariani, *A Commentary on the Complete Poems of Gerard Manley Hopkins* (Ithaca: Cornell University Press, 1970), pp. 212; 218.

13. Virginia Jackson and Yopie Prins, 'General Introduction', in *The Lyric Theory Reader: A Critical Anthology*, ed. by Virginia Jackson and Yopie Prins (Baltimore: Johns Hopkins University Press, 2014), p. 5.

14. Laura Riding and Robert Graves, *A Survey of Modernist Poetry* (London: Heinemann, 1927; repr. 1929), p. 90; F. R. Leavis, *New Bearings in English Poetry* (London: Chatto and Windus, 1932), p. 181.

15. I. A. Richards, 'Gerard Hopkins', *Dial*, repr. in *Hopkins: The Critical Heritage*, p. 145; William Empson, *Seven Types of Ambiguity* (London: Chatto and Windus, 1930), p. 286; and *Selected Letters of William Empson*, ed. by John Haffenden (Oxford: Oxford University Press, 2006), p. 231.

16. Michael Roberts, 'Introduction', in *The Faber Book of Modern Verse* (1936), repr. in *Hopkins: The Critical Heritage*, p. 347.

17. Lichtmann, pp. 214; 209; 192.

18. J. Hillis Miller, *The Disappearance of God: Five Nineteenth-Century Writers* (Cambridge, MA: Harvard University Press, 1963), p. 359.

19. Donald Davie, 'Introduction', in *The New Oxford Book of Christian Verse*, ed. by Donald Davie (Oxford: Oxford University Press, 1981; repr. 1988), xxviii–xxix.

20. Kirstie Blair, *Form and Faith in Victorian Poetry and Religion* (Oxford: Oxford University Press, 2012), p. 87.

21. *CW*, II, 530.

22. See e.g. the maternal quality attributed after the event to the Marian apparitions at Lourdes in 1858, discussed by Ruth Harris in *Lourdes: Body and Spirit in the Secular Age* (London: Allen Lane, 1999), pp. 70–71.

23. See Gillian Beer, *Open Fields: Science in Cultural Encounter* (Oxford: Clarendon Press, 1996), pp. 242–72; and Brown, *Hopkins' Idealism*, pp. 201–2 and 244–46. Brown notes that 'the poem alludes not only to the traditional seven colours of the spectrum but also to the more numerous but definitive gradations of spectral bright lines in which chemical element is registered in a specific wave-length … the sum of which is clear white light, representative of the all-inclusive and ultimate ontological principle of God' (p. 202).

24. *The Raccolta: Or, Collection of Indulgenced Prayers*, trans. by Ambrose St John (London: Burns and Lambert, 1857), pp. 181; 225; 230.

25. I am indebted in my discussion of the poem to Matthew Campbell's unpublished conference paper 'Hopkins, rhyme and audient atmosphere', given at 'Hopkins' Audiences', Newcastle University, April 2014.

26. Yvor Winters, *The Function of Criticism: Problems and Exercises* (London: Routledge & Kegan Paul, 1957), p. 148; also cited in Norman H. MacKenzie, *A Reader's Guide to Gerard Manley Hopkins* (London: Thames and Hudson, 1981), p. 157.

27. *CW*, II, 576.

28. *CW*, II, 587.

29. Letter to Joseph Keating, S.J., 9 February 1918 (Gonzaga MS 1:30).

30. Miller, *Disappearance of God*, p. 285.

31. *CW*, I, 476. 'Peace' (1879) is another curtal sonnet.

32. Beer, p. 255.

33. *CW*, II, 800.

34. Barbara Hardy, *The Advantage of Lyric: Essays on Feeling in Poetry* (London: Athlone Press, 1977), p. 56.

35. McLeod, 'Gerard Hopkins and the Shapes of His Sonnets', pp. 256–57.

36. Susan Chambers, 'Gerard Manley Hopkins and the Kinesthetics of Conviction', *Victorian Studies*, 51 (2008), 7–35 (p. 8).

37. See e.g. *Hearts on Fire: Praying with Jesuits*, ed. by Michael Harter, S.J. (Chicago: Loyola Press, 2004).

38. Helen Vendler, *The Art of Shakespeare's Sonnets* (Cambridge, MA: Harvard University Press, 1997), p. 2.

39. Jonathan Culler, *Theory of the Lyric* (Cambridge, MA: Harvard University Press, 2015), pp. 35; 36.

40. Culler, *Theory of the Lyric*, p. 37.

41. Jahan Ramazani, *Poetry and Its Others: News, Prayer, Song, and the Dialogue of Genres* (Chicago: University of Chicago Press, 2014), pp. 132–34.

42. Ramazani, p. 131.

43. Alfonso Rodriguez, S.J., *The Practice of Christian and Religious Perfection*, 3 vols. (Dublin: Richard Coyne, 1840–41), I (1840), 252.

44. *CW*, I, 116; *CW*, II, 814.

45. The prayer appears in *The Correspondence of Gerard Manley Hopkins and Richard Watson Dixon*, ed. by Claude Colleer Abbott, 2nd edn (London: Oxford University Press, 1955), pp. 159–60.

46. William FitzGerald, *Spiritual Modalities: Prayer as Rhetoric and Performance* (University Park: Pennsylvania State University Press, 2012), p. 6.

47. Among the biblical echoes are 'For thou desirest not the sinner's death, but that he should be converted and live', which is a version of Ezekiel 18.23: 'Is it my will that a sinner should die, saith the Lord God, and not that he should be converted from his ways, and live?' (Douay-Rheims). 'Our better hope' comes from Hebrews 7.19. To Hopkins's surprise and frustration, the orthodoxy manifest in the prayer's overtly doctrinal content appears to have been the reason it was not thought appropriate for publication by Elizabeth Waterhouse, Robert Bridges's stepmother, for whose *Book of Prayers* (1884) it had been written: see *CW*, II, 618–19. I cite the translation of the *Confiteor* from the officially prescribed version given in the *Manual of Prayers for Congregational Use* (London: Thomas Richardson, 1887).

48. Henri Bremond, *Poetry and Prayer: A Contribution to Poetical Theory*, trans. by A. Thorold (London: Burns, Oates & Washbourne, 1927), p. 193; Francesca Bugliani Knox, 'Introduction', in *Poetry and Prayer: The Power of the Word II*, ed. by Francesca Bugliani Knox and John Took (Farnham: Ashgate, 2015), pp. 6–7.

49. See Chapter 4.

50. See my 'The *Month* as Hopkins Knew It', 296–308.

51. *CW*, I, 292.

52. *CW*, I, 282.

53. Elizabeth Jennings, *Every Changing Shape* (London: Andre Deutsch, 1961), pp. 105–6.

54. See Robert V. Caro, S.J., 'Hopkins's Poems in the Breviary', *Studies: An Irish Quarterly Review*, 2 (1995), 173–80.

55. Hopkins mentions his intention to send poems likely to be 'terrible sonnets' to Bridges in a letter of 1885, for which see *CW*, II, 743.

56. *CW*, II, 743; 736.

57. *CW*, VII, 49; 52.

58. A. D. Nuttall, *Overheard by God: Fiction and Prayer in Herbert, Milton, Dante and St John* (London: Methuen, 1980), p. 9.

59. Nuttall, p. 10.

60. *S*, p. 70.

61. William Waters, *Poetry's Touch: On Lyric Address* (Ithaca: Cornell University Press, 2003), p. 5.

62. *LPM*, p. 272.

63. Donald McChesney observes an echo with the Litany of Loreto (with its appeal to Mary as 'Comforter of the afflicted') in *A Hopkins Commentary: An Explanatory Commentary on the Main Poems, 1876–89* (London: University of London Press, 1968), p. 152.

64. Jonathan Culler, *The Pursuit of Signs: Semiotics, Literature, Deconstruction* (Ithaca: Cornell University Press, 1981), p. 146.

65. J27/165, Irish Jesuit Archives.

66. Several versions of the prayer existed in this period; I cite from the version given in the *Manual of Prayers for Congregational Use*.

67. Mary Heimann, *Catholic Devotion in Victorian Britain* (Oxford: Clarendon Press, 1995), p. 98.

68. Yvor Winters, 'The Poetry of Gerard Manley Hopkins (I)', *The Hudson Review*, 1 (1949), 455–76 (p. 461).

69. R. P. Blackmur, 'Mature Intelligence of an Artist', *The Kenyon Review*, 1 (1939), 96–99 (p. 97); Austin Warren, 'Monument Not Quite Needed', *The Kenyon Review*, 6 (1944), 587–89 (p. 588).

70. C. Day Lewis, *A Hope for Poetry* (1934), repr. in *Hopkins: The Critical Heritage*, p. 282.

71. Ballinger, for instance, concentrates on *The Wreck* and the 1877 sonnets, adducing the 'terrible sonnets' only for their biographical relevance. Brown in *Hopkins' Idealism* ranges more widely, but his book is still strongly weighted towards 'The Wreck of the Deutschland' and the 1877 nature sonnets.

72. On allusions to *King Lear*, see especially Norman White, 'Hopkins' Sonnet "No Worst, There is None" and the Storm Scenes in "King Lear"', *Victorian Poetry*, 24 (1986), 83–87.

73. George Tyrrell, *Nova et Vetera: Informal Meditations for Times of Spiritual Dryness* (London: Longmans, 1898), p. 42.

74. Catherine J. Golden, *Posting It: The Victorian Revolution in Letter Writing* (Gainesville: University Press of Florida, 2009), p. 35.

75. John W. O'Malley, S.J., *The Jesuits: A History from Ignatius to the Present* (Lanham: Rowman & Littlefield, 2014), p. 98.

76. Gonzaga MS 30:16.

77. Oliver P. Rafferty, S.J., 'Tyrrell and the English Jesuits', in *George Tyrrell and Catholic Modernism*, ed. by Oliver P. Rafferty, S.J. (Dublin: Four Courts Press, 2010), pp. 153–78 (p. 162).

78. Declan Marmion and Mary E. Hines, 'Introduction', in *The Cambridge Companion to Karl Rahner*, ed. by Declan Marmion and Mary E. Hines (Cambridge: Cambridge University Press, 2005), pp. 1–10 (p. 3).

79. Stephen Prickett, 'Tractarian Poetry', in *A Companion to Victorian Poetry*, ed. by Richard Cronin, Alison Chapman, and Anthony H. Harrison (Oxford: Blackwell, 2002), pp. 279–90 (p. 288). This is an argument developed in detail by Margaret Johnson in *Gerard Manley Hopkins and Tractarian Poetry* (Aldershot: Ashgate, 1997). For an important reappraisal, see Peter Groves, 'Hopkins and Tractarianism', *Victorian Poetry*, 44 (2006), 105–12.

80. [William Braden], 'The Works of George Herbert, in Prose and Verse', *The British Quarterly Review*, 46:91 (July 1867), 97–125 (p. 107).

81. As Kirstie Blair observes, *The Christian Year* drew 'huge numbers of Victorian readers', who chose to 'read, reread, and, crucially, to use Keble's poems, whether as consolation, panacea or religious aid': see her 'Introduction', in *John Keble in Context*, ed. by Kirstie Blair (London: Anthem Press, 2004), p. 8.

82. See e.g. MacKenzie, *A Reader's Guide*, p. 175; Norman White, *Hopkins in Ireland* (Dublin: University College Dublin Press, 2002), pp. 97–104.

83. *PW*, p. 459.

84. Michael D. Hurley, *Faith in Poetry: Verse Style as a Mode of Religious Belief* (London: Bloomsbury Academic, 2017). I am grateful to the author for allowing me to read this book's chapter on Hopkins in draft form.

85. Geoffrey Hill, *Collected Critical Writings*, ed. by Kenneth Haynes (Oxford: Oxford University Press, 2008), p. 106.

86. It does not appear in Brown's *Hopkins' Idealism* and features only for its biographical relevance in Ballinger (pp. 14–15).

87. Hill, *Critical Writings*, p. 105.

88. Ian Ker, *The Catholic Revival in English Literature, 1845–1961: Newman, Hopkins, Belloc, Chesterton, Greene, Waugh* (Notre Dame: University of Notre Dame Press, 2003), p. 41.

89. Ker, *The Catholic Revival*, p. 46.

90. Alphonsus Liguori, *A Short Treatise on Prayer; The Great Means of Obtaining from God Eternal Salvation, and All the Graces of Which We Stand in Need* (Dublin: John Coyne, 1834), pp. 115; 82.

91. André de Bovis, 'L'Église catholique, 16e–19e siècles', from 'Prière', in *Dictionnaire de spiritualité: ascétique et mystique, doctrine et histoire*, ed. by Marcel Viller et al., 17 vols. (Paris: Beauchesne, 1937–95), XII, part 2 (1986), 2295–317 (p. 2315); translation mine.

3 The Soldier

1. *Ivor Gurney: Collected Letters*, ed. by R. K. R. Thornton (Northumberland: Mid Northumberland Arts Group/Manchester: Carcanet Press, 1991), p. 140. Harvey was initially assumed dead but had in fact been captured alive and taken prisoner. John Lucas writes about Hopkins's influence on Gurney in *Ivor Gurney* (Tavistock: Northcote House, 2001), pp. 20–21. See also Michael D. Moore, 'Hopkins and Gurney', in *Hopkins among the Poets*, ed. by R. F. Giles (Hamilton, Ontario: International Hopkins Association, 1985), pp. 36–41.

2. *Gurney: Collected Letters*, p. 140.

3. F. R. Leavis, 'Gerard Manley Hopkins – Reflections after Fifty Years' (1971), repr. in *The Critic as Anti-Philosopher: Essays and Papers by F. R. Leavis*, ed. by G. Singh (London: Chatto & Windus, 1982), 76–97 (pp. 81–82).

4. F. R. Leavis, 'Gerard Manley Hopkins' (1944), repr. in *The Common Pursuit* (Harmondsworth: Penguin, 1952), p. 48.

5. Leavis, 'Reflections after Fifty Years', p. 79.

6. I. A. Richards, 'Gerard Hopkins', *Dial*, repr. in *Hopkins: The Critical Heritage*, p. 142.

7. Letter from Bridges to Joseph Keating, S.J., 31 May 1918 (Gonzaga MS 1:32). The 750 copies of the first edition did not sell out until 1928.

8. 'Our generation already is overpast', in *Poems of Gerard Manley Hopkins*, ed. by Robert Bridges (London: Humphrey Milford, 1918), ll. 9–12.

9. Robert Bridges, *Selected Letters of Robert Bridges*, ed. by Donald E. Stanford, 2 vols. (Newark: University of Delaware Press, 1983), II, 714. See John Schad's creative reimagining of events surrounding the publication of the 1918 edition, which attends to Gurney's reading of Hopkins: 'Queerest Book – A Dramatic Monologue', *Literature and Theology*, 26 (2012), 3–22.

10. Bernadette Waterman Ward, 'Hopkins on Warfare: "the war within"', *Hopkins Quarterly*, 30 (2003), 7–82 (pp. 79; 80).

11. Lucas, *Ivor Gurney*, p. 7.

12. Other alternatives Hopkins proposed in revision for lines 6 and 7 (but had not yet certainly decided upon) were 'It fáncies, féigns, déems, déars the ártist áfter his árt;' and 'Is fain to find (*or* And's fain to find *or* And fain will find)'.

13. Edward M. Spiers, 'War', in *The Cambridge Companion to Victorian Culture*, ed. by Francis O'Gorman (Cambridge: Cambridge University Press, 2010), 80–100 (p. 80). See also Olive Anderson, 'The Growth of Christian Militarism in Mid-Victorian Britain', *English Historical Review*, 86 (1971), 46–72, a subject discussed in relation to the figure of General Havelock in Graham Dawson's *Soldier Heroes: British Adventure, Empire and the Imagining of Masculinities* (London: Routledge, 1994), pp. 79–154, and more generally in John M. MacKenzie, 'Introduction: Popular Imperialism and the Military', in *Popular Imperialism and the Military, 1850–1950*, ed. by John M. MacKenzie (Manchester: Manchester University Press, 1992), pp. 1–24.

14. Matthew Bevis, 'Fighting Talk: Victorian War Poetry', in *The Oxford Handbook of British and Irish War Poetry*, ed. by Tim Kendall (Oxford: Oxford University Press, 2007), pp. 7–33 (p. 24).

15. *CW*, I, 450; *CW*, I, 431.

16. Cicero, *On Duties*, ed. by M. T. Griffin and E. M. Atkins (Cambridge: Cambridge University Press, 1991), p. 25. The Dublin Notebook includes the 1885 lecture 'On Duty', which considers Cicero's text, observing differences and correspondences between it and the Christian understanding of duty (*CW*, VII, 179–83). Waterman Ward observes the influence of classical texts on Hopkins's idea of war in 'Hopkins on Warfare', p. 74, drawing attention to Todd K. Bender's work on Hopkins's reading of the Greek historians Thucydides and Herodotus. See Bender, *Gerard Manley Hopkins: The Classical Background and Critical Reception of His Work* (Baltimore: Johns Hopkins University Press, 1966), pp. 52–57.

17. Joseph Bristow, '"Churlsgrace": Gerard Manley Hopkins and the Working-Class Male Body', *ELH*, 59 (1992), 693–711 (p. 708).

18. Bristow, p. 696. Maureen F. Moran makes the same connection in '"Lovely manly mould": Hopkins and the Christian Body', *Journal of Victorian Culture*, 6 (2001), 61–88.

19. See Norman Vance, *The Sinews of the Spirit: The Ideal of Christian Manliness in Victorian Literature and Religious Thought* (Cambridge: Cambridge University Press, 1985).

20. See James Eli Adams, *Dandies and Desert Saints: Styles of Victorian Masculinity* (Ithaca: Cornell University Press, 1995), pp. 100–2. Hopkins in a letter of 1881 writes that Robert Browning 'has got a great deal of what came in with Kingsley and the Broad Church school, a way of talking (and making his people talk) with the air and spirit of a man bouncing up from table with his mouth full of bread and cheese and saying that he meant to stand no blasted nonsense' (*CW*, I, 477).

21. John Henry Newman, 'Christian Manhood', in *Parochial and Plain Sermons*, 8 vols. (London: Rivingtons, 1875), I, 345.

22. Julia F. Saville, *A Queer Chivalry: The Homoerotic Asceticism of Gerard Manley Hopkins* (Charlottesville: University of Virginia Press, 2000), p. 5. On Hopkins and Keats, see Seamus Heaney, *The Fire i' the Flint: Reflections on the Poetry of Gerard Manley Hopkins* (London: Oxford University Press, 1975).

23. *EPM*, p. 157.

24. See Kirstie Blair's discussion of this poem in the context of the 'Anglo-Catholic sonnet tradition' in *Form and Faith in Victorian Poetry and Religion*, pp. 225–27.

25. John Henry Newman, 'Poetry with Reference to Aristotle's Poetics' (1829), repr. in *Essays Critical and Historical*, 2 vols. (London: Longmans, Green and Co., 1907), I, 23.

26. *CW*, I, 84; *CW*, I, 86–87.

27. Cotter, *Inscape*, p. 56.

28. John Henry Newman, *Sermons*, ed. by Placid Murray, Vincent Ferrer Blehl and Francis J. McGrath, 5 vols. (Oxford: Oxford University Press, 1991–2012), V (2012), 110.

29. Matthew Campbell, *Irish Poetry under the Union, 1801–1924* (Cambridge: Cambridge University Press, 2013), p. 172.

30. See *PW*, p. 459.

31. John Henry Newman, *Meditations and Devotions of the Late Cardinal Newman*, ed. by W. P. Neville (1893; repr. London: Longmans, 1907), p. 185.

32. *LPM*, p. 263.

33. *S*, p. 70.

34. I quote the poem from the version printed as (*b*) in *PW*.

35. David Alderson, *Mansex Fine: Religion, Manliness and Imperialism in Nineteenth-Century British Culture* (Manchester: Manchester University Press, 1998), p. 2.

36. *CW*, II, 889.

37. *CW*, I, 438. Sjaak Zonneveld usefully places this comment in the wider context of Hopkins's response to urbanization in *The Random Grim Forge: A Study of Social Ideas in the Work of Gerard Manley Hopkins* (Assen/Maastricht: Van Gorcum, 1992), pp. 55–57.

38. *CW*, II, 981.

39. Gabriele Taylor, *Pride, Shame, and Guilt: Emotions of Self-Assessment* (Oxford: Clarendon Press, 1985), p. 53.

40. *CW*, II, p. 928.

41. Christopher Saunders and Iain R. Smith, 'Southern Africa, 1795-1910', in *The Oxford History of the British Empire*, ed. by Wm. Roger Louis et al., 5 vols. (Oxford: Oxford University Press, 1998–99), III (1999), pp. 597–623 (p. 608).

42. *CW*, II, 862.

43. Hill, *Critical Writings*, p. 105.

44. Rowan Strong, *Anglicanism and the British Empire, c. 1700–1850* (Oxford: Oxford University Press, 2007), pp. 287–88.

45. *CW*, II, 785.

46. *CW*, II, 715.

47. Alderson, p. 135; *CW*, II, 933.

48. *CW*, II, 951.

49. See Lewis Winstock, *Songs & Music of the Redcoats: A History of the War Music of the British Army, 1642–1902* (London: Leo Cooper, 1970), pp. 274–77.

50. *S*, p. 261.

51. *CW*, II, 950.

52. 'The Superior General in Rome, for instance, 'is "general" only in the sense of the adjective, that is, he is the "overall" superior': see John W. O'Malley, S.J., *The First Jesuits* (Cambridge, MA: Harvard University Press, 1993), p. 45.

53. *S*, p. 261.

54. *S*, p. 234.

55. *S*, p. 17.

56. *CW*, I, 395.

57. *CW*, I, 61.

58. *CW*, I, 375–76.

59. W. H. Auden, review of Elsie Elizabeth Phare's *The Poetry of Gerard Hopkins*, in *The Criterion* (April 1934), repr. in *The Complete Works of W. H. Auden*, ed. by Edward Mendelson, 8 vols. (Princeton: Princeton University Press 1996–), I (1996), p. 68.

60. David Jones, *In Parenthesis: Seinnyessit E Gledyf Ym Penn Mameu* (London: Faber and Faber, 1937; repr. 1975); the debt is acknowledged in a note on p. 193.

61. Jones, *In Parenthesis*, p. 28.

62. Robert Bridges, 'Preface to Notes', in *Poems of Gerard Manley Hopkins*, p. 100.
63. Griffiths, *Printed Voice*, p. 326.
64. McDonald, *Sound Intentions*, p. 261.
65. See e.g. his retreat notes of 1885, on Christ crowned with thorns: 'These men crowned Xt in mockery ... Nevertheless their act was mystical and both the crown and the adorations were types of his true rights and royalty [.] Crown him king over yourself, of your heart [.] Wish to crown him king of England, of English hearts and of Ireland and all Christendom and all the world' (*CW*, VII, 76–77).
66. *CW*, II, 569.
67. *CW*, I, 479. He was not alone in this impression of Jesuit life: Robert Curtis, the Jesuit who was Hopkins's closest friend in Ireland, wrote in notes on moral theology that 'Vocation may be either i Conviction that one ought to leave the world ii an attraction for Religion iii, or a union of both which is best' (S11/2, Irish Jesuit Archives). For another Jesuit contemporary, Henry Schomberg Kerr, 'Among the attractions to him of the Society of Jesus [was] the hatred borne to it by the world': see Mary Monica Maxwell-Scott, *Henry Schomberg Kerr: Sailor and Jesuit* (London: Longmans, Green, and Co., 1901), p. 82.
68. *S*, pp. 34–37. In the sentence beginning 'As Christ lived and breathed and moved in a true and not a phantom human body', 'human' appears in the manuscript as an insertion. Later in the passage, Hopkins has also changed 'a human will' and 'a human genius' for 'his human will' and 'his own human genius' (MS F, fo. 42, Campion Hall, Oxford). All of these changes serve to underline that Christ's humanity was personal, and that it was a human nature like that of other human beings.
69. *LPM*, p. 182.
70. *CW*, I, 368; Robert Bernard Martin, *Gerard Manley Hopkins: A Very Private Life* (London: Flamingo, 1992), p. 298.
71. Probably the remark is not 'half-joking', as Peter Swaab suggests in 'Hopkins and the Pushed Peach', *Critical Quarterly*, 37 (1995), 43–60 (p. 51). Inclinations can be in earnest for Hopkins, e.g. his remark to Bridges on not being allowed to proceed to a fourth year of theology at St Beuno's: 'Much against my inclination I shall have to leave Wales' (*CW*, I, 278).
72. Swaab, p. 53.
73. *CW*, I, 347.
74. Geoffrey H. Hartman, *The Unmediated Vision: An Interpretation of Wordsworth, Hopkins, Rilke, and Valéry* (New Haven: Yale University Press, 1954), p. 49.
75. *J&P*, p. 289.
76. This is a process that defines Hopkins's poetry generally according to Michael D. Hurley in '"Dancing in Chains": Patterns of Sound in the Poetry of Gerard Manley Hopkins', unpub. PhD thesis, University of Cambridge, 2004. See also Hurley's review of Wimsatt's *Hopkins's Poetics of Speech Sound* in *Modern Philology*, 107 (2008), 126–30.

77. Empson, *Seven Types*, p. 285.

78. *CW*, IV, 311.

79. *S*, p. 158; Brown, *Gerard Manley Hopkins*, p. 61.

80. Empson, *Seven Types*, p. 285.

81. *J&P*, p. 278. On Hopkins's debts to the alliterative tradition of Anglo-Saxon verse, see Joseph Phelan, *The Music of Verse: Metrical Experiment in Nineteenth-Century Poetry* (Basingstoke: Palgrave Macmillan, 2012), pp. 118–32.

82. *CW*, I, 362.

83. Clive Scott, *A Question of Syllables: Essays in Nineteenth-Century French Verse* (Cambridge: Cambridge University Press, 1986), p. 130.

84. Robert Bridges, *The Testament of Beauty: A Poem in Four Books* (Oxford: Clarendon Press, 1929; repr. 1930), Book IV, 430–33.

85. Bridges, *Testament of Beauty*, Book IV, 433–38.

4 The Martyr

1. *CW*, I, 244.

2. *CW*, I, 120.

3. See R. L. Starkey, 'Books Hopkins Had Access To', *Hopkins Research Bulletin*, 6 (1975), 17–21 (p. 19). The book is now held at the John J. Burns Library, Boston College.

4. Anon., 'The Persecution in Poland', *The Tablet*, 27 March 1875, 390–92.

5. Geoffrey Grigson, 'Blood or Bran', *New Verse* (1935), repr. in *Gerard Manley Hopkins*, ed. by Walford Davies, pp. 203–6 (pp. 203–4).

6. *CW*, II, 950.

7. In terms of martyrdom specifically, Frederick S. Rosen in *Same-Sex Desire in Victorian Religious Culture* (Basingstoke: Palgrave, 2002) argues that 'Instead of imagining Hopkins' interest in female martyrs as heteroerotic, we should consider his identification with them and their aspirations' (p. 106). Maureen Moran in 'The Art of Looking Dangerously: Victorian Images of Martyrdom', *Victorian Literature and Culture*, 32 (2004), 475–93, discusses this same interest as part of the Victorian fascination with martyrdom, an illicit pleasure which engaged 'the dangers of bodily looking' (p. 475).

8. Asceticism has itself been suggested to have held for Hopkins an erotic charge: see Saville, pp. 58–87.

9. Robert Bridges, 'Preface to Notes', in *Poems of Gerard Manley Hopkins*, p. 104.

10. Ward, *World as Word*, p. 95.

11. *CW*, I, 116.

12. Martin, *The Rise and Fall of Meter*, p. 56.

13. *CW*, I, 282.

14. For their comparison, see Mariaconcetta Costantini, 'A Poem "for Four Hands" and Many Voices: The Myth of St. Dorothy in Christina Rossetti and G.M. Hopkins', in *Widening Horizons: Essays in Honour of Professor Mohit K. Ray*, ed. by Rama Kundu (New Delhi: Sarup, 2005), pp. 75–92.

15. A possibility advanced by Norman H. MacKenzie in 'Hopkins and St. Dorothea: Lines for whose Picture?' in *Vital Candle: Victorian and Modern Bearings in Gerard Manley Hopkins*, ed. by John S. North and Michael D. Moore (Waterloo, Ontario: University of Waterloo Press, 1984), pp. 21–40. Catherine Phillips observes that writing poems in connection with art was a habit Hopkins shared with his father: see *Gerard Manley Hopkins and the Victorian Visual World* (Oxford: Oxford University Press, 2007), pp. 10–11.

16. For 'peculiar beat', see *CW*, I, 187.

17. Phare, p. 67.

18. Owen Chadwick, *The Spirit of the Oxford Movement: Tractarian Essays* (1990; repr. Cambridge: Cambridge University Press, 1995), p. 30; Michael Wheeler, *The Old Enemies: Catholic and Protestant in Nineteenth-Century English Culture* (Cambridge: Cambridge University Press, 2006), pp. 51–76.

19. Stephen J. Davis, *The Cult of Saint Thecla: A Tradition of Women's Piety in Late Antiquity* (Oxford: Oxford University Press, 2001), p. 21.

20. Jude V. Nixon argues that Hopkins may not have intended to tell the entire story of Thecla, and that the poem, rather than being unfinished, is actually a complete work: see his '"St. Thecla," Monastic Transvestitism, and Hopkins's Proto-Feminist Utterance', *Hopkins Quarterly*, 39 (2012), 43–67.

21. Robert Lowell, 'A Note', *The Kenyon Review*, 6 (1944), 583–86 (p. 585).

22. 'Author's Note on the Rhythm in "*The Wreck of the Deutschland*"', *PW*, p. 118.

23. *The Times*, 11 December 1875, 7.

24. Anon., 'A Contemporary Elegy on Edmund Campion', *The Month*, 16 (January–February 1872), 116–20.

25. Maureen Moran, 'Hopkins and Victorian Responses to Suffering', *Revue Lisa/ Lisa e-journal*, 8:3 (2009) http://lisa.revues.org/145 [accessed 15 December 2014]. See also Wheeler, *The Old Enemies*, pp. 77–110.

26. Bernard Basset, S.J., *The English Jesuits: From Campion to Martindale* (London: Burns & Oates, 1967), p. 436.

27. Alison Shell, *Catholicism, Controversy and the English Literary Imagination, 1558–1660* (Cambridge: Cambridge University Press, 1999), p. 226.

28. Peter Gallwey, S.J., *The Beatified Martyrs and Prayers for the Conversion of England* (London: Burns & Oates, 1888), p. 9.

29. John Henry Newman, 'The Second Spring' (1852), repr. in *Sermons Preached on Various Occasions* (London: Burns and Lambert, 1857), pp. 208–9.

30. Anne Dillon, *The Construction of Martyrdom in the English Catholic Community, 1535–1603* (Aldershot: Ashgate, 2008), p. 101.

31. Thomas S. Freeman, '"Imitatio Christi with a Vengeance": The Politicisation of Martyrdom in Early-Modern England', in *Martyrs and Martyrdom in England, c.1400–1700*, ed. by Thomas S. Freeman and Thomas F. Mayer (Woodbridge: Boydell and Brewer, 2007), pp. 35–69 (p. 39).

32. Anon., 'Papal Rome and Catholic Reform', *Edinburgh Review*, 141 (April 1875), 554–84 (p. 577).

33. As Norman MacKenzie observes, 'the body of the superior ....was never recovered, whereas the tall nun's was ... GMH may be excused for wrongly identifying the superior when even scholars with access to their convent records have gone astray' (*PW*, p. 337).

34. Michael Wheeler, *Death and the Future Life in Victorian Literature and Theology* (Cambridge: Cambridge University Press, 1990), p. 349.

35. As reported in the *Tablet*, 18 December 1878, 786–87.

36. Wheeler, *Death and the Future Life*, p. 355.

37. As reported in the *Tablet*, 18 December 1878, 786.

38. John E. Keating, S.J., *'The Wreck of the Deutschland': An Essay and Commentary* (Kent, OH: Kent State University, 1963), p. 97.

39. George Augustus Simcox, review of J. H. Newman's *Letter to the Duke of Norfolk*, *The Academy*, 23 January 1875, 79–80: 80. Hopkins was interested by the article: see *CW*, iii, 610.

40. *S*, p. 43.

41. *MW*, p. 341.

42. *The Times*, 14 August 1875, 10.

43. Hopkins's previously quoted letter to his mother of April 1875, in addition to complaining that 'the daily papers have nothing' of the torment of the Polish Uniates, makes excited reference to a fierce attack on the Jesuits launched by the *Quarterly Review* a few months earlier: see *CW*, i, 243–45.

44. John Rutherford Shortland, *The Corean Martyrs: A Narrative* (London: Burns & Oates, 1869), p. 1.

45. Hartman, p. 57.

46. Dillon, p. 92.

47. Alderson, p. 134; Muller, p. 62.

48. *CW*, i, 190.

49. Mary Douglas, *In the Wilderness: The Doctrine of Defilement in the Book of Numbers* (Oxford: Oxford University Press, 1993; repr. 2001), p. 44.

50. Basil Champneys, *Memoirs and Correspondence of Coventry Patmore*, 2 vols. (London: George Bell, 1900), ii, 26.

51. Walter L. Arnstein, *Protestant versus Catholic in Mid-Victorian England: Mr. Newdegate and the Nuns* (Columbia: University of Missouri Press, 1982), pp. 137–39.

52. *CW*, ii, 503.

53. W. E. Gladstone, *The Vatican Decrees in Their Bearing on Civil Allegiance: A Political Expostulation* (London: John Murray, 1874), p. 48.

54. Cited in *The Times*, 23 June 1876, 8.

55. The poem exists in rough autograph, with only the first three stanzas numbered. The logical sequence of the rest of the poem cannot be known for certain, but the ordering of its fragments given in *PW* appears likely, especially in respect of the final stanza, which evidently closes the story.

56. R. J. Schoeck compares Hopkins's poem to Mush's account in 'Peine Forte et Dure and Hopkins' "Margaret Clitheroe"', *Modern Language Notes*, 74 (1959), 220–24. 'Clitherow' is the usual spelling; Hopkins uses an alternative form.

57. *S*, p. 129.

58. Brown, *Hopkins' Idealism*, pp. 310–11.

59. *CW*, i, 292.

60. Herbert F. Tucker, 'Story', in *The Oxford Handbook of Victorian Poetry*, ed. by Matthew Bevis (Oxford: Oxford University Press, 2013), pp. 130–46 (p. 144).

61. See Brown's discussion of this image in *Hopkins' Idealism*, pp. 208–9.

62. Griffiths, p. 269.

63. Griffiths, p. 270.

64. *CW*, ii, 645. Hopkins was objecting to Patmore's reference to Disraeli as 'Jew' in the poem '1867'.

65. Dillon, p. 293. As a result, its status and accuracy continue fiercely to be debated: see Peter Lake and Michael Questier, *The Trials of Margaret Clitherow: Persecution, Martyrdom and the Politics of Sanctity in Elizabethan England* (London: Continuum, 2011).

66. William Joseph Sheils, 'Mush, John (1552–1612)', *Oxford Dictionary of National Biography*, Oxford University Press, 2004 www.oxforddnb.com/view/article/19669 [accessed 12 September 2014].

67. Anon., Review of Morris's *The Troubles of Our Catholic Forefathers* in *Athenaeum*, 2570 (27 January 1877), 111–13 (pp. 111–12).

68. Her controversial reputation among the Catholics of York becomes in Mush's account another token of her worthiness: 'she suffered persecution, not only for her invincible constancy in the Catholic faith by heretics, but also for her true virtue by some one or other emulous Catholic.' See John Mush, 'A True Report of the Life and Martyrdom of Mrs. Margaret Clitherow' (1586), in *The Troubles of Our Catholic Forefathers Related by Themselves*, ed. by John Morris, S.J., 3rd series (London: Burns and Oates, 1877), pp. 333–440 (p. 404).

69. Phare, p. 15.

70. For a discussion of comic rhyme in Hopkins which comments on 'Margaret Clitheroe' in particular, see James Williams's unpublished conference paper 'Hopkins's Comedy', given at 'Hopkins' Audiences', Newcastle University, April 2014. The paper is available at www.academia.edu/27926178/Hopkinss_Comedy [accessed 23 August 2016].

71. Mush, 'A True Report', in Morris, *Troubles of Our Catholic Forefathers*, p. 432.
72. This is William Nicholson's edition, published as *Life and Death of Margaret Clitherow, the Martyr of York* (London: Richardson, 1849); the manuscript from which Nicholson worked actually reads 'she was in dying about one quarter of an houre' (cited by Dillon, p. 277).
73. Seamus Perry, 'Elegy', in *A Companion to Victorian Poetry*, ed. by Cronin, Chapman, and Harrison, pp. 115–33 (p. 128).
74. Christopher Ricks, review of Robert Bernard Martin, *Gerard Manley Hopkins: A Very Private Life*, *New Criterion* (September 1991), repr. in *Reviewery* (London: Penguin, 2002), pp. 3–10 (pp. 5–6).
75. *CW*, I, 456.
76. Hill, *Critical Writings*, p. 525.

5 Death and Judgement

1. *S*, p. 244.
2. *CW*, I, 284. The death of his sister's fiancé was the occasion for another such token, as he told her in a letter of 1883: 'I said mass for Henry Weber this morning and during the mass I felt strongly those motions from God (as I believe them to be) which I have often before now received touching the condition of the departed, by which was signified that it was well with him. I have also warnings sometimes of an approaching death: I had such a one lately, but it was slight and I paid little attention to it' (*CW*, II, 580). See also Hopkins's remark in 1873 that he had 'received as I think a great mercy about [Digby] Dolben', the cousin of Robert Bridges with whom Hopkins had been fascinated; Dolben had died some years earlier (*CW*, III, 558).
3. *CW*, I, 117.
4. Michael Wheeler writes about the particular significance of John 19.26–27 (the Virgin Mary and St John at the foot of the Cross) for Roman Catholic Marian devotion in *St John and the Victorians* (Cambridge: Cambridge University Press, 2012), pp. 169–79, also citing this letter.
5. *CW*, I, 127.
6. Mariaconcetta Costantini, '"To his Watch": Gerard Manley Hopkins and the Rhythm of Mortal Life', *Hopkins Quarterly*, 39 (2012), 88–106 (p. 88). For Hopkins's 'apocalyptic angst', see Jude V. Nixon, '"Death blots black out": Thermodynamics and the Poetry of Gerard Manley Hopkins', *Victorian Poetry*, 40 (2002), 131–55; I cite from p. 145.
7. John Morris, S.J., retreat notes of 1886 (Gonzaga MS 22:50).
8. Joseph Sollier, 'Final Perseverance', in *The Catholic Encyclopedia* (1911), www.newadvent.org/cathen/11711a.htm [accessed 20 September 2013].

9. Alphonsus de Liguori, *The Practice of the Love of Jesus Christ* (1768), cited from *Selected Writings*, ed. by Frederick M. Jones (New York: Paulist Press, 1999), p. 149. See also Jill Muller's comments on Liguori as a 'mainstay of Ultramontanist popular Catholicism', pp. 120–21.

10. See his comments on Leo XIII's *Spectata Fides* (1885), 'a really beautiful letter … the most liberally worded in dealing with those outside the Church that ever Pope, I shd. fancy, yet penned': *CW*, II, 753.

11. Pius IX, from the encyclical *Quanto conficiamur moerore* (1863); I quote from *The Sources of Catholic Dogma* (St Louis: Herder, 1957), which is Roy J. Deferrari's translation from Heinrich Denzinger's *Enchiridion Symbolorum* (30th edn, 1954), p. 425.

12. Pius IX, *Syllabus Errorum* (1864), cited from the English translation at www .papalencyclicals.net/Pius09/p9syll.htm [accessed 4 April 2016].

13. *CW*, I, 97–98.

14. *CW*, I, 181.

15. A concise explanation of the same notion is provided by Geoffrey Brown, 'Praying about the Past', *The Philosophical Quarterly*, 35 (1985), 83–86 (pp. 85–86): 'divine activity cannot properly be ascribed to particular times or periods of time at all … language about God is, strictly speaking, bound to be tenseless. Thus the prayer P, though in a sense "addressed to God at time t" would nevertheless *not* be regarded as addressed to "God at time t", for "God at time t" is alleged to make no sense.'

16. Sobolev, *The Split World*, p. 242. Writing in 1882 about the death of the father of a fellow convert, Hopkins comments: 'He died a Protestant; still prayers may do much, all that is necessary in fact: in these cases I always pray backwards, if you understand, and God allows discount. It is really a great light. You ask him to have granted the grace and the difference of tense is only to you' (*CW*, II, 534).

17. W. A. M. Peters, *Gerard Manley Hopkins: A Critical Essay towards the Understanding of His Poetry* (London: Oxford University Press, 1948), p. 130.

18. *CW*, I, 316.

19. *CW*, II, 568.

20. Michael D. Hurley, 'Passion and Playfulness in the Letters of Gerard Manley Hopkins', in *Letter Writing among Poets: From William Wordsworth to Elizabeth Bishop*, ed. by Jonathan Ellis (Edinburgh: Edinburgh University Press, 2015), pp. 141–54 (p. 147).

21. *The Catechism of the Council of Trent*, trans. by J. Donovan (Dublin: W. Folds, 1829), p. 77.

22. Frederick William Faber, *Notes on Doctrinal and Spiritual Subjects*, 2 vols. (London: Thomas Richardson, 1866), II, 374.

23. *S*, p. 140.

24. *CW*, II, 840.

25. Helen Vendler, *The Breaking of Style: Hopkins, Heaney, Graham* (Cambridge, MA: Harvard University Press, 1995), p. 37.

26. Sometimes suggested to be a Scottish word by commentators on Hopkins, 'throughther' has also been claimed by Cary H. Plotkin to be one of Hopkins's dialect words which 'by their form ... are recognizably English words' (*The Tenth Muse*, p. 87). The issue with 'disremember' is at least a little more clear-cut given that the instances given for 'disremember' in Joseph Wright's *English Dialect Dictionary*, to which Hopkins contributed, indicate its prevalence in Ireland. On the meaning of 'disremember', see Geoffrey Hill's insistence that instead of '"failing to remember", "forgetting"; it is "dismembering the memory"' (*Critical Writings*, p. 266). Matthew Campbell enlists these words as evidence for his claim that '"Spelt from Sibyl's Leaves" ... is not just a poem set in Ireland, but an Irish poem': see his *Irish Poetry under the Union*, p. 167.

27. *CW*, I, 364; *CW*, II, 809; *CW*, I, 365.

28. Valentine Cunningham, *Victorian Poetry Now: Poets, Poems, Poetics* (Oxford: Wiley-Blackwell, 2011), p. 145.

29. *CW*, II, 842.

30. *CW*, II, 650.

31. The remark appears in notes on Hill's annotated photocopy of 'Spelt from Sibyl's Leaves', held at the Brotherton Library, University of Leeds, and cited in Matthew Sperling, *Visionary Philology: Geoffrey Hill and the Study of Words* (Oxford: Oxford University Press, 2015), p. 30.

32. Geoffrey Hill, 'XLIX' in *The Orchards of Syon*, cited from *Broken Hierarchies: Poems 1952–2012*, ed. by Kenneth Haynes (Oxford: Oxford University Press, 2013), ll. 13–14.

33. Peter McDonald, 'Truly Apart', *Times Literary Supplement*, 1 April 2005, 13.

34. Muller, p. 117.

35. Augustine, *The City of God against the Pagans*, trans. by R. W. Dyson (Cambridge: Cambridge University Press, 1998), p. 909.

36. Wheeler, *Death and the Future Life*, p. 364.

37. Wheeler, *Death and the Future Life*, p. 342.

38. Francis O'Gorman, 'Hopkins' Yonder', *Literature and Theology*, 27 (2013), 81–97 (p. 83).

39. Michael D. Hurley, 'What Sprung Rhythm Really Is NOT', *Hopkins Quarterly*, 23 (2006), 71–94 (p. 89).

40. *J&P*, p. 284.

41. *S*, p. 244.

42. See *PW*, p. 347.

43. Wheeler, *Death and the Future Life*, p. 349.

44. See, variously, Phillips, note in *MW*, pp. 341–42; MacKenzie, *Reader's Guide*, p. 55; Elisabeth W. Schneider, *The Dragon in the Gate: Studies in the Poetry of G.M. Hopkins* (Berkeley: University of California Press, 1968), p. 34.

45. *S*, p. 74.

46. See Paul S. Fiddes, *Past Event and Present Salvation: The Christian Idea of Atonement* (London: Darton, Longman and Todd, 1989).

47. Schneider, p. 71.

48. *CW*, I, 292.

49. Paul H. Fry, *The Poet's Calling in the English Ode* (New Haven: Yale University Press, 1980), p. 6. Fry sees the ode as divided between such offices and 'the arrogation of divinely cosmogonic powers', namely 'invention, exorcism, mythopoeia'.

50. Louis de Ponte, S.J., *Meditations on the Mysteries of Our Holy Faith; Together with a Treatise on Mental Prayer*, trans. by John Heigham, 6 vols. (London: Richardson and Son, 1852–54), I (1852), 133.

51. See the discussion of 'sandal' in Chapter 1.

52. Seamus Perry, 'Elegy', in *A Companion to Victorian Poetry*, ed. by Cronin, Chapman; and Harrison, p. 128.

53. *CW*, II, 963.

54. *CW*, IV, 206. Another essay observes that the philosopher felt 'beyond any of his predecessors the chaos, uncertainty, and illusion of all things', yet 'spoke nevertheless of a rhythm, something imposed by mind as an air on the notes of a flute' (*CW*, IV, 210).

55. Phillips, *Hopkins and the Victorian Visual World*, p. 260.

56. *S*, p. 146.

57. *S*, p. 122.

58. *PW*, p. 495.

59. *S*, p. 123.

60. White, *Hopkins in Ireland*, p. 179.

61. Lesley Higgins, 'Heraclitean Fire and Eucharistic Flame: The Poetry of Transformation in Hopkins', *The Month*, 22 (1989), 423–28 (p. 425).

62. Hill, *Critical Writings*, pp. 570–71.

63. *CW*, VII, 162–63. The relevant biblical passage is from Luke 18.9–14 (Douay-Rheims): 'Two men went up into the temple to pray: the one a Pharisee, and the other a publican. The Pharisee standing, prayed thus with himself: O God, I give thee thanks that I am not as the rest of men, extortioners, unjust, adulterers, as also is this publican. I fast twice in a week: I give tithes of all that I possess. And the publican, standing afar off, would not so much as lift up his eyes towards heaven; but struck his breast, saying: O God, be merciful to me a sinner. I say to you, this man went down into his house justified rather than the other: because every one that exalteth himself, shall be humbled: and he that humbleth himself, shall be exalted.'

64. Anon., 'Father Gerard Hopkins', p. 179.
65. *CW*, II, 1002.

6 Heaven and Hell

1. Finn Fordham, *I Do I Undo I Redo: The Textual Genesis of Modernist Selves in Hopkins, Yeats, Conrad, Forster, Joyce, and Woolf* (Oxford: Oxford University Press, 2010), p. 87.
2. Fordham, p. 87.
3. Anthony Burgess, 'Gash gold-vermilion', *The Spectator*, 21 September 1967, 10–11 (p. 10).
4. Richard Ellmann, *James Joyce*, rev. edn (New York: Oxford University Press, 1982), p. 27.
5. James Joyce, *Ulysses*, ed. by Jeri Johnson (Oxford: Oxford University Press, 1993; repr. 1998), p. 8.
6. James Joyce, *A Portrait of the Artist as a Young Man*, ed. by Seamus Deane (London: Penguin, 2000), p. 137.
7. Joyce, *A Portrait*, p. 131.
8. Joyce, *A Portrait*, p. 143.
9. *S*, pp. 136–37. This comes explicitly as part of a reflection on *pœna damni*, considered separately from the *pœna sensus*. As such it does not, as Jill Muller argues, connote a rejection of hell's materiality that 'places him squarely in the camp of such Victorian eschatological liberals as Newman, Manning, and Joseph Rickaby' (p. 119), but rather an insistence on the materiality of the intellectual suffering known in hell.
10. Hill, *Critical Writings*, p. 393.
11. O'Gorman, p. 5.
12. *S*, p. 263.
13. Geoffrey Rowell, *Hell and the Victorians* (Oxford: Clarendon Press, 1974), p. 153.
14. Henry James Coleridge, *The Prisoners of the King: Thoughts on the Catholic Doctrine of Purgatory* (London: Burns and Oates, 1882), p. 177.
15. Susan Stewart, *Poetry and the Fate of the Senses* (Chicago: University of Chicago Press, 2002), p. 93.
16. John Casey, *After Lives: A Guide to Heaven, Hell, and Purgatory* (Oxford: Oxford University Press, 2009), p. 8. Hopkins affirmed that hell was a real physical location: 'Not known where Hell is; many say beneath our feet. It is at all events *a place of imprisonment*, a prison; *a place of darkness*; and *a place of torment*' (*S*, p. 241).
17. Patricia M. Ball, *The Science of Aspects: The Changing Role of Fact in the Work of Coleridge, Ruskin and Hopkins* (London: Athlone Press, 1971), p. 119.

18. *S*, p. 123.
19. *CW*, ii, 835.
20. *S*, p. 138.
21. *S*, p. 201.
22. Casey, p. 194.
23. George Tyrrell, 'A Perverted Devotion' (1899), repr. in *Essays on Faith and Immortality*, arranged by M. D. Petre (London: Edward Arnold, 1914), pp. 158–71 (pp. 165; 166).
24. Alphonsus Liguori, *Preparation for Death*, ed. by Orby Shipley (London: Rivingtons, 1868), p. 215. Muller comments that 'Hopkins's eschatological writings are notable for their silence on the subject of an intermediate state and for their strenuous efforts to preserve and justify Ignatian and Liguorian views of hell' (p. 129).
25. John Eusebius Nieremberg, S. J., *Of Adoration in Spirit and Truth*, trans. by R. S. (London: Burns and Oates, 1871), p. 56.
26. Phillipe Ariès, *The Hour of Our Death*, trans. by Helen Weaver (London: Allen Lane, 1981), p. 449.
27. Manley Hopkins, 'Rest', in *Spicilegium Poeticum* (London: Leadenhall Press, 1892), ll. 25–30.
28. Henry Parry Liddon, *The Divinity of Our Lord and Saviour Jesus Christ* (London: Rivingtons, 1867), p. 87. Hopkins attended the lectures on which Liddon's book is based.
29. *LPM*, pp. 262–63.
30. Genesis 32.30 (King James).
31. John Saward, *Sweet and Blessed Country: The Christian Hope for Heaven* (Oxford: Oxford University Press, 2005), p. 28.
32. The six other instances given in Robert J. Dilligan and Todd K. Bender's *A Concordance to the English Poetry of Gerard Manley Hopkins* (Madison: University of Wisconsin Press, 1970) are all from early poems.
33. See Jason R. Rudy, *Electric Meters: Victorian Physiological Poetics* (Athens: Ohio University Press, 2009), pp. 127–36.
34. Jane Wright, 'Hopkins's Dividing Errors', *Literary Imagination*, 17 (2015), 183–97 (p. 190).
35. Cited in Norman White, *Hopkins: A Literary Biography* (Oxford: Clarendon Press, 1992; repr. 1995), p. 387.
36. Harris, p. 117.
37. See on the rhyme of 'hell' and 'spell' McDonald, *Sound Intentions*, p. 289.
38. *S*, p. 201.
39. Jeffrey Burton Russell, *Lucifer: The Devil in the Middle Ages* (Ithaca: Cornell University Press, 1984), p. 172.

40. Mary Beth Ingham and Mechthild Dreyer, *The Philosophical Vision of Duns Scotus: An Introduction* (Washington, DC: Catholic University of America Press, 2004), p. 95.

41. Muller, p. 111.

42. Miller, *Disappearance of God*, pp. 323–24; 353.

43. *EPM*, p. 37.

44. Entry for 'Devil and Evil Spirits' in William E. Addis and Thomas Arnold, *A Catholic Dictionary, Containing Some Account of the Doctrine, Discipline, Rites, Ceremonies, Councils, and Religious Orders of the Catholic Church* (London: Kegan Paul, 1884).

45. J. H. Newman, *The Catholic Sermons of Cardinal Newman*, ed. by Birmingham Oratory (London: Burns and Oates, 1957), pp. 64–65.

46. *S*, p. 92.

47. *CW*, i, 363.

48. Cotter, *Inscape*, pp. 63–64; 65.

49. Nieremberg, p. 58.

50. *CW*, i, 181.

Bibliography

Adams, James Eli, *Dandies and Desert Saints: Styles of Victorian Masculinity* (Ithaca: Cornell University Press, 1995)

Addis, William E., and Thomas Arnold, *A Catholic Dictionary, Containing Some Account of the Doctrine, Discipline, Rites, Ceremonies, Councils, and Religious Orders of the Catholic Church* (London: Kegan Paul, 1884)

Alderson, David, *Mansex Fine: Religion, Manliness and Imperialism in Nineteenth-Century British Culture* (Manchester: Manchester University Press, 1998)

Alter, Robert, *The Art of Biblical Narrative* (London: George Allen & Unwin, 1981)

Anderson, Olive, 'The Growth of Christian Militarism in Mid-Victorian Britain', *English Historical Review*, 86 (1971), 46–72

Anon., 'A Contemporary Elegy on Edmund Campion', *The Month*, 16 (January–February 1872), 116–20

Anon., 'Father Gerard Hopkins', *Letters and Notices*, 20 (1890), 173–79

Anon., 'Papal Rome and Catholic Reform', *Edinburgh Review*, 141 (April 1875), 554–84

Anon., 'The Persecution in Poland', *The Tablet*, 27 March 1875, 390–92

Anon., Review of John Morris S.J.'s *The Troubles of Our Catholic Forefathers*, *Athenaeum*, 2570 (27 January 1877), 111–13

Ariès, Phillipe, *The Hour of Our Death*, trans. by Helen Weaver (London: Allen Lane, 1981)

Armstrong, Isobel, *Victorian Poetry: Poetry, Poetics and Politics* (London: Routledge, 1993; repr. 1996)

Arnstein, Walter L., *Protestant versus Catholic in Mid-Victorian England: Mr. Newdegate and the Nuns* (Columbia: University of Missouri Press, 1982)

Atwan, Robert, and Laurance Wiener, eds., *Chapters into Verse: Poetry in English Inspired by The Bible*, 2 vols. (New York: Oxford University Press, 1993)

Auden, W. H., *The Complete Works of W. H. Auden*, ed. by Edward Mendelson, 8 vols. (Princeton: Princeton University Press 1996–)

Augustine, *The City of God against the Pagans*, trans. by R.W. Dyson (Cambridge: Cambridge University Press, 1998)

Ball, Patricia M., *The Science of Aspects: The Changing Role of Fact in the Work of Coleridge, Ruskin and Hopkins* (London: Athlone Press, 1971)

Ballinger, Philip A., *The Poem as Sacrament: The Theological Aesthetic of Gerard Manley Hopkins* (Louvain: Peeters Press, 2000)

Basset, Bernard, S.J., *The English Jesuits: From Campion to Martindale* (London: Burns & Oates, 1967)

Beard, John R., 'Lessons in English', *The Popular Educator*, 2 (1853), 378–80

Beer, Gillian, *Open Fields: Science in Cultural Encounter* (Oxford: Clarendon Press, 1996)

Bender, Todd K., *Gerard Manley Hopkins: The Classical Background and Critical Reception of His Work* (Baltimore: Johns Hopkins Press, 1966)

Bevis, Matthew, ed., *The Oxford Handbook of Victorian Poetry* (Oxford: Oxford University Press, 2013)

Bishop, Elizabeth, *Prose*, ed. by Lloyd Schwarz (London: Chatto & Windus, 2011)

Blackmur, R.P., 'Mature Intelligence of an Artist', *The Kenyon Review* 1 (1939), 96–99

Blair, Kirstie, *Form and Faith in Victorian Poetry and Religion* (Oxford: Oxford University Press, 2012)

ed., *John Keble in Context* (London: Anthem Press, 2004)

Bloom, Harold, ed., *Gerard Manley Hopkins* (New York: Chelsea House, 1986)

The Book of J (London: Faber and Faber, 1991)

Bottalla, P., G. Marra, and F. Marucci, eds., *Gerard Manley Hopkins: Tradition and Innovation* (Ravenna: Longo Editore, 1991)

[Braden, William], 'The Works of George Herbert, in Prose and Verse', *The British Quarterly Review*, 46:91 (July 1867), 97–125

Bremond, Henri, *Poetry and Prayer: A Contribution to Poetical Theory*, trans. by A. Thorold (London: Burns, Oates & Washbourne, 1927)

Bridges, Robert, *Selected Letters of Robert Bridges*, ed. by Donald E. Stanford, 2 vols. (Newark: University of Delaware Press, 1983)

The Testament of Beauty: A Poem in Four Books (Oxford: Clarendon Press, 1929; repr. 1930)

Bristow, Joseph, '"Churlsgrace": Gerard Manley Hopkins and the Working-Class Male Body', *ELH*, 59 (1992), 693–711

Brittain, Clark M., 'Logos, Creation, and Epiphany in the Poetics of Gerard Manley Hopkins', unpub. PhD thesis, University of Virginia, 1988

Brown, Daniel, *Gerard Manley Hopkins* (Tavistock: Northcote House, 2004)

Hopkins' Idealism: Philosophy, Physics, Poetry (Oxford: Clarendon Press, 1997)

Brown, Geoffrey, 'Praying about the Past', *The Philosophical Quarterly*, 35 (1985), 83–86

Brueggemann, Walter, *The Psalms and the Life of Faith*, ed. by Patrick D. Miller (Minneapolis: Fortress Press, 1995)

Bugliani Knox, Francesca, and John Took, eds., *Poetry and Prayer: The Power of the Word II* (Farnham: Ashgate, 2015)

Burgess, Anthony, 'Gash gold-vermilion', *The Spectator*, 21 September 1967, 10–11

Campbell, Matthew, *Irish Poetry under the Union, 1801–1924* (Cambridge: Cambridge University Press, 2013)

Rhythm and Will in Victorian Poetry (Cambridge: Cambridge University Press, 1999)

Caro, Robert V., S.J., 'Hopkins's Poems in the Breviary', *Studies: An Irish Quarterly Review*, 2 (1995), 173–80

Casey, John, *After Lives: A Guide to Heaven, Hell, and Purgatory* (Oxford: Oxford University Press, 2009)

The Catechism of the Council of Trent, trans. by J. Donovan (Dublin: W. Folds, 1829)

Chadwick, Owen, *The Spirit of the Oxford Movement: Tractarian Essays* (1990; repr. Cambridge: Cambridge University Press, 1995)

Chambers, Susan, 'Gerard Manley Hopkins and the Kinesthetics of Conviction', *Victorian Studies*, 51 (2008), 7–35

Champneys, Basil, *Memoirs and Correspondence of Coventry Patmore*, 2 vols. (London: George Bell, 1900)

Cicero, *On Duties*, ed. by M. T. Griffin and E. M. Atkins (Cambridge: Cambridge University Press, 1991)

Clare, James, S.J., *The Science of Spiritual Life, According to the Spiritual Exercises* (London and Leamington: Art and Book Company, 1896)

Cook, Eleanor, *Against Coercion: Games Poets Play* (Stanford: Stanford University Press, 1998)

Costantini, Mariaconcetta, '"To his Watch": Gerard Manley Hopkins and the Rhythm of Mortal Life', *Hopkins Quarterly*, 39 (2012), 88–106

Cotter, James Finn, 'Hopkins and Job', *Victorian Poetry*, 33 (1995), 283–93

'Apocalyptic Imagery in Hopkins' "That Nature is a Heraclitean Fire and of the Comfort of the Resurrection"', *Victorian Poetry*, 24 (1986), 261–73

Inscape: The Christology and Poetry of Gerard Manley Hopkins (Pittsburgh: University of Pittsburgh Press, 1972)

Cronin, Richard, Alison Chapman, and Anthony H. Harrison, eds., *A Companion to Victorian Poetry* (Oxford: Blackwell, 2002)

Culler, Jonathan, *The Pursuit of Signs: Semiotics, Literature, Deconstruction* (Ithaca: Cornell University Press, 1981)

Theory of the Lyric (Cambridge, MA: Harvard University Press, 2015)

Cummings, Brian, *The Literary Culture of the Reformation: Grammar and Grace* (Oxford: Oxford University Press, 2002)

Cunningham, Valentine, *Victorian Poetry Now: Poets, Poems, Poetics* (Oxford: Wiley-Blackwell, 2011)

D'Amico, Diane, *Christina Rossetti: Faith, Gender, and Time* (Baton Rouge: Louisiana State University Press, 1999)

Davie, Donald, ed., *The New Oxford Book of Christian Verse* (Oxford: Oxford University Press, 1981; repr. 1988)

ed., *The Psalms in English* (London: Penguin, 1996)

Davis, Stephen J., *The Cult of Saint Thecla: A Tradition of Women's Piety in Late Antiquity* (Oxford: Oxford University Press, 2001)

Dawson, Graham, *Soldier Heroes: British Adventure, Empire and the Imagining of Masculinities* (London: Routledge, 1994)

Denzinger, Heinrich, *The Sources of Catholic Dogma*, trans. by Roy J. Deferarri (St Louis: Herder, 1957)

De Ponte, Louis, S.J., *Meditations on the Mysteries of Our Holy Faith; Together with a Treatise on Mental Prayer*, trans. by John Heigham, 6 vols. (London: Richardson and Son, 1852–54)

Dickstein, Morris, 'Is Religious Poetry Possible?' *Literary Imagination*, 2 (2000), 135–51

Dilligan, Robert J., and Todd K. Bender, *A Concordance to the English Poetry of Gerard Manley Hopkins* (Madison: University of Wisconsin Press, 1970)

Dillon, Anne, *The Construction of Martyrdom in the English Catholic Community, 1535–1603* (Aldershot: Ashgate, 2008)

Douglas, Mary, *In the Wilderness: The Doctrine of Defilement in the Book of Numbers* (Oxford: Oxford University Press, 1993; repr. 2001)

Downes, David Anthony, *The Ignatian Personality of Gerard Manley Hopkins* (Lanham: University Press of America, 1990)

Dubois, Martin, 'The *Month* as Hopkins Knew It', *Victorian Periodicals Review*, 43 (2010), 296–308

Eliot, T. S., *After Strange Gods: A Primer of Modern Heresy* (New York: Harcourt, Brace and Company, 1934)

For Lancelot Andrewes: Essays on Style and Order (London: Faber and Gwyer, 1928)

Selected Essays, 3rd edn (London: Faber and Faber, 1951; repr. 1999)

Ellis, Jonathan, ed., *Letter Writing among Poets: From William Wordsworth to Elizabeth Bishop* (Edinburgh: Edinburgh University Press, 2015)

Ellmann, Richard, *James Joyce*, rev. edn (New York: Oxford University Press, 1982)

Empson, William, *Selected Letters of William Empson*, ed. by John Haffenden (Oxford: Oxford University Press, 2006)

Seven Types of Ambiguity (London: Chatto and Windus, 1930)

Endean, Philip, S.J., 'The Spirituality of Gerard Manley Hopkins', *Hopkins Quarterly*, 8 (1981), 107–29

Faber, Frederick William, *Notes on Doctrinal and Spiritual Subjects*, 2 vols. (London: Thomas Richardson, 1866)

Feeney, Joseph J., S.J., 'Hopkins' "Failure" in Theology: Some New Archival Data and a New Reevaluation', *Hopkins Quarterly*, 13 (1986–87), 99–114

The Playfulness of Gerard Manley Hopkins (Aldershot: Ashgate, 2008)

Fiddes, Paul S., *Past Event and Present Salvation: The Christian Idea of Atonement* (London: Darton, Longman and Todd, 1989)

FitzGerald, William, *Spiritual Modalities: Prayer as Rhetoric and Performance* (University Park: Pennsylvania State University Press, 2012)

Fraser, Hilary, *Beauty and Belief: Aesthetics and Religion in Victorian Literature* (Cambridge: Cambridge University Press, 1986)

Freeman, Thomas S., and Thomas F. Mayer, eds., *Martyrs and Martyrdom in England, c.1400–1700* (Woodbridge: Boydell and Brewer, 2007)

Froude, James Anthony, *Short Studies on Great Subjects*, 4 vols. (London: Longmans, 1877–83)

Fry, Paul H., *The Poet's Calling in the English Ode* (New Haven: Yale University Press, 1980)

Gallwey, Peter, S.J., *The Beatified Martyrs and Prayers for the Conversion of England* (London: Burns & Oates, 1888)

Gardner, W. H., and N. H. MacKenzie, eds., *The Poems of Gerard Manley Hopkins* (Oxford: Oxford University Press, 1970)

Giles, R. F., ed., *Hopkins among the Poets* (Hamilton, Ontario: International Hopkins Association, 1985)

Gillingham, S. E., *The Poems and Psalms of the Hebrew Bible* (Oxford: Oxford University Press, 1994)

Ginzburg, Carlo, 'Morelli, Freud and Sherlock Holmes: Clues and Scientific Method', *History Workshop*, 9 (1980), 5–36

Gladstone, W. E., *The Vatican Decrees in Their Bearing on Civil Allegiance: A Political Expostulation* (London: John Murray, 1874)

Golden, Catherine J., *Posting It: The Victorian Revolution in Letter Writing* (Gainesville: University Press of Florida, 2009)

Goody, Jack, *The Domestication of the Savage Mind* (Cambridge: Cambridge University Press, 1977)

Grafe, Adrian, ed., *Ecstasy and Understanding: Religious Awareness in English Poetry from the Late Victorian to the Modern Period* (London: Continuum, 2008)
Gerard Manley Hopkins: la profusion ténébreuse (Lille: Septentrion, 2003)

Griffiths, Eric, *The Printed Voice of Victorian Poetry* (Oxford: Clarendon Press, 1989)

Groves, Peter, 'Hopkins and Tractarianism', *Victorian Poetry*, 44 (2006), 105–12

Gurney, Ivor, *Ivor Gurney: Collected Letters*, ed. by R. K. R. Thornton (Northumberland: Mid Northumberland Arts Group/Manchester: Carcanet Press, 1991)

Hall, Jason David, ed., *Meter Matters: Verse Cultures of the Long Nineteenth Century* (Athens: Ohio University Press, 2011)

Hardy, Barbara, *The Advantage of Lyric: Essays on Feeling in Poetry* (London: Athlone Press, 1977)

Harris, Daniel A., *Inspirations Unbidden: The 'Terrible Sonnets' of Gerard Manley Hopkins* (Berkeley: University of California Press, 1982)

Harris, Ruth, *Lourdes: Body and Spirit in the Secular Age* (London: Allen Lane, 1999)

Harter, Michael, S.J., ed., *Hearts on Fire: Praying with Jesuits* (Chicago: Loyala Press, 2004)

Hartman, Geoffrey H., *The Unmediated Vision: An Interpretation of Wordsworth, Hopkins, Rilke, and Valéry* (New Haven: Yale University Press, 1954)

Heaney, Seamus, *The Fire i' the Flint: Reflections on the Poetry of Gerard Manley Hopkins* (London: Oxford University Press, 1975)

Heimann, Mary, *Catholic Devotion in Victorian Britain* (Oxford: Clarendon Press, 1995)

Higgins, Lesley, 'Heraclitean Fire and Eucharistic Flame: The Poetry of Transformation in Hopkins', *The Month*, 22 (1989), 423–28

Hill, Geoffrey, *Broken Hierarchies: Poems 1952–2012*, ed. by Kenneth Haynes (Oxford: Oxford University Press, 2013)

    Collected Critical Writings, ed. by Kenneth Haynes (Oxford: Oxford University Press, 2008)

    'What you look hard at seems to look hard at you', Oxford Professor of Poetry lecture, 6 May 2014, www.english.ox.ac.uk/news-events/regular-events/professor-poetry [accessed 21 September 2014]

Holder, Arthur, ed., *The Blackwell Companion to Christian Spirituality* (Oxford: Blackwell, 2005)

Hollahan, Eugene, ed., *Gerard Manley Hopkins and Critical Discourse* (New York: AMS Press, 1993)

Hopkins, Gerard Manley, *The Collected Works of Gerard Manley Hopkins*, general eds. Lesley Higgins and Michael F. Suarez, S.J. (Oxford: Oxford University Press, 2006–)

    The Correspondence of Gerard Manley Hopkins and Richard Watson Dixon, ed. by Claude Colleer Abbott, 2nd edn (London: Oxford University Press, 1955)

    The Early Poetic Manuscripts of Gerard Manley Hopkins in Facsimile, ed. by Norman H. MacKenzie (New York and London: Garland, 1989)

    Gerard Manley Hopkins: The Major Works, ed. by Catherine Phillips, rev. edn (Oxford: Oxford University Press, 2002)

    Gerard Manley Hopkins: Poetry and Prose, ed. by Walford Davies (London and Vermont: J. M. Dent, 2002)

    The Journals and Papers of Gerard Manley Hopkins, ed. by Humphry House and Graham Storey (London: Oxford University Press, 1959)

    The Later Poetic Manuscripts of Gerard Manley Hopkins in Facsimile, ed. by Norman H. MacKenzie (New York and London: Garland, 1991)

    Poems of Gerard Manley Hopkins, ed. by Robert Bridges (London: Humphrey Milford, 1918)

    The Poetical Works of Gerard Manley Hopkins, ed. by Norman H. MacKenzie (Oxford: Clarendon Press, 1990)

    The Sermons and Devotional Writings of Gerard Manley Hopkins, ed. by Christopher Devlin (London: Oxford University Press, 1959)

Hopkins, Manley, *Spicilegium Poeticum* (London: Leadenhall Press, 1892)

Housman, A. E., *The Letters of A. E. Housman*, ed. by Archie Burnett, 2 vols. (Oxford: Clarendon Press, 2007)

Humphries, Simon, 'Hopkins's Silent Men', *ELH*, 77 (2010), 447–76

Hurley, Michael D., '"Dancing in Chains": *Patterns of Sound in the Poetry of Gerard Manley Hopkins*', unpub. PhD thesis, University of Cambridge, 2004

    Faith in Poetry: Verse Style as a Mode of Religious Belief (London: Bloomsbury Academic, 2017)

    Review of James I. Wimsatt's *Hopkins's Poetics of Speech Sound*, *Modern Philology*, 107 (2008), 126–30

'What Sprung Rhythm Really Is NOT', *Hopkins Quarterly*, 23 (2006), 71–94

Ignatius of Loyola, *Spiritual Exercises*, trans. by Charles Seager (London: Charles Dolman, 1847)

Ingham, Mary Beth, and Mechthild Dreyer, *The Philosophical Vision of Duns Scotus: An Introduction* (Washington, DC: Catholic University of America Press, 2004)

Jackson, Virginia, and Yopie Prins, eds., *The Lyric Theory Reader: A Critical Anthology* (Baltimore: Johns Hopkins University Press, 2014)

James, William, *The Varieties of Religious Experience*, ed. by Matthew Bradley (Oxford: Oxford University Press, 2012)

Jennings, Elizabeth, *Every Changing Shape* (London: Andre Deutsch, 1961)

Jodock, Darrell, ed., *Catholicism Contending with Modernity: Roman Catholic Modernism and Anti-Modernism in Historical Context* (Cambridge: Cambridge University Press, 2000)

Johnson, Margaret, *Gerard Manley Hopkins and Tractarian Poetry* (Aldershot: Ashgate, 1997)

Jones, David, *In Parenthesis: Seinnyessit E Gledyf Ym Penn Mameu* (London: Faber and Faber, 1937; repr. 1975)

Josipovici, Gabriel, *The Book of God: A Response to the Bible* (New Haven: Yale University Press, 1988)

Joyce, James, *A Portrait of the Artist as a Young Man*, ed. by Seamus Deane (London: Penguin, 2000)

Ulysses, ed. by Jeri Johnson (Oxford: Oxford University Press, 1993; repr. 1998)

Karlin, Daniel, 'Victorian Poetry and the English Poetry Full-Text Database: A Case Study', *Literature Online*, 6 May 2014, http://collections.chadwyck .co.uk/marketing/karlin.jsp [accessed 28 June 2016]

Keating, John E., S.J., *'The Wreck of the Deutschland': An Essay and Commentary* (Kent, OH: Kent State University, 1963)

Kendall, Tim, ed., *The Oxford Handbook of British and Irish War Poetry* (Oxford: Oxford University Press, 2007)

Ker, Ian, *The Catholic Revival in English Literature, 1845–1961: Newman, Hopkins, Belloc, Chesterton, Greene, Waugh* (Notre Dame: University of Notre Dame Press, 2003)

Kermode, Frank, *The Genesis of Secrecy: On the Interpretation of Narrative* (Cambridge, MA: Harvard University Press, 1979)

Knight, Mark, and Emma Mason, *Nineteenth-Century Religion and Literature: An Introduction* (Oxford: Oxford University Press, 2006)

Knox, Ronald, *On Englishing the Bible* (London: Burns and Oates, 1949)

Kundu, Rama, ed., *Widening Horizons: Essays in Honour of Professor Mohit K. Ray* (New Delhi: Sarup, 2005)

Lahey, G. F., S.J., *Gerard Manley Hopkins* (Oxford: Oxford University Press, 1930)

Lake, Peter, and Michael Questier, *The Trials of Margaret Clitherow: Persecution, Martyrdom and the Politics of Sanctity in Elizabethan England* (London: Continuum, 2011)

Landow, George P., *Victorian Types, Victorian Shadows: Biblical Typology in Victorian Literature, Art, and Thought* (Boston: Routledge and Kegan Paul, 1980)

Lawler, Justus George, *Hopkins Re-Constructed: Life, Poetry, and the Tradition* (New York: Continuum, 1998)

Leavis, F. R., *The Common Pursuit* (Harmondsworth: Penguin, 1952)

The Critic as Anti-Philosopher: Essays and Papers by F. R. Leavis, ed. by G. Singh (London: Chatto & Windus, 1982)

New Bearings in English Poetry (London: Chatto and Windus, 1932)

Lemon, Rebecca, Emma Mason, Jonathan Roberts, and Christopher Rowland, eds., *The Blackwell Companion to the Bible in English Literature* (Chichester: Wiley-Blackwell, 2009)

Lichtmann, Maria R., *The Contemplative Poetry of Gerard Manley Hopkins* (Princeton: Princeton University Press, 1989)

Liguori, Alphonsus, *Preparation for Death*, ed. by Orby Shipley (London: Rivingtons, 1868)

A Short Treatise on Prayer; The Great Means of Obtaining from God Eternal Salvation, and All the Graces of Which We Stand in Need (Dublin: John Coyne, 1834)

Selected Writings, ed. by Frederick M. Jones (New York: Paulist Press, 1999)

Liddon, Henry Parry, *The Divinity of Our Lord and Saviour Jesus Christ* (London: Rivingtons, 1867)

Sermons Preached before the University of Oxford, 3rd edn (London: Rivingtons, 1869)

Loomis, Jeffrey B., *Dayspring in Darkness: Sacrament in Hopkins* (Lewisburg: Bucknell University Press, 1988)

Louis, Wm. Roger, et al., eds., *The Oxford History of the British Empire*, 5 vols. (Oxford: Oxford University Press, 1998–99)

Lowell, Robert, 'A Note', *The Kenyon Review*, 6 (1944), 583–86

Lucas, John, *Ivor Gurney* (Tavistock: Northcote House, 2001)

MacKenzie, John M., ed., *Popular Imperialism and the Military, 1850–1950* (Manchester: Manchester University Press, 1992)

MacKenzie, Norman H., *Hopkins* (Edinburgh: Oliver and Boyd, 1968)

A Reader's Guide to Gerard Manley Hopkins (London: Thames and Hudson, 1981)

Manual of Prayers for Congregational Use (London: Thomas Richardson, 1887)

Mariani, Paul L., *A Commentary on the Complete Poems of Gerard Manley Hopkins* (Ithaca: Cornell University Press, 1970)

Marmion, Declan, and Mary E. Hines, eds., *The Cambridge Companion to Karl Rahner* (Cambridge: Cambridge University Press, 2005)

Martin, Meredith, 'Hopkins's Prosody', *Hopkins Quarterly*, 38 (2011), 1–30

The Rise and Fall of Meter: Poetry and National Culture, 1860–1930 (Princeton: Princeton University Press, 2012)

Martin, Robert Bernard, *Gerard Manley Hopkins: A Very Private Life* (London: Flamingo, 1992)

Martz, Louis L., *The Poetry of Meditation: A Study in English Religious Literature of the Seventeenth Century* (New Haven: Yale University Press, 1954)

Maxwell-Scott, Mary Monica, *Henry Schomberg Kerr: Sailor and Jesuit* (London: Longmans, Green, and Co., 1901)

McChesney, Donald, *A Hopkins Commentary: An Explanatory Commentary on the Main Poems, 1876–89* (London: University of London Press, 1968)

McDermott, John, ed., *Hopkins' Lancashire: Sesquicentennial Essays* (Wigan: North West Catholic History Society, 1994)

McDonald, Peter, *Sound Intentions: The Workings of Rhyme in Nineteenth-Century Poetry* (Oxford: Oxford University Press, 2012)

'Truly Apart', *Times Literary Supplement*, 1 April 2005, 13

McGrath, Alister E., *Iustitia Dei: A History of the Christian Doctrine of Justification*, 2 vols. (Cambridge: Cambridge University Press, 1986)

Miller, J. Hillis, *The Disappearance of God: Five Nineteenth-Century Writers* (Cambridge, MA: Harvard University Press, 1963)

The Linguistic Moment: From Wordsworth to Stevens (Princeton: Princeton University Press, 1985)

Milroy, James, *The Language of Gerard Manley Hopkins* (London: André Deutsch, 1977)

Modiano, Raimonda, Leroy F. Searle, and Peter Shillingsburg, eds., *Voice, Text, Hypertext: Emerging Practices in Textual Studies* (Seattle: University of Washington Press, 2004)

Moran, Maureen, *Catholic Sensationalism and Victorian Literature* (Liverpool: Liverpool University Press, 2007)

'Hopkins and Victorian Responses to Suffering', *Revue Lisa/Lisa e-journal*, 8:3 (2009) http://lisa.revues.org/145 [accessed 15 December 2014]

'"Lovely manly mould": Hopkins and the Christian Body', *Journal of Victorian Culture*, 6 (2001), 61–88

'The Art of Looking Dangerously: Victorian Images of Martyrdom', *Victorian Literature and Culture*, 32 (2004), 475–93

Morris, John, S.J., *The Troubles of Our Catholic Forefathers Related by Themselves*, 3rd series (London: Burns and Oates, 1877)

Muller, Jill, *Gerard Manley Hopkins and Victorian Catholicism: A Heart in Hiding* (New York and London: Routledge, 2003)

Newman, John Henry, *An Essay in Aid of a Grammar of Assent* (London: Burns & Oates, 1870)

Essays Critical and Historical, 2 vols. (London: Longmans, Green and Co., 1907)

Meditations and Devotions of the Late Cardinal Newman, ed. by W.P. Neville (1893; repr. London: Longmans, 1907)

Parochial and Plain Sermons, 8 vols. (London: Rivingtons, 1875)

Sermon Notes of John Henry Cardinal Newman, 1849–1878, ed. by The Fathers of the Birmingham Oratory (London: Longmans, 1913)

Sermons, ed. by Placid Murray, Vincent Ferrer Blehl, and Francis J. McGrath, 5 vols. (Oxford: Oxford University Press, 1991–2012)

Sermons Preached on Various Occasions (London: Burns and Lambert, 1857)

The Catholic Sermons of Cardinal Newman, ed. by Birmingham Oratory (London: Burns and Oates, 1957)

The Letters and Diaries of John Henry Newman, ed. by Charles Stephen Dessain et al., 32 vols. (Oxford: Clarendon Press, 1973–2008)

Nicholson, William, *Life and Death of Margaret Clitherow, the Martyr of York* (London: Richardson, 1849)

Nieremberg, John Eusebius, S.J., *Of Adoration in Spirit and Truth*, trans. by R. S. (London: Burns and Oates, 1871)

Nixon, Jude V., '"Death blots black out": Thermodynamics and the Poetry of Gerard Manley Hopkins', *Victorian Poetry*, 40 (2002), 131–55

Gerard Manley Hopkins and His Contemporaries: Liddon, Newman, Darwin, and Pater (New York: Garland, 1994)

'"Goldengrove unleaving": Hopkins' "Spring and Fall," Christina Rossetti's "Mirrors of Life and Death," and the Politics of Inclusion', *Victorian Poetry*, 43 (2005), 473–84

'"St. Thecla," Monastic Transvestitism, and Hopkins's Proto-Feminist Utterance', *Hopkins Quarterly*, 39 (2012), 43–67

North, John S., and Michael D. Moore, eds., *Vital Candle: Victorian and Modern Bearings in Gerard Manley Hopkins* (Waterloo, Ontario: University of Waterloo Press, 1984)

Nowell Smith, David, *On Voice in Poetry: The Work of Animation* (Basingstoke: Palgrave Macmillan, 2015)

Nuttall, A. D., *Overheard by God: Fiction and Prayer in Herbert, Milton, Dante and St John* (London and New York: Methuen, 1980)

O'Gorman, Francis, ed., *The Cambridge Companion to Victorian Culture* (Cambridge: Cambridge University Press, 2010)

'Hopkins' Yonder', *Literature and Theology*, 27 (2013), 81–97

O'Malley, John W., S.J., *The First Jesuits* (Cambridge, MA: Harvard University Press, 1993)

The Jesuits: A History from Ignatius to the Present (Lanham: Rowman & Littlefield, 2014)

Ong, Walter J., S.J., *Hopkins, the Self, and God* (Toronto: University of Toronto Press, 1986)

Parham, John, *Green Man Hopkins: Poetry and the Victorian Ecological Imagination* (Amsterdam: Rodopi, 2010)

Peters, W. A. M., *Gerard Manley Hopkins: A Critical Essay towards the Understanding of His Poetry* (London: Oxford University Press, 1948)

Phare, Elsie Elizabeth, *The Poetry of Gerard Manley Hopkins: A Survey and Commentary* (Cambridge: Cambridge University Press, 1933)

Phelan, Joseph, *The Music of Verse: Metrical Experiment in Nineteenth-Century Poetry* (Basingstoke: Palgrave Macmillan, 2012)

Phillips, Catherine, *Gerard Manley Hopkins and the Victorian Visual World* (Oxford: Oxford University Press, 2007)

Pick, John, *Gerard Manley Hopkins: Priest and Poet* (London: Oxford University Press, 1942)

Pius IX, *Syllabus Errorum* (1864), www.papalencyclicals.net/pius09/p9syll.htm [accessed 4 April 2016]

Pizza, Joseph, 'Hopkins' Counter Stress', *Literature and Theology*, 25 (2011), 47–63

Plotkin, Cary H., ed., *Soundings: Hopkins Studies in Transition* (Philadelphia: St Joseph's University Press, 2007)

   The Tenth Muse: Victorian Philology and the Genesis of the Poetic Language of Gerard Manley Hopkins (Carbondale: Southern Illinois University Press, 1989)

Pomplun, Trent, 'The Theology of Gerard Manley Hopkins: From John Duns Scotus to the Baroque', *The Journal of Religion*, 95 (2015), 1–34

Prickett, Stephen, *Words and The Word: Language, Poetics and Biblical Interpretation* (Cambridge: Cambridge University Press, 1986)

The Raccolta: Or, Collection of Indulgenced Prayers, trans. by Ambrose St John (London: Burns and Lambert, 1857)

Rafferty, Oliver P., S.J., ed., *George Tyrrell and Catholic Modernism* (Dublin: Four Courts Press, 2010)

Ramazani, Jahan, *Poetry and Its Others: News, Prayer, Song, and the Dialogue of Genres* (Chicago: University of Chicago Press, 2014)

Rickaby, Joseph, S.J., *Scholasticism* (London: Archibald Constable, 1908)

Ricks, Christopher, *Reviewery* (London: Penguin, 2002)

Riding, Laura, and Robert Graves, *A Survey of Modernist Poetry* (London: Heinemann, 1927; repr. 1929)

Roberts, Gerald, ed., *Gerard Manley Hopkins: The Critical Heritage* (London: Routledge, 1987)

Roberts, Michael Symmons, 'Poetry in a Post-Secular Age', *Poetry Review*, 98 (2008), 69–75

Roden, Frederick S., *Same-Sex Desire in Victorian Religious Culture* (Basingstoke: Palgrave, 2002)

Rodriguez, Alfonso, S.J., *The Practice of Christian and Religious Perfection*, 3 vols. (Dublin: Richard Coyne, 1840–41)

Roothaan, Jan, S.J., *How to Meditate*, trans. by Louis J. Puhl (Wesminster, MD: The Newman Bookshop, 1945)

Rowell, Geoffrey, *Hell and the Victorians* (Oxford: Clarendon Press, 1974)

Rudy, Jason R., *Electric Meters: Victorian Physiological Poetics* (Athens: Ohio University Press, 2009)

Russell, Jeffrey Burton, *Lucifer: The Devil in the Middle Ages* (Ithaca and London: Cornell University Press, 1984)

Saville, Julia F., *A Queer Chivalry: The Homoerotic Asceticism of Gerard Manley Hopkins* (Charlottesville: University of Virginia Press, 2000)

Saward, John, *Sweet and Blessed Country: The Christian Hope for Heaven* (Oxford: Oxford University Press, 2005)

Schad, John, 'Queerest Book – A Dramatic Monologue', *Literature and Theology*, 26 (2012), 3–22

Schneider, Elisabeth W., *The Dragon in the Gate: Studies in the Poetry of G. M. Hopkins* (Berkeley: University of California Press, 1968)

Schoeck, R. J., 'Peine Forte et Dure and Hopkins' "Margaret Clitheroe"', *Modern Language Notes*, 74 (1959), 220–24

Scott, Clive, *A Question of Syllables: Essays in Nineteenth-Century French Verse* (Cambridge: Cambridge University Press, 1986)

Sermons by Fathers of the Society of Jesus, 3 vols. (London: Burns & Oates, 1869–75)

Shea, Victor, and William Whitla, eds., *Essays and Reviews: The 1860 Text and Its Reading* (Charlottesville: University Press of Virginia, 2000)

Simcox, George Augustus, Review of J. H. Newman's *Letter to the Duke of Norfolk*, *The Academy*, 23 January 1875, 79–80

Sheldrake, Philip, *A Brief History of Spirituality* (Oxford: Blackwell, 2007)

Spirituality and History: Questions of Interpretation and Method, rev. edn (London: SPCK, 1995)

Shell, Alison, *Catholicism, Controversy and the English Literary Imagination, 1558–1660* (Cambridge: Cambridge University Press, 1999)

Sheils, William Joseph, 'Mush, John (1552–1612)', *Oxford Dictionary of National Biography*, Oxford University Press, 2004 www.oxforddnb.com/view/article/19669 [accessed 12 September 2014]

Shortland, John Rutherford, *The Corean Martyrs: A Narrative* (London: Burns & Oates, 1869)

Smith, Jonathan Z., *Imagining Religion: From Babylon to Jonestown* (Chicago and London: University of Chicago Press, 1982)

Map Is Not Territory: Studies in the History of Religions (Leiden: E. J. Brill, 1978)

Smith, Sydney Fenn, 'Our English Catholic Bible', *The Month*, 90 (1897), 43–62

Sobolev, Dennis, 'Inscape Revisited', *English*, 51 (2002), 219–34

'Semantic Counterpoint and the Poetry of Gerard Manley Hopkins', *Victorian Literature and Culture*, 35 (2007), 103–19

The Split World of Gerard Manley Hopkins: An Essay in Semiotic Phenomenology (Washington, DC: Catholic University of America Press, 2011)

Sollier, Joseph, 'Final Perseverance', *in The Catholic Encyclopedia* (1911), www.newadvent.org/cathen/11711a.htm [accessed 20 September 2013]

Sperling, Matthew, *Visionary Philology: Geoffrey Hill and the Study of Words* (Oxford: Oxford University Press, 2015)

Starkey, R. L., 'Books Hopkins Had Access To', *Hopkins Research Bulletin*, 6 (1975), 17–21

Stewart, Susan, *Poetry and the Fate of the Senses* (Chicago: University of Chicago Press, 2002)

Storey, Graham, *A Preface to Hopkins* (Harlow: Longman, 1981)

Strong, Rowan, *Anglicanism and the British Empire, c.1700–1850* (Oxford: Oxford University Press, 2007)

Sundermeier, Michael, and Desmond Egan, eds., *Gerard Manley Hopkins Annual 1993* (Omaha: Creighton University Press, 1993)

Swaab, Peter, 'Hopkins and the Pushed Peach', *Critical Quarterly*, 37 (1995), 43–60

Taylor, Gabriele, *Pride, Shame, and Guilt: Emotions of Self-Assessment* (Oxford: Clarendon Press, 1985)

Thomas, Alfred, S.J., 'Hopkins's "Felix Randal": The Man and the Poem', *Times Literary Supplement* (19 March 1971), 331–32

   Hopkins the Jesuit: The Years of Training (London: Oxford University Press, 1969)

Thornton, R. K. R., *Gerard Manley Hopkins: The Poems* (London: Edward Arnold, 1973)

Trench, R. C., *English, Past and Present: Five Lectures* (London: Parker, 1855)

Tynan, Katharine, *Memories* (London: Eveleigh Nash & Grayson, 1924)

Tyrrell, George, *Essays on Faith and Immortality*, arranged by M. D. Petre (London: Edward Arnold, 1914)

   Nova et Vetera: Informal Meditations for Times of Spiritual Dryness (London: Longmans, 1898)

Vance, Norman, *The Sinews of the Spirit: The Ideal of Christian Manliness in Victorian Literature and Religious Thought* (Cambridge: Cambridge University Press, 1985)

Vendler, Helen, *The Art of Shakespeare's Sonnets* (Cambridge, MA: Harvard University Press, 1997)

   The Breaking of Style: Hopkins, Heaney, Graham (Cambridge, MA: Harvard University Press, 1995)

   'I have not lived up to it', *London Review of Books* (3 April 2014), 13–18

Viller, Marcel et al., ed., *Dictionnaire de spiritualité: ascétique et mystique, doctrine et histoire*, 17 vols. (Paris: Beauchesne, 1937–95)

Von Balthasar, Hans Urs, *The Glory of the Lord: A Theological Aesthetics*, 7 vols. (Edinburgh: T & T Clark, 1982–91)

Walhout, Donald, *Send My Roots Rain: A Study of Religious Experience in the Poetry of Gerard Manley Hopkins* (Athens: Ohio University Press, 1981)

Ward, Bernadette Waterman, 'Hopkins on Warfare: "the war within"', *Hopkins Quarterly*, 30 (2003), 7–82

   World as Word: Philosophical Theology in Gerard Manley Hopkins (Washington, DC: Catholic University of America Press, 2002)

Ward, Thomas, *Errata of the Protestant Bible* (Dublin: James Duffy, 1841)

Warren, Austin, 'Monument Not Quite Needed', *The Kenyon Review* 6 (1944), 587–89

Waters, William, *Poetry's Touch: On Lyric Address* (Ithaca: Cornell University Press, 2003)

Wheeler, Michael, *Death and the Future Life in Victorian Literature and Theology* (Cambridge: Cambridge University Press, 1990)

The Old Enemies: Catholic and Protestant in Nineteenth-Century English Culture (Cambridge: Cambridge University Press, 2006)

St John and the Victorians (Cambridge: Cambridge University Press, 2012)

White, Norman, *Hopkins: A Literary Biography* (Oxford: Clarendon Press, 1992; repr. 1995)

Hopkins in Ireland (Dublin: University College Dublin Press, 2002)

'Hopkins' Sonnet "No Worst, There is None" and the Storm Scenes in "King Lear"', *Victorian Poetry*, 24 (1986), 83–87

Williams, Isaac, *The Cathedral, or the Catholic and Apostolic Church in England* (Oxford: John Henry Parker, 1838)

Wimsatt, James I., *Hopkins's Poetics of Speech Sound: Sprung Rhythm, Lettering, Inscape* (Toronto: University of Toronto Press, 2006)

Winstock, Lewis, *Songs & Music of the Redcoats: A History of the War Music of the British Army, 1642–1902* (London: Leo Cooper, 1970)

Winters, Yvor, *The Function of Criticism: Problems and Exercises* (London: Routledge & Kegan Paul, 1957)

'The Poetry of Gerard Manley Hopkins (I)', *The Hudson Review*, 1 (1949), 455–76

Worcester, Thomas, ed., *The Cambridge Companion to the Jesuits* (Cambridge: Cambridge University Press, 2008)

Wright, Jane, 'Hopkins's Dividing Errors', *Literary Imagination*, 17 (2015), 183–97

Wright, Joseph, *English Dialect Dictionary* (London: Henry Frowde, 1898–1905)

Zonneveld, Sjaak, *The Random Grim Forge: A Study of Social Ideas in the Work of Gerard Manley Hopkins* (Assen/Maastricht: Van Gorcum, 1992)

Index

CAMBRIDGE STUDIES IN NINETEENTH-CENTURY LITERATURE AND CULTURE

GENERAL EDITOR: Gillian Beer, University of Cambridge

Titles published

CPSIA information can be obtained
at www.ICGtesting.com
Printed in the USA
LVOW13*1742020718
582513LV00009B/209/P